THE ROMANCE
OF TRISTRAN

THE ROMANCE
OF TRISTRAN

by BEROUL

Edited by
A. EWERT
Formerly Professor of the Romance Languages,
University of Oxford

VOLUME II

INTRODUCTION, COMMENTARY

BASIL BLACKWELL
OXFORD
1970

Cloth edition 0 631 12360 1

Paperback edition 0 631 12770 4

Library of Congress Catalog Card No. 40-671

Printed in Great Britain by
Alden & Mowbray Ltd.
at the Alden Press, Oxford

PREFACE

It is a matter of much regret to me that the appearance of this second volume has been so long delayed: a variety of circumstances and preoccupations explain, without entirely excusing, the tardiness of its completion and some of its deficiencies. In the interim much has been written about this text, various passages have been elucidated and a considerable number of emendations have been proposed. Some of these had already occurred to me and were not adopted, others have proved interesting and illuminating but did not qualify for incorporation in an edition conceived on the lines of the present one: all have rendered assistance which I gratefully acknowledge. I have tried to take due account of them in the Commentary and to exploit them for exegetical purposes, my aim being to explain, as far as I can, a text which, in spite of its obscurities—and no doubt often because of them—continues to hold the attention of students and critics. I have therefore been led to give priority to explanatory comment and to leave aside for the present a more detailed treatment of the questions of authorship, date, language and general Tristan problems. To the same end I have made a liberal use of translation, which I have kept as literal as possible, even at the risk of some loss in readability.

I fully share the indebtedness of successive generations of scholars to Muret's editions, and not least to the first, published in 1903 for the Société des Anciens Textes Français, and of course to the fundamental and imperishable publications of Joseph Bédier.

Of the colleagues to whom I owe both assistance and encouragement I must mention particularly Professor R. C. Johnston, who read the typescript and the proofs, and Mr. R. C. D. Perman, who also read the proofs:

both saved me from error and favoured me with constructive suggestions. To Professor T. B. W. Reid I owe valuable help in the interpretation of difficult words and constructions.

The Publisher has placed me under a heavy obligation by his kindly interest and by the patience with which he has borne my dilatoriness. To the Printers I am particulary indebted for the readiness with which they have accommodated the rules of their craft to the special requirements of this edition and for the care which they have bestowed upon its presentation.

Oct. 1969   A.E.

PUBLISHER'S NOTE

At the time of his death Professor Ewert was about to pass the proofs of this volume for press, subject to a few last corrections which I had discussed with him two days previously. To satisfy his exact scholarship he would have wished to see a last revise; in acting as his deputy I hope I have not failed him.

10th Nov. 1969   Basil Blackwell

CONTENTS

INTRODUCTION[1]

I. AUTHORSHIP

It is generally assumed that at lines 1268 and 1790 of our text the author refers to himself (in the third person) by name as *Berox* (which we may take to be the nominative form of an oblique *Berol* or *Beroul*); but this is not certain, and in any case he remains unidentified (see the notes to these lines). Muret's edition of 1903 described our romance as *Le roman de Tristan par Béroul et un anonyme.* Post-1922 editions in the Classiques français du moyen âge abandoned the assumption of dual authorship, but it continues to find its adherents, most recently in the persons of M. G. Raynaud de Lage[2] and Professor T. B. W. Reid.[3] The former based his conclusions chiefly on the nature and distribution of the rhymes and the handling of the octosyllabic couplet in the two parts[4] and on differences in the use of the direct address to the public (*Oiez!*, *Seignors!* and the like) and parenthetic interventions by the author. His arguments were reviewed seriatim by Signor Vàrvaro who, after a rapid summary of the debate from R. Heinzel to Muret and beyond, concluded that the case for dual authorship as stated by Raynaud de Lage remained not proven. In an article published in 1965 Professor Reid produced a substantial body of evidence (chiefly details of vocabulary and style) in support of the thesis of dual authorship.

While one may concede the statistical value of such analyses, it is clear that when it comes to interpreting and

---

[1] For full details of the publications cited in abbreviated form, see the Select Bibliography at the end of the Introduction. For other abbreviations and sigla, see pp. 58–59.

[2] In *Le Moyen Age*, 1958.   [3] In *Mod. Lang. Rev.*, 1965.

[4] The second part beginning, as originally proposed by Muret, at l. 3028; alternatively at l. 2754.

seeking to account for the relative prevalence or absence of certain features of pronunciation, vocabulary, syntax, versification and style, the proponents of dual authorship are constrained to rely very largely on subjective judgements. This has been well brought out by Vàrvaro, and Mlle Hanoset has shown how the application of Raynaud de Lage's criteria to the romances of *Erec*, *Cligés* and *Yvain* produces similar results and similar presumptions of dual or multiple authorship.[1] One hesitates to think what might result if a similar comparison were undertaken of other and smaller sections of the Beroul text with each other: we might find ourselves back at the stage represented by R. Heinzel's 'cantilène' theory of multiple authorship.

In the last resort such comparisons between two parts of the Beroul text are inspired and conditioned by the fact that, whereas the first 2752 lines show a close correspondence, both in general and in detail, between Beroul and Eilhart (see below), the latter part of Beroul (ll. 3028–4485) differs radically from Eilhart and all other versions, although showing here and there a familiarity with one or more of them. Moreover, the contradictions and inconsistencies which the narrative presents are by no means completely accounted for by a presumed dual authorship, since they are to be found within each of the two parts, and there remains the problem of the attribution of the link passage (ll. 2765–3027) and of the so-called interpolations (ll. 1656–1746 and 3985–4072).

Various explanations of the differences between Beroul and Eilhart have been advanced, and it has perhaps been too readily assumed that when they differ it is not Eilhart who deviates. It has also been suggested that the latter part of our text was composed by Beroul after an interval

[1] It should however be noted that Raynaud de Lage, in a further article (*Le Moyen Age*, 1961), questions the validity of Mlle Hanoset's procedure and of M. Delbouille's concurrence in it (*Rom.*, 1960). F. Lecoy *Rom.*, 1959 and *Rom.*, 1965) agreed with Raynaud de Lage's conclusions.

of many years or by a collaborator or pupil of his. Yet it is equally possible that certain changes in manner and treatment are attributable not to the passage of time but to a change of source or merely of preoccupation and manner of composition.[1]

For present purposes I therefore confine myself to a commentary on the relevant passages, the more readily as I find myself on the side of Signor Vàrvaro.[2] His demonstration and that of Mlle Hanoset confirm the view which determined my conservative editorial procedure, namely that the version preserved in B.N. MS fr. 2171 is probably the work of a single author and that its contradictions and inconsistencies are chiefly attributable to his having composed his romance by episodic instalments (possibly corresponding to successive sessions in its public recital), each treated in a knowledge of current variations in the narrative and showing the eclectic procedure of a poet with an independent and strongly marked personality.[3]

II. VERSIFICATION

Our poem is written entirely in rhyming octosyllabic couplets, which frequently show a departure from the older practice of avoiding a break in sense or construction elsewhere than at the end of the couplet. In this the poet continues a practice which would seem to have been

---

[1] Mrs. Whitteridge, in an article contributed to the *Vinaver Miscellany* (1965), arrived independently at the same general conclusion as Vàrvaro and went on to show how Beroul might have been led into the major contradictions and inconsistencies, and reduces them to their just proportions. A similar view had been expressed by M. K. Pope in 1913.

[2] Since the above was written A. Holden has contested, in the article mentioned in the Bibliography, Professor Reid's findings and has strengthened the case for single authorship. His article also contributes some discerning remarks on Beroul's syntax, which the scribe of MS fr. 2171 is not alone in having found baffling or misleading.

[3] The article published by M. Le Gentil in *Romance Philology*, 1953–4, is particularly relevant and telling in this connection.

initiated by Chrétien de Troyes, and it has been argued that Beroul must therefore postdate Chrétien and more specifically his *Erec*, in which this departure is first observed. Professor Frappier has recently demonstrated tellingly (in *Romania* LXXXVI (1965), pp. 1–21) the literary implications of this innovation, and we might add that they are fully exploited by Beroul.

Beroul's reluctance to be bound by traditional rules is reflected in other 'irregularities'. On two occasions the same rhyme is found in consecutive couplets (725–8, 2703–6),[1] to which one might add ll. 1117–20 and 1891–4, having regard to the attested reduction of *ui* in the language of the poet (655–6, 851–2, 2017–8, 4437–8), and possibly 2315–8 and 3947–50, where the scribe would seem to have omitted a (fourth) line or incorporated a variant (third) line.

Having regard to the fact that the poet appears upon occasion to have been content to link two lines by mere assonance (e.g. 331–2, 2627–8 (?); and perhaps 2821–2, 3579–80), it is difficult to decide what significance is to be attached to the much more numerous instances where the rhymes of two or more successive couplets have the same tonic vowel followed by consonants which are either similar (e.g. 1051–4 *-ois* : *-oiz*; 713–8 *-oit* : *-ois* : *-oit*; 1205–8 *-ier* : *-iers*; 2061–4 *-ist* : *-iz*) or dissimilar, or are distinguished by a feminine *-e* (543–6 *-ier* : *-iere*; 1563–6 *-is* : *-ise*; 2925–30 *-oie* : *-oi* : *-oie*).

As preserved in the MS, our text shows a large number of 'repetitive' rhymes (commonly called 'identical').[2] Ten of these are instances of homoeoteleuton and have accordingly been corrected:—974 (cf. 1010), 1392 (cf. 1390 and 2347), 1553, 1693, 1892, 3462, 4000, 4086; also

[1] This feature is found in Norman and particularly Anglo-Norman, where the same rhyme may be employed in more than two consecutive couplets (e.g. *Gui de Warewic*, 10431–50).
[2] See the illuminating article by P. Rickard, 'Semantic Implications of Old French Identical Rhyme', *Neuphilologische Mitteilungen* LXVI (1965), 355–401, where references to earlier contributions will be found.

418 and 4066, where some corruption of the text is involved.

Of the 'repetitive' rhymes classified by Rickard as 'homonymic', our text shows a considerable number in which the two rhyme-words are 'of different origin and therefore different meaning' (Rickard's B2), which were regarded as legitimate in the literary usage of the time and which are clearly attributable to the poet:—1121, 1969, 2203, 2577, 2793, 3429, 3611, 3745, 3777, 4293; to which may be added 2863 (*sueffre*, vb. : *soffre*, subst.) and 3489 (*foiz* : *fois*).

'Repetitive' rhymes linking words of the same origin but differing in meaning or grammatical function are of similar frequency:—1381, 1849, 1871, 2001, 2181, 2571, 2651, 3347, 3613, 3785, 3909, 4363; to which one might add 3177 (*l'aseüre* : *aseüre*) and perhaps 2557 (*Irlande* : *Horlande*). Such rhymes were also regarded as legitimate and are preserved in Muret's editions. (M⁴ restores the MS reading at 2571 and 3177, which had been emended in M⁰.)

The remaining 'repetitive' rhymes are 'identical' in the strict sense of the term:—193, 1301, 1783, 2121, 3057, 3421, 3677, 3963, 4079. Editors of Old French texts have in the past tended to condemn such rhymes as scribal imperfections and to resort to emendation. But we cannot be certain that such identical rhymes were not tolerated if 'the grammatical or functional implications were different' or that the poet was not 'concerned to produce a simple figure of iteration'[1] and motivated by rhetorical considerations. Alternatively, he may have allowed himself the licence of maintaining such imperfections.

Bearing this in mind, modern editors are inclined to

---

[1] Cf. Robert Browning's *Pippa Passes*, Part II, six lines from the end:
> Some unsuspected isle in the far seas!

and the last two lines:

> Some unsuspected isle in the far seas!
> Some unsuspected isle in far-off seas!

allow the MS reading to stand in such cases, and it is significant that, whereas M⁰ emended at lines 1301, 2121, 3057, 3421, 3677, the MS reading is restored in M⁴. At l. 957 there is obviously scribal corruption and I have adopted a reading which keeps as close as possible to the MS.

There is a similar number of instances of rhymes between a simple word and its compound:—*retraire* : *traire* 483, 3349; *saine* : *ensaigne* 731; *assez* : *sez* 1941; *voie* : *convoie* 2929; *vint* : *avint* 4409; *tost* : *tantost* 4397. Such rhymes were freely admitted in Old French, as was also the rhyming of two compounds of the same root:— *parçoivre* : *deçoivre* 2111.

Of the lacunae which may be observed or inferred the majority are clearly attributable to our scribe, but some may be the result of the 'episodic' method of composition of the poet, the lacuna representing a break in the narrative, corresponding perhaps to the end of an instalment of the public recital. Leaving aside those portions of the MS which are wholly or partly illegible (13–15, 45–48, 81–82, 111–16, 255–8), we may postulate the omission of one or more couplets at the following points:—208–9 (resulting in corruption of 208; cf. Eilhart), 1174–5, 2495–6, 2836–7, 2866–7, 3224–5, 4313–4. Between 1055 and 1056 the scribe would seem to have omitted one or more couplets, unless one accepts one or other of the emendations indicated in the Notes. At 3171 the suppression of *Q'* as a scribal error would make the postulation of a lacuna unnecessary, and at 2821–2 it is possible that the poet allowed the assonating *faire* : *moleste* to stand and that there is no lacuna.

The scribe's omission of single lines has left the couplet incomplete at the following points:—343, 534, 1795, 2599, 3941, 4078, 4213, 4445. At 697–8 he appears to have misread 698 in his source and produced two versions, both imperfect, while at 1834–5 he added (or transcribed from his source) a supernumerary line repeating *destrier* of l. 1833. On two occasions the omission of a line occurs when two successive couplets have the same rhyme:—2315–8, 3947–50.

In addition to the instances of homoeoteleuton already mentioned, scribal corruption or distortion of rhyme-words or their replacement by other words must be assumed in some 105 instances, and these I have corrected in the light of a close study of the scribe's practice and habits (see *Pope Miscellany*, pp. 88–98). About half of these affect single letters (including intrusive final -*s* and involving a change of tense in a dozen instances), and in some 50 instances the scribe has replaced the rhyme-word by another, of which some 40 may be described as palaeographically motivated.

III. LANGUAGE

The vast majority of our poet's rhymes are 'normal' in the sense that they conform to the regular phonetic development of what is called Central French or Francien of the latter part of the twelfth century and the beginning of the thirteenth; but his practice shows, in large measure, the 'tolérances' which characterize the standard literary language of the time. Of such are:—

(*a*) Variant forms of particular words:—

pitié : *pechié* 1549, etc.
pité : *trové* 2023, : *Damledé* 909.
reigné (scribal for *reignié*) : *menacié* 3500.
reigné : *esté* 2566.
quitié : *pechié* 2346.
aquiter : *parler* 227, *aquité* : *herité* 3272, etc.
degiez : *plungiez* [3843].
deget : *vaslet* [3932].
sanglent : *gesant* 4404. (No rhyme showing unlowered
    $\bar{e}$.)

molanc : *fanc* 3793. (No rhyme showing unlowered *ẽ*.)
talent : *omnipotent* 31, : *mandement* 2283.
talent : *dedenz* 1750.
(*h*)*us* (< *ŪSTIUM) : *lasus* [1209], : *plus* 528, 1492. (No rhyme showing *ui*.)
bois : *vois* 595, : *blois* 2762.
bos : *os* 2597.
estait : *fait* 1700. (No rhyme showing *esta*.)
fut : *dut* 821, : *connut* 2059.
fu : *feru* 3548.
ostel : *el* 507. (But see below, No. 2.)
ostal : *Governal* 3577.
huz : *paluz* 3699. (No rhyme showing *hus*.)
plaignes : *conpaignes* 4028. (No rhyme showing *plaine*.)
mervelle : *selle* 3799.
merville : *vile* [2456].
tristre : *magistre* 345. (No rhyme showing *triste*.)
celestre : *destre* 4161. (No rhyme showing *celeste*.)
vie : *druerie* 129, : *die* 4254, etc.
vite : *ermite* 1422, : *merite* 1120.

The poet avails himself of (or creates) variant forms of the following proper names:—

Tristran : *ban* 1431, etc.
Tristrain : *anjen* 407 (?) (See notes to ll. 5 and 407.)
Frocin : *matin* 320, etc.
Frocine : *roïne* 469, 1349; : *espine* 1327.
Loenois : *mois* [2310].
Loenoi : *toi* 2868.[1]
Morrois : *voirs* 2090.
Morroi : *moi* 1900.[1]

---

[1] *Loenoi* and *Morroi* are to be interpreted as oblique forms created by analogy, but *Loenois* and *Morrois* are also used as oblique forms. Within the line the scribe uses only *Morrois*, and in every case as an oblique form (1275, 1648, 1662, 2127).

(*b*) Variant pronunciations representing either dialectal features or features which are survivals of an earlier pronunciation.

A. *Vowels*

1. Palatalization of *a* before *ts* (and *tš*) would account for *trace* : *berserece* 1581. This is a specifically Eastern trait but is attested sporadically from other regions (cf. Pope, p. 494).

2. The rhyme *ostal* : *Governal* (3577, 4299) points to the S.W. It is possible that *ostel* (: *el* 507, 3609; : *sel* 1297) is scribal for the poet's *ostal* since the alternative forms *al* and *sal* are normal in the S.W. and occur sporadically in N.W. and in Anglo-Norman texts.

3. The nom. sg. of *tel* appears as *tex* (: *Dex* 377) and this may be an example of the widespread effacement of praeconsonantal *l* after *e* (<tonic free *a*); cf. *Dé* : *armé* 803, etc. (See Pope, § 391 and Suchier, 17c, 22b); an alternative interpretation is *t(i)eus* : *D(i)eus* (cf. Suchier, 61b).

4. *set* (<SAPIT) is linked with the analogical pple. *ameit*[1] at l. 69; elsewhere it rhymes with *het* (511, 561, 1687).

5. In linking *afaire* with *mare* (3615) the poet may be availing himself of dialectal pronunciation[2] or of an archaic survival. The latter is more likely if we accept *faire* : *moleste* (2821) as representing an assonance.

6. The reduction of blocked *ai* to *ę* is amply attested (*plest* : *forest* 1881, etc.). The analogical 3 sg. pres. ind. of *ester* appears once in rhyme:—*estait* : *fait* 1699.

7. The linking of *ie* with *e* is found, not only in the doublets or alternative forms mentioned above, but in *depeciez* : *rez* 1019; *depecier* : *per* 1041 (beside *depecier* : *l'ier*

---

[1] Such forms are found in E. and N.E. French and also in Anglo-Norman (cf. Fouché, *Le Verbe français*, p. 351).

[2] The original pronunciation *ái* is retained rather late in N. dialects; cf. Pope, § 533. M³ cites a form *maire* from a Norman document (Godefroy X, 123).

811); *soudeier* : *loer* 2669; and perhaps in *anter* (for *entier*) : *entrer* 4422.[1]

8. The reduction of *iée* to *ie*, which is characteristic of the scribe (except in *alegiee* : *meschiee* 3443–4), is nowhere attested by a rhyme in our text.

9. Various rhymes suggest that the change blocked *ẹ* > *ẹ* had already taken place or was taking place in the language of the poet:—*met* : *est* 2049, : *atret* 4407; *berseret* : *prez* 1441; *brachetz* : *prez* 1457; *festes* (<Germ. *first*) : *testes* 3331; *Castele* : *sele* 3987; *Tudele* : *bele* 3409. Before *l'* we find the *e* of *merveille* rhyming on one occasion with *ẹ* (: *selle* 3799).

10. The Northern differentiation of *eau* to *iau* is exemplified by the rhymes *roiaume* : *Dureaume* 2231, : *Durelme* 4263. On the wide dissemination of this feature in later twelfth-century texts, see G. Wacker, *op. cit.* Note that *joiaus* (: *meseaus* 3772) is the plural of *joiel* (cf. G. Paris, in *Rom.* XXII, 617).

11. Tonic *ẹ* + yod > *i*, which rhymes only with itself (*pire* : *eslire* 1187 etc.) or with *ui* (*pris* : *puis* 4437, etc.).

12. *ei* rhymes with *oi* on only two occasions:—*conbatroient* : *oient* (<AUDIANT) 3261 and *gerroie* : *joie* 2925;[2] possibly also in *rois* : *lois* (<LUSCUS ?) 2813 (emended by Muret to *voirs*). Other apparent instances are clearly due to scribal corruption and have been emended (921, 3071, 3783, 4017). For *esquoi* (: *amedoi*) see the note to l. 1678.

13. There are a considerable number of instances of free *ọ* rhyming with blocked *ọ*: in *jor* (25, etc.: 17 examples), *tor* (: *veneor* 3149), *retor* (: *chaceor* 3551), *entor*

---

[1] Muret tentatively proposed (in M⁰ glossary) emendation to *et soudeer* (vb.). As for *anter*, it is true that elsewhere the poet uses the form *entier* (452, 3031, 3432, 3967), i.e. the form with analogical suffix -*ier* (for etymological *entir*). The existence of an alternative *enter* (under the influence of *enterin*, etc. ?) would seem to be attested in *Erec* 1154 var. Muret's emendation of the scribe's *ancer* to *Li ber* is conjectural. It would seem more prudent to class these two instances with the certain *ie* : *e* rhymes and interpret them in the way proposed by Bédier in *Rom.* XLVII, 465, and *Roland* II (Commentaires p. 291), viz. as poetic licences.

[2] Readings rejected in M⁰, but restored in M⁴.

(: *flor* 3593), *dedesoz* (: *noz* 3301), *seceure* (: *eure* 3231), *fole* (: *sole* 3879), *cort* (: *avot* 209), or with the *o* of *nos*, *vos* (225, etc.; 10 examples); cf. *estros* : *vos* 513 and *sous* : *vos* 389.

14. There is one example of free *ǫ* rhyming with blocked *ǫ* (*dolors* : *cors* 843), which may be due to the opening influence of the following *r*. The evidence would indicate a monophthongal pronunciation (*u*) for the product of tonic free *ǫ*. The levelling of *ou* (<*ǫ*) is characteristic of the Western region; cf. Pope § 230 (i).

15. Blocked *ǫ* rhymes with free *ǫ* on one occasion (*mole* : *vole* 4479), with *eu* (<*ǫl* before cons.) in *fors* : *deus* (nom. sg. of *duel*) 1455.

16. There are two examples of the rhyme blocked *ǫ* : blocked *ǫ*:—*desconfort* : *cort* 1211, *loche* : *boche* 3821.[1]

17. The effacement of praeconsonantal *l* after *ǫ* is indicated by the rhyme *Morhout*[2] : *javelot* 855, and perhaps also by *destot* : *estot* 3101; cf. Pope § 391.

18. Free *ǫ*+atonic *u* appears in the MS as *eu* and rhymes with itself (*feu* : *queu* 1295; : *leu* 1429); on one occasion it rhymes with *ü* (*feu* : *vestu* 153).

19. *ue* (<*ǫ*) when brought into contact with *u* (<*l* or *l'*+consonant) likewise appears as *eu*, which rhymes with itself (*veus* : *deus* (nom. sg. of *duel*) 405; *veut* : *Iseut* 607, 829, 2117, 2659, 2673; *seut* : *Yseut* 3775; *deus* (nom. sg. of *duel*) : *chevreus* 1425), with *ę*+*u* (<*l* before consonant) (*deus* : *eus* 1993), with *ǫ* in *fors* (: *deus* 1455), and with *eu* in *porseut* : *aqeut* (<AD-COLLIGIT through a stage *akueut*) 2155.

20. Free *ǫ* (graphies *ue*, less frequently *o*) normally rhymes with itself only (*pueple* : *moble* 955), but on one occasion with blocked *ǫ* (*vole* : *mole* 4479).

21. *ǫ*+yod appears in the MS as *ui* and rhymes with

---

[1] The quality of the *o* of *mot* varied, the pronunciation with close *o* predominating in the S.W.:—*mot* : *tot* 65, 398; *moz* : *toz* 216; *mot* : *dot* (<DŪBITET) 3333.

[2] The scribe writes *Morhout* (28, 848, 855) or *Morhot* (136, 2038).

itself (*ennuit* : *nuit* 2819; *ennui* : *pui* 3145, 3469, : *sui* 2421; *ancui* : *sui* 3225), with the sound resulting from ū + yod (*nuit* : *quit* (*CŪGITO) 721, and with *i* (see below).

22. The reduction of *üi* to *ẅi* is attested by the rhymes *nuit* : *lit* 655; *lui* : *hardi* 851, : *endormi* 2017; *puis* : *pris* 4437 (cf. *puis* : *ruis* 1407).[1] This reduction is reflected in the graphies *aprisme* (< *apruisme*) 3, and *aprime* (: *dime* 3563); but *ui* also rhymes with *ü* in the following instances:— *pertus* : *nus* 4321; *us* (< *ŪSTIUM): *plus* 527, 1491, : *lasus* [1209].[2]

23. ǫ + yod > ǫi, which rhymes with ǫi (< ǫ + yod) in *angoise* : *parroise* 1433 and *doiz* (< DŬCTUS) : *jagloiz* (< GLADIŎLUS) 4317. The form *anoie* (: *joie* 1007) shows the weak form of the radical by analogy; cf. *apoie* : *ennoie* (for *apuie* : *ennuie*) 3927. The interpretation of the rhyme *amedoi* : *esquoi* 1677 is rendered difficult by the obscurity of the form *esquoi*. Assuming that it is a compound of *coi* (Suchier proposed the emendation to *recoi*), the normal result would be *esquei in the West, which would have evolved to *esquoi* in Central French. According to Suchier (p. 95) *oi* for *ei* is found in Norman texts only in *coi* (< QUIĒTUM) and *coivre* (< CŬPREUM), but with close ǫ; and he explains these forms as a development of earlier *cuei*, *cueivre*; *amedoi* could be explained as a remodelling on the oblique *dous*. Yet at l. 3312, we have *coie* rhyming with *voie*, and it would therefore seem possible to accept the pronunciation *esquoi* and equate the rhyme with that of *angoise* : *parroise*. See note to l. 1678.

24. The nasal vowels ã and ẽ are linked in rhyme only in the following instances:—(*mal*)*talent* : *meslant* 539, : *itant* 2363, : *alent* 3533, beside (*mal*)*talent* : *omnipotent* 31, : *dedenz* 1749, : *mandement* 2283, : *acordement* 2225, : *entent*

---

[1] For the rhyme *cuite* : *voitre* 3685, see below, No. 28, note 2.

[2] The change *üi* < *ẅi* is in the main a thirteenth-century change, but it took place earlier in the S.W., while in the N.E. it was late and the reduction was to *ü* (Pope, §§ 515–7); the latter is, however, found also in Western texts, where it resulted from the absorption of glide *i* from final palatalized *s* by the preceding *ü*.

3217; *sanglent* : *gesant* 4403; *sarmenz* : *tenant* 869; *durement*
: *maintenant* 3841; *molanc* : *fanc* 3793; *ensenble* : *chanbre*
597; *prenent* : *chanbre* 771. The rhyming of $\tilde{e}$ with $\tilde{a}$ would
not be expected in a poet hailing from the N.E., N. or
W. regions or in an A.N. writer; but the testimony of
the above examples is weakened by the fact that the
majority are actually attested in writers from those
regions and may be explained as recognized alternative
pronunciations or as permitted licences. *Sanglent* appears
(like *serjanz* 3023) to have been assimilated to the present
participles in *-ant*,[1] and it alternates in Norman and A.N.
texts with *sanglant*, as does also *talent* with *talant*. Muret[2]
has pointed out that *tenant* and *maintenant* sometimes
appear with etymological $\tilde{e}$. *Molanc* appears as *molenc* in
the *Roman de Thèbes* 8875, which would seem to be the
original form; but the suffix *-enc* (<Germ. *-ing*) early
began to be replaced by more common suffixes (*-ant*,
etc.), and the remodelling of the very rare word *molenc* to
molanc may have been further facilitated by the influence
of *estanc* and *fanc* (cf. M[0], p. xliii).

Before *m* the lowering of $\tilde{e}$ to $\tilde{a}$ was general in Old
French, and *ensenble* : *chanbre* 597 therefore presents a
normal rhyme in $\tilde{a}$. *Chanbre* : *prenent* 771 is probably not
to be attributed to the poet and may result from the
omission of two or more lines by the scribe or scribes.
For *cane* : *feme* 3067, see below, No. 25, note 1.

25. $\tilde{a}i$ rhymes freely with $\tilde{e}i$ and there is considerable
confusion in spelling:—*semaine* : *paine* 1597, 2163; *vaine* :
peine 2131; *laine* : *maine* 4095; *mainte* : *çainte* 1963; *remaint* :
faint 2475; *main* : *frain* 3893. Similarly $\tilde{a}i$ ($<a+n'$) rhymes
with $\tilde{e}i$ ($<\varrho+n'$):—*Montaigne* : *enseigne* 4015, *saine*
(= *saigne*) : *enseigne* 777.[3] The form *fange* (: *enseigne* 3797)
has undoubtedly been substituted by the scribe for the

---

[1] Waters, *Brendan*, p. cxlix.   [2] M[0], p. xli.
[3] The development of a glide *i* before intervocalic *n'* was fairly general
in Old French after ϱ (*enseigne* = àsẽin'ə), but after other vowels it was
a feature of E., S., and S.W. dialects (cf. Pope, §§ 408, 465).

poet's *faigne*, which is characteristic of the S.W. and
spread north as far as the Loire.[1]

It is therefore clear that *ãi* had already reached the
stage *ẽi*, and there are indications that the further development to *ẽ* had also begun although not yet generalized.
The rhyme *anjen* : *Tristrain* 407 is inconclusive: it can be
easily regularized by emendation, as applied in M⁰ (but
since abandoned), *anjen* being treated as the scribe's
rendering of *enjan* (verbal subst. from *enjaner* < *IN-
GANNARE) and his substitution of *Tristrain* for *Tristran*.
But it is possible that the poet wrote *engien*, a W. and
S.W. dialectal variant of *engin* (< INGĔNIUM)[2] and an
alternative 'popular' form *Tristrain* (found nowhere else
in the poem). On the other hand, the form *Brengain* may
mask the poet's use of the common alternative form
Brengien at l. 523 (: *bien*) and l. 553 (: *mien*); but there
remain:—*plaine* : *rencïene* 3723, *grisens* (= *grisains*?) : *pens*
3721, *vilaine* : *reigne* 57.[3] The tendency to keep *ẽi* and *ẽ*
apart in the rhyme may therefore be interpreted as to
some extent a survival of an earlier (real) distinction; a
more striking archaism is the linking of *ãi* and *a* in
mains : *francs* 3323.[4]

26. *ïẽ* rhymes with *ẽ* (*esscïent* : *maltalent* 521) or with
ïẽ (*lïen* : *chien* 1507, *celestïen* : *bien* 2285). *Lencïen* (*Lancïen*)
rhymes with *bien* (2394, 2437) and *Ivein* (1155), the latter
(spelt *Ivain*) rhyming with *vilain* (1265) and *main* (1219);
Urïen rhymes with *Dinoalen* [3483], which in its turn

---

[1] See Wartburg, *Frz. Etym. Wb.*, p. 410, s.v. *fani*.

[2] Cf. Andresen's edition of Wace's *Roman de Rou*, p. 520, footnote 2,
and E. Goerlich, *Die südwestlichen Dialecte der Langue d'oïl* (1882), p. 52.

[3] The loan-word *reigne* was pronounced *rẽnə*. The poet must therefore
be assumed to have used the form *fenne* (scribal *feme*) at ll. 287, 883, 1092,
[1115,] 4124 (: *reigne*) and at l. 3067 (: *cane* < Germ. *kenna*). Variants of
this form *fenne* (i.e. with -*n*- or -*nn*-) are characteristic of the S.E. region,
are frequent in the S. and are also found in the S.W. (Toulouse, etc.);
see Wartburg, *Frz. Etym. Wb.*, p. 449, s.v. FEMINA. The change *mn* > *nn*
is also found in S. Normandy (Pope, § 371:—*St. Martin* 5533, *fenne* :
Vienne).

[4] Such rhymes are attested in other poems; cf. Waters, *Brendan*, p.
cxxxix. For another explanation of the present instance, see M⁰, p. xliv.

rhymes with *suen* (4433). These rhymes would seem to lend support to the view that *ãi* and *ẽi* had by this time been currently reduced to *ẽ*.

ĩ rhymes only with itself, except *roïne* : *oïe* 2627, which suggests that the nasalization was not very marked (cf. Pope, § 455), unless there is here a lacuna in the MS, as suggested in M⁰ (though not in M⁴).

Tonic free *ǫ* before *m* or *n* appears as *ue*:—*suen* : *suen* 3745, *buen* : *suen* 2109, *buens* : *suens* 465, 2029. The rhymes *buen* : *bien* 3583[1] and *suen* : *Denoalen* 4433 suggest that the *ue* had the value *wẽ*; this was no doubt also the value of the diphthong in *loinz* (: *denz* 3165); at l. 1878, *loin* rhymes with *besoin*.

It is clear therefore that in the poet's usage *ãi*, *ẽi*, *ẽi*, *uẽ*, *ẽ* freely rhyme with each other.

B. *Consonants*

27. Among the rhymes which are 'imperfect' in respect of consonant or consonants following the tonic vowel, a certain number are 'tolérances' of which other twelfth-century poets also avail themselves:—

> *mbr* : *mbl* (*chanbre* : *ensenble* 597)
> *p* : *b* (*chape* : *gabe* 2879)
> *l'* : *l* (*mervelle* : *selle* 3799, *merville* : *vile* [2455])

The rhymes *reigne* : *vilaine* 57, : *feme* (pronounced *fẽnǝ*, see above) 287, 883, 1092 [1115], 4124, and *signe* : *roïne* 3581, are accounted for by the fact that the learned words *reigne* and *signe* were regularly pronounced with *n*. At line 4368, *poine* (: *esloigne*) is scribal for *poigne* (< PUG- NA). For *fange* (= *faigne*) : *enseigne* 3797, and *feme* : *cane* 3067, see Nos. 24 and 25.

28. On a number of occasions the poet avails himself of the common licence of neglecting *r* before a consonant:—

---

[1] For rhymes of this type, see Waters, *Brendan*, p. cxlviii and note; cf. Pope, § 478.

rs : *s* (*pas* : *ars* 1099, 1499; *fiers* : *niés* 1103; *fors* : *deus* 1455, : *dos* 2051; *voirs* : *Morrois* 2089; *mes* : *ners* 3847).

The poet links *Artus* (nom.) with *seürs* (3273, 3701), *tafurs* (3345), and also with *plus* (3285, 4025), *druz* (4109); *Artur* (obl.) with *seür* (obl. sg. 3397, for nom. sg. 3495), *mur* (649), *asur* (4251). Within the line the scribe always uses *Artur* as an oblique form, *Artus* generally as a nom. (16 exs.), but occasionally for the oblique (8 exs.).[1]

rt : *t* (*cort* : *avot* 209, *vet* : *sert* 4343).

The poet also links *tr* with *t*:—*metre* : *regrete* 1943, *voitre* : *cuite* 3685.[2] He also uses the current alternative forms *tristre* (: *magistre* 345) and *celestre* (: *destre* 4161).

29. *-che* : *-ce*. The rhyme *sace* (scribal for *sache*) : *enbrace* 2803 implies the Northern pronunciation *embrache*.[3] This derives some support from the rhyme *biches* (dialectal for *bisses*) : *chiches* 3021. At l. 3965, the very plausible correction proposed by Muret implies the pronunciation *guiche* (: *apetiche*), a doublet of *guige* which is the form introduced by the scribe.

30. *-che* : *-que*. The rhyme *riche* : *tunique* 2881 indicates the characteristic Northern pronunciation *rike*.[4]

The MS shows much confusion in the notation of final dentals: -*s*, -*z* (= *ts*), *st*, *t*. The poet generally observed the twelfth-century distinctions, and many of the apparent exceptions observable in the rhymes can be explained as analogical remodellings or as tolerated

---

[1] The rhyme *premierz* : *oiez* (2531) is of doubtful authenticity.

[2] At l. 3686, *cuite* may be scribal for *coite* (verbal noun from *coitier* (< *cŏctare*?) under the influence of *cuite* (< *cŏcta*) and rhyming with the alternative form *vuitre* (see the examples in Godefroy). The phonetic history of *voitrer* (and of Mod. Fr. *vautrer* < *volutulare*) is very confused; but the poet's rhyme was probably *coite* : *voitre*, the latter showing (according to Pope, p. 504) the S.W. palatalization of praeconsonantal *l* and its reduction to *i*.

[3] Cf. M⁰, p. xlviii. It is possible, however, that *sace* is what the poet wrote, since in the Western region *sache* was replaced by *sace* under the influence of *face*; cf. Pope § 957.

[4] Cf. Pope, p. 487.

variants; but there remain a number of imperfect rhymes which are attributable to a relaxed articulation of *s* in final or praeconsonantal position, the equivocal role of final -*s* as a sign of the decadent declensional system, and the poet's utilization of dialectal pronunciations. I have therefore been reluctant to introduce into the text the regularizing and uniformizing emendations which suggest themselves in many instances and which are indicated for the most part in what follows or in the Notes.

31. -*s* : -*ʒ*(= *ts*). The poet normally maintains the distinction between these endings. Most of the apparent exceptions are to be explained as analogical remodellings:—*seʒ* (: *priveʒ* 1907) and *doiʒ* (: *foiʒ* 2943) show -*ʒ* by analogy with verbs which regularly have -*ʒ* in the 2nd sg. (e.g. *croiʒ* : *foiʒ* 411) and they are regularly employed by Chrétien de Troyes; *retiens* (: *criens* 2871) may be scribal for a similar analogical *retienʒ*;[1] the form *druʒ* (: *Artus* 4109) may be scribal for *drus* (formed on *dru*), and *pans* (: *frans* 3019) may be similarly explained; *soutiʒ* (: *filʒ* 1939) results from the common substitution of -*il* (= *l'*) for -*il* (<ILEM), and the same change accounts for *gentis* (for *gentiʒ*) : *endormis* 2105. *Pais* always rhymes in -*s*, although the scribe frequently writes -*ʒ* (*peʒ* : *jameʒ* 621, etc.); *plaiʒ* (: *palais* 1863) is no doubt scribal for *plais* formed on *plai*.

Tristrans (nom.) appears twice in rhyme (: *chans* 1423, : *ahans* 1637); *Tristran* appears as the oblique form on nine occasions and as the nominative on two (1717, 2901).[2] *Tristranʒ* appears once only in the MS, viz. at l. 2960, where the scribe would appear to have created the form to rhyme with *enfanʒ*, wrongly substituted by him for the poet's correct nom. pl. *enfant*. M⁰ emended to *enfant* : *Tristrant*,[3] but M⁴ restores the MS reading.

---

[1] Alternatively the past participle *criens* (for *crienʒ*) may be an analogical form created under the influence of -*s* participles (e.g. *sous*< SOLSUM), or the poet may have written *retien* : *crient*.

[2] For *Tristrain* (407), see above, No. 25.

[3] A form found nowhere else in the MS.

There would further remain as imperfect rhymes:—
deduis : *Malpertis* 4285 and *premierz* : *oiez* 2531 (the
authenticity of which is doubtful) and *foiz* : *fois* 3489. In
any case such occasional linkings of *-s* with *-z* can be
paralleled from writers like Chrétien de Troyes and are
to be classed as tolerated imperfections, or dialecta-
lisms reflecting the early reduction of *-ts* to *-s* in N.
dialects.

32. *-t* : *-z* (= *ts*). In a number of instances the MS
links these sounds. Some of them can be attributed to the
scribe with certainty:—*couchiez* (for *couchiet*) : *chiet* 1815,
fonz (for *font*) : *mont* 3809. Others were eliminated by
emendation in M⁰ (but not in M⁴):—*berseret* (: *prez* 1441)
resulting from a misinterpretation of *berserez* as a nominative and the creation of an oblique form *berseret* which
the scribe substituted for the author's *berserez*;[1] *mesfez*
(: *vet* 2171) corrected to *mesfet*; *dedanz* : *decent* (3383),
dedenz : *garnement* (4023), : *talent* (1749); *sarmenz* : *tenant*
(869). At l. 3278, *baniz* (: *dit*) must be attributed to the
poet as a mistake in declension (*banit*) corrected by the
scribe or as an approximate rhyme.

33. *-st* : *-t*. While the regular effacement of *s* before
voiced consonants is attested by such a rhyme as *meïmes* :
dimes (599), its effacement before a voiceless consonant is
quite exceptional:—*est* : *met* 2049, *dist* : *abit* 2267. A
further example may be furnished by *fist* : *bolli* 2139,
where the poet may have resorted to a form *bollit* with
analogical *-t*. The form *donst* (: *respont* 505, : *mont* 2185)
may be scribal for the alternative and regular *dont* (not
found anywhere in the MS).

34. *-t* : (-). Unsupported final *t* (and *d*) had long since
ceased to be sounded.[2] Apparent exceptions affect forms
of the 3 pret. and past participle with analogical *-t*:—
fut (: *dut* 821) (cf. *fu* : *feru* 3547), *oït* (: *dit* 459), *pendit*

---

[1] The MS shows *berseret* (as a nom.) on two occasions (1551, 2697).
[2] See G. Straka, 'Sur la date de l'amuïssement du *-t* final non appuyé
en ancien français', *Mélanges Gardette*, 449–68.

(: *escrit* 2649);[1] *banit* (: *petit* 1883), *gerpi*[t] (: *escrit* 2503).[2]

35. Supported final -*t* persists, although the supporting consonant may have been vocalized or lost:—*plait* (<PLAC(I)TUM) : *desfait* 1158, etc., but its effacement is a Southern trait which is found in S.W. dialects (cf. Pope, p. 504) and also in Norman texts:—*doi* (<DIG(I)TUM) : *roi* 1811, 2084, : *moi* 2031, 2709; (but note the obl. pl. *doiz* : *estroiz* 1053); *quit* (<*CŪG(I)TO) : *lui* 123, 1891, but *quit* : *nuit* 721, : *destruit* 781.

On two occasions the poet links -*st* with -*s*:—*fist* : *pris* 2209, *froidis*[t] : *vis* 3167.

C. *Declension*

36. The breakdown of the two-case system, though much less advanced than the scribe's handling of it would suggest, is reflected in a considerable number of 'mistakes' guaranteed by rhyme or, less conclusively, by syllable-count.[3] The majority of these consist in the use of the masc. obl. sg. for the nom. sg. form in -*s*:—*roi* 109, *losengier* 1060, *mal* 1343, *chastel* 2798, *penon* 3603, *siglaton* 3868, *covert* (?) 4313, *mariage* 126, *corage* 2270, *terme* 3564 (but *termes* 2494, 3447), etc. etc.

This appears often to have been induced by special circumstances[4] favouring the use of an oblique or un-inflected (neuter) form:—(i) Predicative use: *fol* 127, *loial* 222, *desfait* 1157, 3922, *aumosnier* 3629, *baé* 4061, *roi* 2314, *lait* 2350, *seür* 3496, *mignon* 3635, *ort* 3804, *sage* 118, 3592, 3648, *oncle* 1104. (ii) Adverbial or semi-adverbial use: *chier* 790, *lent* 1696, *seür* 2442,[5] *fort* 4048, *prochain* 4190.

---

[1] Cf. Pope § 998.   [2] See below, Nos. 48 and 50.
[3] For statistics, see M⁰, pp. li–lvi.
[4] See G. G. Laubscher, *The syntactical causes of case-reduction in Old French* (Princeton, 1921); *Brendan*, ed. E. G. R. Waters, pp. clxiv–clxvi; B. Woledge, 'La déclinaison des substantifs dans la *Chanson de Roland*', *Rom.* LXXXVIII (1967), 145–74 and XC (1969), 174–201.
[5] At ll. 1661–2 the obl. pl. *eschis* (for nom. pl. *eschif*) was corrected by emendation (*li naïf* : *eschif*) in M⁰, but M⁴ restores the MS reading. At 2802 the obl. *gré* may be interpreted as an instance of the oblique used as

(iii) Used predicatively with an impersonal verb or as the 'logical' subject: *fait* 671, *gent* 1098, *bel* 3242, *voir* 4305, *meschoiet* 1809, *dit* 3044, *asouagié* 3179, *fin* 1346.[1] (iv) After *sembler*: *contret* 3622, *ome* 1874; after *faire que*: *vilains* 900; after *devenir*: *noir* 1068.

The substitution of the oblique for the nominative affects proper names earlier and more extensively than it does common nouns, and our poet conforms in this to the general practice of writers of the latter half of the twelfth century. The rhymes show that the distinction between nom. *Artus* (3274, 3285, 3346, 4026, 4109) and the obl. *Artur* (649, 3398, 3495, 4251) is correctly observed. In eight other instances nom. *-s* forms of proper names are correctly used, while the oblique form is substituted for the nominative in twenty (41, 278, etc.).

The oblique form is used for the vocative on three occasions (238, 2288, 2333), the nominative somewhat more frequently (845, 907, 2699, 2811, 2829, 3403, 3538). After exclamatory *es vos* the nominative occurs at l. 3702 and the oblique at ll. 570 and 2101.

37. The rhymes do not reveal the use of the nom. sg. in *-s* for the oblique, except *filz* (1939) and possibly *fulliers* (1838) and *pensis* (139), or of the obl. pl. in *-s* for the nom. pl., except *certains* (1242) and *dras* (3512).[2]

After impersonal (*il i*) *a* the poet, in common with other writers, employs the nom. (137, 3426, 4175), beside the oblique (209, 581, 879, 2056(?), 2058, 3499, 3711); both in l. 3426; cf. Sneyders de Vogel, *Syntaxe historique*, § 186.[3]

---

a dative (= *a vostre gré*), and the same interpretation would apply to *vostre pleisir* (2604).

[1] At l. 2089, *voirs* may be, as suggested in M⁰, p. lvii, the adjective used as a substantive; cf. *ce est grant deus* (1425).

[2] At l. 2918 the form *pensis* may be an obl. pl. agreeing with the poet's *tanz cuers* (replaced by scribal *tant cuer*?), and at 2865–6 *saus* : *chaus* may be scribal for *sauf* : *chauf*. At 3877 *Andrez* : *nez* may also be scribal, the uninflected form *Andret* having been used by the poet to form a compound subject with *lui* and rhyming with a correct nom. pl. *net*.

[3] The nominative appears regularly after *tenir por* (1178) and *avoir a non* (1444).

38. Our poet, like other Old French writers, treats the polite *vous* as grammatically either singular (390, 905, 2381) or plural (54, 3592); cf. notes to ll. 856-7.

39. Exceptions to the rule that the past participle conjugated with *estre* agrees with the subject are not unknown in Old French (cf. Sneyders de Vogel, § 286), and our poem presents examples of this at ll. 1019 (?), 2425, 3205, 3272(?), 3547(?). Reflexive verbs show no such exception (cf. 98, 233, 2129, 2346, 3204). If conjugated with *avoir*, the participle may remain uninflected or agree with the direct object, particularly when the latter precedes (96, 103, 234, etc.), but there are instances of non-agreement (153, 362, 960, 2130, 2728).

40. Feminine substantives of the Latin third declension appear without -*s* in the nom. sg. (17 instances), except:— *dolors* 844, *fois* 3490, *paluz* 3700,[1] *doiz* 4317, and *pitiez* 1227.

41. The rhymes attest no instance of the restoration of the final consonant of the stem before flexional -*s*, such as the scribe's practice shows. Thus:—*hauberc* (: *merc*) 2771, *haubers* (: *sers*) 3007; *loncs* (: *nons*) 3227, etc.

42. The imparisyllabic declension is also in process of disruption, as can be seen from the evidence of both rhyme and syllable-count. The oblique singular forms are occasionally used for the nom. sg.:—*home* 188, 4205, *felon* 470, *pastor* [3974]. An analogical nom. sg. is formed by adding -*s* to the oblique form:—*garçons* 3888 and perhaps *Guenelons* [3462].

The nominatives *ber*, *pire*, *sire*, *Saisne*, *fel* are dissociated from the obl. sg. and the plural forms, and are treated as independent words which tend to be used adjectivally:—*ber* 834, 1178, 2984; *pire*, *sire*, *Saisne* used as obl. sg. at ll. 1187, 4212, 3254 respectively; *fel* is used as a nom. sg. (862, 4401), obl. sg. (4368) and nom. pl. (121, 786, 3190, 3339, 4222), while the analogical *feus* is used as nom. sg. (3139) and obl. pl. (4466).

---

[1] Cf. *palu* : *feru* 3897. At l. 3095 the scribe added -*s* to the poet's *fin* : *chemin*).

43. Adjectives of the *grant* type normally preserve the original feminine form without *-e*: *elgal* (: *mal*) 1649, *grant* 157, 2519, etc., *paior* 1194, *quel* 643, *tel* 84, etc. The only exceptions, attested by the syllable-count, are: *crüele* 2760, *verte* 3726 (beside *vert* 4128), *dolente* (: *jovente*) 2201, *brive* (= *brieve*) 4076.

44. The poet's practice in respect of pronouns conforms closely to later twelfth-century usage, except the occurrence of *son* (: *gerredon* 2730) as tonic obl. sg. of the possessive pronoun (elsewhere *suen* 2110, etc.). The use, at l. 2347, of the obl. tonic *aus* (N. and E. dialectal equivalent of *eus* 3140, etc.) as the subject of a verb is not necessarily the poet's (cf. M⁰, p. lvi), although his fondness for what may be called a 'rhetorical' use of the tonic forms of pronouns[1] may incline one to attribute *aus* (or *eus*?) to him.

The text shows considerable confusion between *li* and *lui* (for examples see the glossary). This is mainly due to the development of the diphthong *üi* to *wi*[2] which, as we have seen above (Vowels, 22), rhymes freely with *i*. It is therefore possible that the poet made little or no distinction between the forms and was content to rely on the context to make the distinction between masc. and fem. (cf. the modern use of dative *lui* masc. or fem.). Consequently I have refrained from regularizing the two forms and have adhered to the MS reading; see below, p. 59n.

The enclitic *os* (reduction of *vos*) is a W. and S.W. feature (cf. Pope, § 832 and p. 504), which is attested in our text by the syllable-count:—*qos* 2813, *n'os* 1243, *jos* 424 and possibly 4252.

D. *Conjugation*

45. The etymological forms of the 1st sg. pres. ind.

[1] See the pertinent observations of A. Holden in *Rom.* LXXXIX (1968), 387–98.
[2] This reduction is frequent in the thirteenth century, but it is found earlier in the S.W. and in the first half of the twelfth century in W. dialects (cf. Pope, p. 501 and §§ 515–7).

of -er verbs are preserved throughout (*demor* 92, *pens* 1190, *afi* 3550, *mervel* 219, etc.), with the exception of *somelle* (: *mervelle*) 1402 and *grate* (: *escarlate*) 3728.[1]

The rhymes show no trace of analogical -*s* in the 1st sg. (*vif* 108, *croi* 1018, *sui* 2421, *voi* 2715, etc.), except *ruis* which is formed on the analogy of *puis*, with which it rhymes at l. 1407; *vois* appears regularly as the 1st sg. pres. ind. of *aler* (596, 715).[2] The 2nd sg. ending -*s* has been replaced by -*z* (by analogy with such forms as *croiz* 412) in *doiz* 2943 and *sez* 1907; for these forms and for *ves*, see above, under Consonants. The 2nd sg. imperative shows regular forms (*pren* : *sen* 2625, *talle* : *falle* 447, etc.). It is replaced by the subjunctive in *esploites* 2479 and probably by the indicative in *retiens* 2871;[3] *lai* (1st sg. of *laier*) alternates with *laise*, *lesse* (*laissier*): 667. The 3rd sg. *lait* (2092), *let* (2055, 2876) alternates with *laise* (4403). The 3rd sg. of *chaloir* always appears as *chaut* (409, 787, 981), that of *aler* as *vait* or *vet* (672, 748, 866, 959, 1285, 1123, 1521, 1707, 1711, etc.),[4] except in the compound *tresva* (: *leva* 1991), that of *ester* as *estait* (1700).[5] The ending of the 1st pl. appears as -*on* (614, 2262, 3382, 3430) or -*ons* (4060, [4063]);[6] *somes* (1554, 3117), *dimes* (600), *diromes* (599) are assured by rhyme or syllable-count[7]; for the 2nd pl. the ending -*ez*, whether etymological or analogical, is the only one attested, with the exception of

[1] *adoise* (: *prooise*) 208 is uncertain; *jure* : *aseüre* 4199–4200 may be scribal (cf. *jur* 660 and *asur* (or *aseür*) 4252).

[2] *doi* (: *roi* for *rois*) 2313 is doubtful.

[3] See above, under Consonants.

[4] On at least three occasions written *voit* (1271, 1511, 1606).

[5] At l. 350 the scribe wrote *estoit*, which I have corrected, somewhat inconsistently, to *estait*.

[6] -*on* points to the Western region, but it is encountered also in Central French. The testimony of the rhymes *conpaigno*[*n*]*s* : *ferons* (4059–60) and *connoisson*[*s*] : *bricons* (4063–4) is suspect since at l. 4059 the reference may be to Andrez only, the forester being mentioned in 4061 (hence the poet's *conpaignon* : *feron*?), and at 4064 the poet may have written *bricon*, the nom. pl., which would be regular after *tenir por* ; see No. 36 above and l. 1178.

[7] -*omes* is characteristic of the N.E. but was widespread in the twelfth century.

metroiz (: *destroiz* 2641);[1] the 3rd pl. *mengüent* is attested by the rhyme with *müent* 1645–6.

46. The sg. pres. subj. forms of *-er* verbs appear without *-e* (*ost* 2578, *envoi* 2691, *lais* 2187, *avot* 210, *criet* 1916, *plort* 1046, *ennuit* 2819, etc.), except *moigne* 1934 (beside *meint* 1959 and *ameint* 2638), *anorte* 2108, *angoise* 1434, *conmande* 2420; the 3rd subj. of *haïr* appears as *hast* (: *chast* 601), but it is possible that the poet wrote *hace* : *chace* (with analogical *-e*); for *aidier* we find regularly *aït* (628, 4201, 4310); for *aler* the alternative forms *aut* (1501, 4319) and *voist* (3454, 4321), the scribe also using the form *alle* (3344), wrongly in l. 651; the 3rd subj. of *doner* appears as *donge* and as *donst*, perhaps for *dont* (: *respont* 506, : *mont* 2186). The MS also shows the forms *doinst* (2373, 2542) and on one occasion *done* (3806); cf. also *doignes* (1222). Subjunctive forms in *-ge* (<-EAM, -IAM), which are particularly common in Norman, are assured by *donge* (: *mençonge* 292, [430], 2568, 2860) and *prenge* (: *venge* 785, : *arenge* 3924).

47. The characteristic Western form of the imperfect indicative endings of *-er* verbs is attested by the following rhymes:—*dotot* : *ot* (<AUDIT) 1746, *prioit* : *pot* 2483, *bohordot* : *pout* 3779, *amot* : *esjot* 2520, *gardoit* : *tripot* 4345. The replacement of *-out* (*-ot*) and *-ouent* (*-oent*) by *-oit* and *-oient* is abundantly reflected in the scribe's practice (e.g. in the forms *prioit* and *gardoit* just cited), but only one rhyme attests the poet's use of this ending (*devisoit* : *savoit* 323–4). For *estre* the attested imperfect forms are:— 1 *estoie* 2598, *ere* 1062; 2 *eres* 71; 3 *ert* 701, *estoit* 717; 6 *erent* 3418, *estoient* 1854: the following also appear in the text as transmitted:—3 *iere* 1112; 5 *erïez* 54, *estïez* 1005; 6 *eirent* 914; *iert* at l. 422 may be scribal for *ert*.[2]

48. A number of rhymes indicate perfects with analogical *-t* in the 3rd sg.:—*fut* 821, [1368], 1844, 2059 (cf.

---

[1] The subjunctive ending *-ez* is attested by *tendez* (: *bendez*) 4439.
[2] For *estot* (impf. of *ester*) the scribe occasionally wrote *estoit* (973, 2200).

fu : *feru* 3547–8), *oït* 460, *pendit* 2650 and perhaps *bolli*[*t*]
(: *fist* 2139). Beside *sot* (: *ot* 3208) the later analogical *sut*
is attested by the rhyme with *connut* 1541. *Aperceut* 975
for *aperçut* (cf. 367) is scribal; on the other hand *feüst*
(299, 300) beside normal *fust* (1587, etc.) seems assured
by the syllable-count.

49. The future forms of *estre* in our text are of the *serai*
type, except in the third person sg. *iert* 294, etc., *ert* 466,
etc. At l. 846 Muret's emendation *seroiz* has been adopted,
although there is no other example of this form in our
text (but cf. *metroiz* 2641, and see Notes). The syllable-
count confirms the Northern form *averez* (2340) beside
avrez (999, etc.), and the analogical *tornera* (2919) beside
torra (3461); cf. *charra* 1171, *dorra* 2920, *pardorrai* 554,
durra (*durer*) 1168, *ferrai* (*ferir*) 843, *jurra* 4161, *merrai* 1319,
parra 1252, the only form of the future shown by those
verbs; *laira* (fut. of *laier*) 296 is found beside *laisera* 515.

50. The following analogical past participles are
attested by rhymes:—*toloit* 1281 (beside *toluz* 4396), *ameit*
70 (beside *amé* 21, etc.), *meschoiet* 1809, *criens* 2872, *banit*
1884, *baniz* 3278, *gerpi* (: *escrit*) 2503. Cf. No. 34.

E. *The Counting of Syllables*

51. The unstressed final *-e* of polysyllabic words is
normally elided before words beginning with a vowel.
In 19 instances the scribe noted the elision by suppressing
-e, and this has been indicated in the edition by an apostrophe. On the other hand, the poem as preserved in the
MS, shows 26 instances of non-elision: the majority of
these occur before monosyllabic words (21 exs.), but a
few before words of two or more syllables (665, 726, 975,
1135, 3766). While it would be possible to reduce this
number by making minor emendations, it is clear that
the poet did upon occasion allow himself a licence which
can be paralleled from *L'Escoufle* (as pointed out in M[0],
p. xxxi) and other Old French poems.

For the fem. pron. *ele* the poet employed the shortened

form *el* (common in Western texts, but by no means confined to them) on 19 occasions. Before vowels it is normally written *ele*, the final *-e* being elided, except in l. 1048, but occasionally *el* (459, 1300, 2033, 3291, 4163).

The following monosyllabic words regularly show elision before a vowel:—*de*, *la* (def. art. and pron.), *le* (def. art.), *me*, *ma*, *se* (pron.), *sa*, *te*, *ta*; (*de hui* 3447 is scribal). The pron. object *le* is elided except in l. 1369 (*Araisne le, oiez comment*), where the pron. follows the verb and comes before a pronounced break in the sense (cf. *fiert l'en l'escu* 4041 and *prist l'a la main* 3157). The neg. particle *ne* (<NON) undergoes elision or is replaced by its doublet *nen* (76, 137, 1131, 1501, 2324, 2573, 4103).

52. Of the masc. nom. forms of the definite article, the singular *li* shows optional elision: before the indefinite *on* it is regularly elided; before *un* used as nominative it is elided 15 times (490, etc.), unelided once (641); before *uns* (nom.) it stands in hiatus regularly (1256, 1968, 4092, 4262); it also stands in hiatus before *hermite* (1367, 2657), *hermites* (1395, 1417, 2435, 2733), *avoirs* (466), *escriz* (2528), while it is elided before *ermite* (1393, 1398, 2428, 2492, 2741, 2885), *ermites* (2331), *autre* (1256, 3642), *anel* (2043), *evesque* (2981), *uel* (3994). As suggested in M⁰, optional elisions of this type may be due to the substitution of the acc. (*le*) for the nom. (*li*). The pl. *li* occurs eight times before a vowel and in each instance is unelided.

53. The pron. *li* (dat. sg.) is uniformly elided before *en* (<INDE) and is elided in five other instances (444, 798?, 1206, 1946, 3434); before forms of the auxiliary *avoir* it normally stands in hiatus (20 exs. against two of elision), and there are ten further instances of non-elision (1054, 2200, 2399, 2421, 2669, 2985, 3158, 3323, 3579, 4410). The pron. *ce* undergoes elision in 16 instances, including one in which the scribe failed to indicate the elision (3263), against 7 cases of non-elision; for *je* (*ge*) the figures are 35 and 17, for *ne* (<NEC) 13 and 10, for *se* (<SI) 64 (+1) and 29, for *si* (*se*) (<SIC) 12 (+1) and

16, for *que* (*qe, c'*) conj. and rel. adv. 161 (+13) and 46, for *que* (*qe, c'*) pron. 38 (+2) and 18 respectively.[1]

54. In the following instances the apostrophe denotes not elision but synizesis, i.e. the contraction of two contiguous vowels into one syllable:—*qu'i* = *qui i* 2208, *qu'il* = *qui il* 4013, *qu'il* = *qui* (*cui*) *il* 1675; (cf. *qui i* 890, *qui il* 1733, 4032). Aphaeresis of initial *e-* is to be assumed in *qui'st* (MS *quest*) 2192, *qui* (*e*)*st* 3518, *quoi* (*e*)*st* 1003, *qui* (*en*)*n* 732; (cf. *qui est* 650, 3775).

55. Enclisis, or the process whereby an unstressed word loses its vowel and combines with a preceding word, is found in the following conditions:—

> *de* + *le* produces *du* regularly, with the exception of two instances of *del* (1644, 3838);
> *de* + *les*, *a* + *le*, *a* + *les*, *en* + *les* appear throughout as *des*, *au*, *as*, *es* respectively.
> *en* + *le* produces *el* (58 exs.) or *u* (9 exs.);
> *ne* (<NON) + *le* produces *nel* (5 exs.) or *nu* (14 exs.) or *nul* (59, 663); but enclisis has not taken place in ll. 791, 1408, 1522, 3492. There is one example of *nul* = *ne li* (810);
> *ne* (<NON) + *les* produces *nes* (12 exs.), but *ne les* on two occasions (824, 825). There is one example of *nes* resulting from *ne* (<NEC) + *les* (1107);
> *je* (*ge*) + *le* normally produces *jel* (*gel*) (28 exs.), but occasionally *je le* (*ge le*) 275, 1941, 2703; while *je* (*ge*) + *les* appears regularly as *jes* (*ges*) (5 exs.).

There are few examples of enclisis after *se, si, qui, que*:—

> *sel* = *se* (<SI) + *le* 1971; *sel* = *se* (<SIC) + *le* 2542;
> *sil* = *si* (<SIC) + *le* 2467, 4427; (cf. *si le* 2420, 3079);
> *ses* = *se* (<SI) + *les* 1994; *ses* = *se* (<SIC) + *les* 1113, 3587, 3887;

---

[1] The figures in brackets signify elisions made by the poet but not indicated by the scribe.

qel = que + le 2193, 2398, 4160; (cf. *que le* 1317);
quil = qui + le 428, 952, 1282, 1643, 2435, 3662; (cf.
qui le 2139, 3902);
qui(e)s = qui + les 756, 2759, 4066; (cf. *qui les* 2826).

For *jos, n'os, qos,* see above, No. 44. There are no cases of
enclisis with *tu* or *te.*

56. The poet makes a very liberal use of the alternative
forms available to him in order to obtain the correct
number of syllables: *con(com)—conme, encor—encore, or—
ore, onc—onques, donc—donques, donc—adonc, lors—lores,
avoc—avoques, anevois—anevoies, mais—imais, ci—ici, tant—
itant, ce—ice, cil—icil, cist—icist, tel—itel, andui—amedoi,
mont—monde, verté—verité, reigne—reigné, areisne—araisone,
lait—laisse, ert—esteit.*[1]

57. I have allowed *contor* (1265) and *asur* (4252) to
stand as possible isolated instances of the reduction
conteör and *aseür,* a reduction which began in the North[2]
before the end of the twelfth century, though essentially
a thirteenth-century phenomenon in Central French.

F. *Conclusion*

The combination of archaisms and innovations revealed by a study of the rhymes and syllable-count, rein-
forced by comparison with other texts, entitles us to place
the composition of our romance in the last third of the
twelfth century. It is impossible to date it more precisely
on linguistic grounds alone.

The dialectal features[3] show a definite preponderance
of Western traits, i.e. belonging to the region lying to
the west of a line running very roughly from Rouen to
Tours, and to the north of the Loire:—

Preservation of *ei* which differentiated to *oi* in Central French. (12 and 23)
Free $\varrho > ou > u$. (14)

---

[1] For references to line-numbers, see the glossary.　　[2] Pope, p. 488.
[3] Figures in brackets refer to the linguistic analysis given on pp. 7–28.

Free *ǫ* rhyming with blocked *ǫ*. (13)
Early disintegration of the declensional system. (36)
Early loss of *-s* in the nom. sing. of feminine substantives of the Latin third declension. (40)
Imperfect indicative in *-oue*, *-oe* (<-ABAM). (47)
Present subjunctive forms in *-ge*. (46)

Possibly also:—

Early change of *ę* to *ę̣*. (9)
Early reduction of *ü̃i* to *ẅi*. (22)
Shortened form *el* for *ele*. (51)
sace for *sache*. (29)
Early substitution of 2 pl. ending *-ez* for *-oiz* by analogy. (45)

In the S.W., i.e. the extension of the Western region beyond the Loire and roughly to the line of the Charente, there developed features[1] which in some cases reflect the influence of border districts to the south of that line:—

Early change from *ãi* through *ẽi* to *ẽ*. (25)†
Development of glide *i* before intervocalic *n'* after vowels other than *a*. (25)†
Use of enclitic *os* (for *vos*). (44)†
-alem persisting as *-al*. (2)

Perhaps also:—

Palatalization of praeconsonantal *l* in *vuitre*. (28)
Effacement of final supported *-t*. (35)
mǫt. (16n)
fenne (<FEMINA). (25n)
engien (for *engin*). (25)
traallier. (See l. 1524n)

On the other hand, there are isolated features which point to the northern part of the Western region or to adjoining regions to the east:—*ca-* for *cha-* (30); *iau* for

[1] Features shared with adjoining northerly regions of the West are distinguished by an obelus.

eau (10); *fu* for *feu* (18); each of which is attested by a single example. The rhyme *sace* : *embrace* 2803 is doubtful evidence for the Northern pronunciation *embrache* (see No. 29 above), and while *porseut* (< *PROSEQUIT) is normal in the Northern dialects, it is also found in the S.W. according to Pope § 328. The evidence for the loss of *e* in hiatus with a following tonic vowel is also doubtful (see above, No. 57). None of these features justifies localization elsewhere than in the Western region and more specifically the southern part of it. They, and the other aberrant features indicated in the summary analysis (pp. 7–28), represent *tolérances* of which Beroul made a characteristically free use.

Muret (M⁰, pp. lix–lxiii) was led to conclude that the author's native dialect was 'un des parlers en usage dans la Normandie orientale, à l'est du Calvados, dans les départements de l'Eure et de la Seine-Inférieure', and to add in a footnote (p. lx): 'La Picardie occidentale n'est même pas exclue'.[1] Miss Pope, in her article of 1913, placed the home of the poet in S.W. Normandy, and in her *From Latin to Modern French* she included Beroul in the list of illustrative texts for the Western region, with the qualification '(provenance South? Norman)'. A. Holden, in his recent article (*Rom.* 89, pp. 387–98), concluded similarly that the language points to Southern Normandy and 'la région plus au sud', and that 'les textes qui offrent la plus grande parenté linguistique avec le poème de Beroul sont incontestablement le *Roman du Mont Saint Michel*, le *Livre des Manières*, le *Roman de Thèbes* et les œuvres de Benoît de Saint-Maure'. The conclusion is reasonable in its broad terms, although Gertrud Wacker[2] has demonstrated the fragility of the linguistic

---

[1] In M⁴ no mention is made of Picardy, but it is conceded that 'pour les besoins de la rime, le poète a quelquefois recouru à des formes d'un autre dialecte que le sien: participes en *-et* et *-it* (70, [1816], 1884, peut-être 3278), *conbatroient* (3262), *faigne* [3797]'.

[2] *Über das Verhältnis von Dialekt und Schriftsprache im Altfranzösischen*, Halle, 1916.

evidence frequently adduced to establish the precise localization of Old French texts. The comparative freedom with which Beroul availed himself of dialectal variants may be held to have favoured his resort to forms and pronunciations of his native speech and therefore to support the conclusion that, if he was not a native of the South-West, he received his training in one or other of the famous schools of the region and found his models in such writers as those mentioned by Dr. Holden. For, it would be a mistake to regard Beroul as an untutored *conteur*, content to write according to the book or slavishly to imitate his models. On the contrary, his handling of rhyme and syllable-count, his syntax and style, and his treatment of his subject-matter, narrative and characters combine to reveal a sophisticated writer, of marked independence and originality. Thus, he appears upon occasion to have been content with mere assonance (*faire : moleste* 2821–2, *asente : enfle* 331–2, *dit : bric* 3579–80, *ator : corz* 4101–2)[1] or imperfect rhymes (*entre : estre* 3151–2, *roïne : oïe* 2627–8)[2] or impossible 'rhymes' (*chanbre : prenent* 771–2, *prie : parole* 2495–6, *toi : hui* 1035–6).[3]

We should therefore be on our guard against assuming too readily that the eccentricities and rugosities of the text are attributable to the ignorance or carelessness of a scribe. Taking these considerations into account, it seems prudent to conclude that Beroul's medium is a more or less standardized literary language with a

[1] At 2821–2 M⁰ introduced extensive emendation and assumed two lacunae, but M⁴ and the present edition merely postulate a lacuna; but as there is no clean break in the narrative, this assumption may be questioned (see the remarks on lacunae on p. 6 above). M⁰ regularized the rhyme at 4101–2 by emendation, but the MS reading is restored in M⁴. Emendation of 3579–80 is tentatively proposed in M⁰ and M⁴.

[2] The emendations made by M⁰ in l. 2627 and the assumption of a lacuna between 2627 and 2628 are abandoned in M⁴.

[3] A break in the sense indicates a lacuna between 2495 and 2496; this is not true of 771–2, where M⁰ assumed a lacuna. At 1035 the emendation *qu'autrui* (for *que toi*) adopted by Muret is eminently reasonable.

Western (and more specifically South Norman) colouring and that his work is therefore, linguistically and basically, in the broad tradition of the *Vie de Saint Alexis* and the *Chanson de Roland*.

The possibility that, like Marie de France, Beroul may have been a writer of Continental origin domiciled in England cannot be ruled out. One can hardly maintain that the casual mention of *Costentin* in l. 2386 necessarily points to composition on the Continent, even if one identifies it with le Cotentin and not, as J. Loth (*Contributions . . .*, p. 86) suggested, with Constantine (formerly Custentin) in Cornwall.

Then again, it has been held that lines 3132–3 ('Par saint André, que l'en vet querre Outre la mer, jusque en Escoce') could hardly have been written by an author domiciled in England; but J. Loth (p. 75), while favouring the Continental origin of Beroul, observed that 'pour aller de Cornwall en Écosse, on prenait sans doute la voie de mer', and Miss Legge has recently pointed out (*Anglo-Norman Literature*, p. 59) that 'the route across the "Sea of Scotland" by the Queensferry Passage was taken by pilgrims from England in the twelfth century, as the Monk of Durham relates'. These lines might therefore be regarded as more readily attributable to a writer domiciled in England and hence more likely to be familiar with the pilgrimage route in question.

A similar conclusion may be drawn from the familiarity our author shows with the Cornish scene and the topography of S.W. England, and the heavy incidence of place-names which have been identified by J. Loth as Cornish, some of which are localities unlikely to have been known to a Continental writer.[1] Even if we accept his view that these existed in Beroul's source, it is surely significant that they have been preserved so fully and in general correctly. Other English place-names come to

---

[1] Note, for example, that *Lancien* occurs only in Beroul and in *Tristan Ménestrel* (see J. Loth, p. 72, and the note to ll. 1943 ff., below).

him readily: *Nicole* (= Lincoln), *Frise* (= Dumfries ?), *Dureaume*, *Durelme* (= Durham), described as a seat of King Arthur (4264). If we add to these the naming of one of the hostile barons as *Godoïne* (= Godwin), the introduction of the English *lovendrant* 2159, *lovendrins* [2138], and of the 'arc qui ne faut' with its specifically English associations, Beroul must be regarded as having at least as strong a claim to English domicile as Marie de France.

IV. DATE

A comparison of the poet's language with that of other works which can be dated (such as Wace's *Roman de Rou* and Benoît de Sainte-Maure's *Chronique des ducs de Normandie*) led H. Warnecke to conclude (p. 57) that he wrote in the last quarter of the twelfth century.

This dating receives some support from the poet's handling of the octosyllabic couplet, in which he follows the example set by Chrétien de Troyes, in his *Erec*, of abandoning the earlier practice of normally avoiding a break in sense or construction elsewhere than at the end of the couplet.[1] Yet Raynaud de Lage has recently discerned[2] a reminiscence or imitation of ll. 35–38 and 1169–70 of Beroul in ll. 3328–52 of *Erec*, considering that 'les mots de Béroul ont un sens concret et terrible pour correspondre à une situation concrète et terrible . . . ceux de Chrétien ne sont qu'une réminiscence heureuse'. But there is no real parallelism with ll. 1169–70, where the lepers point out that once Iseut is consumed by fire nothing will be left but ashes which will quickly be dispersed by the wind. The parallel is with ll. 35–38,

---

[1] See P. Meyer, 'Le couplet de deux vers', *Rom.* XXIII (1894), 1–35 and the article entitled 'La brisure du couplet dans *Erec et Enide*', *Rom.* LXXXVI (1965), 1–21, in which Professor Frappier has demonstrated tellingly the literary implications of Chrétien's innovation.

[2] 'Trois notes sur le *Tristan* de Béroul', *Rom.* LXXXIII (1962), 522–6.

where we have a conventional form of asseveration: 'Rather would I be burnt and my ashes scattered down the wind than that I should ever in all my days have borne love to any man save my lord!'[1] There is nothing in the context of this passage to indicate that Beroul borrowed from Chrétien: the latter might equally well have borrowed from the former, or the resemblance may be fortuitous, having regard to the fondness shown by both writers, and particularly by Beroul, for asseverations of this type.

A somewhat more promising indication of date is furnished by l. 4285, where a spy, by way of characterizing Tristran's deceitful cunning, declares: 'Tristran set molt de malpertis.' This is clearly a reference to Malpertuis, the lair of the fox, first so named in Branch I of the *Roman de Renart*, which was composed, according to L. Foulet, about 1180.[2]

But a decisive *terminus a quo* would seem to be provided by the terms in which Tristran, disguised as a leper at the ford, describes his disabling afflictions (3847–52). It has been generally held that the *mal d'Acre* refers to the epidemic which ravaged the army of the Crusaders during the siege of Acre in 1190 and 1191.[3] Mrs. Whitteridge

---

[1] Cf. the following passage from *Le Comte de Poitiers* (composed about 1180, according to G. Paris), cited by A. Tobler under the title 'Vom Verwünschen' in *Vermischte Beiträge* IV, 122 (reprinted from *Commentationes philologae in honorem Th. Mommseni*, Berlin, 1877, p. 180):—

> De male flame soit brüie
> Ma chars et a porre ventee
> S'onques d'ome fui adesee
> Carneument ainc se de vous non.

See the extensive classified lists given by Tobler (art. cit.), by K. Tolle, *Das Betheuern und Beschwören in der altromanischen Poesie* (Diss. Göttingen), Erlangen, 1883, and by R. Busch, *Über die Beteuerungs- und Beschwörungsformeln in den* 'Miracles de Notre Dame par personnages', Diss. Marburg, 1886.

[2] Cf. W. A. Tregenza, 'The relation of the oldest Branch of the *Roman de Renart* to the Tristan poems', *MLR* XIX (1924), 301 ff.

[3] See Muret's Introductions and his important review of Röttiger, *Der heutige Stand . . .*, in *Rom.* XXVII (1898), 617.

has rightly reminded us (in *Medium Aevum* XXVIII, 167–79) that this assumption requires us to accept the emendation of the manuscript reading *dagres* to *dacres* (interpreted as *d'Acre*) and of *poacres* of the following line to *poacre*. She points out that weakness or numbness of the hands (*les mains gourdes*) is not mentioned in the list of symptoms given by the chroniclers; but her thesis invites us to make rather too much of this omission. Although the medical aspects of the problem are explored carefully, the interpretation of *le mal d'agres* (of which no other mention is recorded) as the name of an unknown disease and signifying 'the disease of the catching pains' cannot be said to carry conviction.

It is not to be denied that the leper's description of his disability shows a remarkable general similarity to that given by Ambroise and others of the 'maladie' which decimated the besieging army before Acre.[1] It is more than probable that the term *maladie* covers two or more diseases induced by the dietary deficiencies and the appalling weather conditions so vividly described by the chroniclers.[2] The afflictions and sufferings of the Cru-

---

[1] For a full account of the siege and references to chronicles and other sources, see S. Runciman, *A History of the Crusades* (Cambridge, 1955), Vol. III, particularly pp. 27–33. The relevant passage in Ambroise, *Estoire de la Guerre Sainte* (ed. G. Paris, 1897), ll. 4265–74, reads:—

> La curut une maladie,
> Si atendez que jo la die:
> Par unes pluies qui donc plurent
> Que tantes ne teles ne furent,
> Ke tote l'ost d'iaue naiot,
> Chescons tusset e enroot,
> E emfloent jambes e chieres.
> Le jor aveit en l'ost mil bieres,
> E de l'emfle qu'es chiefs avoient
> Les denz des buches lor chaieient.

[2] Scurvy was undoubtedly the major element; but some of the symptoms mentioned by chroniclers could have been produced by acute rheumatism or streptococcal infection, or what the First World War taught us to designate by the terms trench feet and trench fever. It is true that, as already pointed out, the chronicles make no mention of numbness of the hands, but one can hardly expect a rigid adherence to the symptoms

saders before Acre must have been so well known at the time that for a contemporary *le mal d'Acre* would be a perfectly intelligible designation.[1] One may assume that this designation fell into disuse fairly quickly and gave place to a more 'scientific' nomenclature. This might explain why no other example of its use has come to light and why a scribe writing more than half a century later should have failed to recognize it.[2] One may therefore conjecture that these lines must have been written not long after the year 1191.

Taken together, these various pieces of evidence justify one in concluding, with a high degree of plausibility, that Beroul composed his romance in the last decade of the twelfth century.[3]

V. THE PRIMARY VERSIONS

Beroul's romance is one of the four primary versions[4]

associated with the Acre epidemic in Tristan's 'explanation' of why he was forced to release his hold on the staff, thus causing Donoalen to fall back into the mire.

It is significant that, while *maladie* serves to cover the complex of diseases which decimated the army, when it comes to describing the illness which struck down the kings Richard I and Philip Augustus not long after their arrival before Acre, Ambroise has no difficulty in giving it a name: *leonardie* (ll. 4608 and 9650) = *arnaldia* of the Latin texts.—See also the *Anglo-Norman Crusade and Death of Richard I* (ed. R. C. Johnston, 1961), pp. 27–30.—Gilbertus Anglicus visited Syria during the 1191 siege and describes in his *Compendium medicinae* the treatment of one of the Crusaders there (a reference which I owe to the kindly interest of Dr. F. N. L. Poynter).

[1] Cf. the modern use of such terms as 'trench feet' and 'trench fever'.

[2] It is possible that the fault was not entirely our scribe's. The existence of the alternative form *Acres* (used consistently in the Anglo-Norman text cited in note 2 above) and the variant forms *poacre—poagre* invited confusion and corruption of the text. For the author's *dacre : le poacre* a first scribe might well have substituted *dacres : le poacres*, and the alternative pronunciation *poagres* may have induced *dagres*, the spelling with *c* being maintained in *le poacres*.

[3] This conclusion is shared, among others, by M. Delbouille (*Rom.* LXXXI), H. Newstead (*Arthurian Literature*, p. 122), and F. Whitehead (*Arthurian Literature*, pp. 134–5).

[4] For particulars of editions see the Select Bibliography (pp. 46–56).

to which, as Bédier has shown, all later versions of the Tristan story go back, the other three being:—

O. The Middle High German romance by Eilhart von Oberge (9524 lines in the Lichtenstein edition, which is based upon three fifteenth-century MSS). Date of composition 1190–1200 according to Lichtenstein; but the earlier date (ca. 1170–80) proposed by K. Wagner seems more likely.

The Eilhart version was used by the two continuators of Gottfried, Ulrich von Türheim (ca. 1250) and Heinrich von Freiberg (ca. 1300). Gottfried's own indebtedness to Eilhart is doubtful. Eilhart is also the basis of a German prose adaptation printed in 1483 and of a partial Czech translation (ca. 1300).

T. The Anglo-Norman romance by Thomas, of which nine fragments (from the latter part) are preserved, amounting to about 3144 lines (about one-sixth of the whole). Composed after 1155, and perhaps as early as 1165 according to some scholars; but a *terminus ad quem* remains difficult to determine.[1]

Derivatives include: Gottfried von Strassburg's *Tristan und Isolt* (ca. 1210), the Norwegian Prose *Saga* by the Monk Robert (1226), the Middle English *Sir Tristrem* (between 1294 and 1330, and probably in the last decade of the thirteenth century).

R. The French Prose Romance (First Version) composed between 1215 and 1230. Analyzed by E. Loeseth (with transcription of extracts). Those portions which may be considered 'primitive' were printed (from two MSS) by Bédier (Vol. II, pp. 321–95). An edition by Renée L. Curtis is in course of publication.

Preserved in a large number of MSS and many *remaniements*, its prodigious popularity is further attested by

[1] Vol. I of Bédier's edition gives the text of the extant fragments and a reconstruction of the rest on the basis of derivatives. See also the editions by B. H. Wind.

translations and adaptations in English, German, Italian, Russian, Spanish, of which the following merit particular attention:—*Il Tristano Riccardiano* (end of thirteenth century?), *La Tavola Ritonda*, cc. 63–67 (ca. 1300), Malory's version in his *Morte d'Arthur* (completed in 1469–70 and printed by Caxton in 1485).

Of the episodic poems dealing with one or more incidents,[1] two present Tristran returning in the guise of a court fool and recalling to Iseut past events in their lives:—

Fb. *La Folie Berne*, a Norman poem of 572 lines, so called because it is preserved in the library of Bern, Switzerland, where it bears the number 354. Its allusions are based, if not upon Beroul, upon a version very close to Beroul, whose immediate source may well have been the same as that of the *Folie Berne*.[2] The latter is of uncertain date but was probably composed about the end of the twelfth century.

Fo. *La Folie Oxford*, an Anglo-Norman poem of 998 lines preserved in MS Douce d. 6 of the Bodleian Library. It alludes to the principal episodes in the order in which they appear in Thomas, who was clearly its main source. It was probably composed not long after *Fb* which, according to Hoepffner, inspired *Fo*.

The Middle High German poem published under the title *Tristan als Mönch* presents Tristran as gaining access to the queen by an elaborate intrigue involving his assumption of the habit of a monk.

---

[1] Cf. F. Whitehead, in *Arthurian Literature* (ed. Loomis), p. 144, and the unpublished thesis of the late Miss Jean M. Telfer. Editions are indicated in the Select Bibliography.

[2] Hoepffner's demonstration, in his 1949 edition (pp. 12–19), leaves little doubt that, although the author of *Fb* may not have had the text of Beroul before him, he carried it in his memory: indeed, Hoepffner concludes: 'Pour nous, c'est bien le roman même de Béroul qui lui a servi de modèle.'

In Gerbert de Montreuil's continuation of the *Perceval* of Chrétien de Troyes occurs an episode (published under the title *Tristan Ménestrel*) in which Tristan achieves a meeting with Iseut by disguising himself as a minstrel, while in the *Donnei des Amanz* (453–662, 667–74) Tristran's skill in imitating bird-songs, and in this instance the nightingale's, enables him to apprise the queen of his presence and to ensure their meeting.

In Marie de France's *Lai du Chievrefeuil* Tristran is credited with having composed the original *lai* in remembrance of the message he had written at the behest of the queen and of the piece of hazelwood bearing his name which, left in the way taken by the queen, enabled the lovers to meet.

For other reminiscences and allusions, see L. Sudre, Bédier II, 57–64, 397–400, and H. F. Williams.

Bédier's classification of the four primary versions and their derivatives has been accepted, in the main, by most scholars; but it is less rigid than his genealogical tree (II, 309) might suggest, even after allowing for the dotted or broken lines which it bears. There is substantial agreement that they all derive ultimately from a common source (now lost) generally designated the *Estoire* (*Ur-Tristan* by Golther and other German scholars). Bédier's main conclusions (II, 192) may be tabulated as follows:

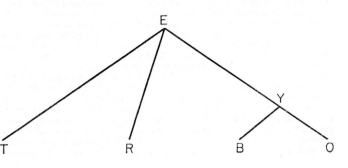

The existence of an 'estoire' (E) must continue to be posited, but whether it was a fully constituted French romance in all its textual detail is less certain; nor can the existence of an intermediate version (Bédier's γ) from which B and O were derived be regarded as firmly established: they do not derive from each other, but they may be independent derivatives from the *Estoire* (as maintained by Golther and Gertrude Schoepperle), and the claims of R and T to be independent and direct derivatives from the *Estoire* have also been called in question.[1] The derivation of Gottfried, the *Saga* and *Sir Tristrem* from Thomas must be accepted as proven, provided only that one grants to the authors of these

[1] For a genealogical tree comprising all the early texts, see Bédier II, 309: it shows Fb as an independent derivative from the *Estoire* through an intermediate x; but, in view of its close affinity with B, it is not clear why Bédier did not relate it to γ rather than to the *Estoire*.

G. Schoepperle's reconstitution of the *Estoire* differs considerably from Bédier's and she regards Eilhart as a direct and much the most faithful derivative. Golther's classification will be found in ZFSL XXII, 23. Muret (in *Rom.* XXVII, 619, and in his Introductions) distinguishes between a 'version commune' (represented by Eilhart and Beroul, and more loosely by the Prose Romance) and the 'version courtoise' of Thomas. More recent classifications are those proposed by J. van Dam, in *Neophilologus* XV (1930), p. 105, and by B. Panvini, *La Leggenda di Tristano e Isotta. Studio critico* (Bibliotheca dell'Archivum Romanicum 32), Florence, 1951. F. Whitehead reviews the present state of the question in his chapter on 'The Early Tristan Poems' in *Arthurian Literature* (ed. R. S. Loomis).

For the development of the legend and the sources of the romances, see particularly Bédier II and G. Schoepperle's *Tristan and Isolt*, of which the second volume is almost entirely devoted to an examination of the *Estoire* for traces of Celtic tradition: the analogies presented by Old Irish literature are studied with great thoroughness, though at times with insufficient differentiation between analogues and sources. Reference should now be made to J. Carney, *Studies in Irish Literature and History*, published by the Dublin Institute for Advanced Studies in 1955, particularly Ch. VI entitled 'Irish Affinities of *Tristan*' (pp. 189–242) and the account of the compulsions under which the authors of the Old Irish tales worked; for the Welsh texts to Mrs. Rachel Bromwich's paper, 'Some Remarks on the Celtic sources of *Tristan*' published in the *Transactions of the Honourable Society of Cymmrodorion for 1953* (London, 1955), pp. 32–60. Miss Helaine Newstead has contributed an informative and judicious re-assessment in her chapter on 'The Growth of the Tristan Legend' in *Arthurian Literature* (ed. R. S. Loomis). Those features of

secondary versions a certain measure of independence and eclecticism. Thus, for example, Bédier himself (I, 199, note 3, etc.) admits the possibility that Gottfried was at times influenced by Eilhart. In fact, one must assume that the authors of the various versions, whether primary or secondary, even when they followed one particular recension, generally had knowledge of variants, whether through having one or more alternative texts accessible or through recollections of and familiarity with traditions or treatments of particular incidents. Confirmation of this is furnished by such statements as that made by Beroul at ll. 1265–70, where he inveighs against story-tellers who say that Tristan and Governal killed Yvain, the leader of the lepers, and who thus betray their ignorance of the 'estoire', of which he has a better recollection and which he claims, according to ll. 1787–92, to have read. We have however no way of telling whether the 'estoire' in question was Beroul's sole or even his principal source.[1]

The uncertainty which continues to envelop the questions of authorship, date and place of composition of our text is thus matched by a similar difficulty in dating other primary versions of the Tristan story and in determining with precision their relation to each other and to their source or sources.

In view of what we have learnt in recent times of the

Beroul's romance which may be considered as additions made by him to received tradition or to the *Estoire* furnish no evidence that he had access to Celtic sources or possessed any Celtic tongue. The question of Celtic sources therefore falls largely outside the scope of this commentary.

[1] Cf. the striking passage in which Thomas enlarges upon the diversity of the accounts, both oral and written, of Tristran known to him: 'Seignurs, cest cunte est mult divers . . . Entre ceus qui solent cunter E del cunte Tristran parler, Il en cuntent diversement . . .' (Bédier edn., 2107 ff. and Wind edn., 835 ff.). Gottfried, while claiming and justifying Thomas as his source, avers that he consulted 'romance' and 'Latin' books as well (ll. 131–4). Eilhart similarly claims to follow 'the book' and finds it necessary to reject other accounts as untrustworthy (e.g. at ll. 4730 ff. and 9452 ff.).

prodigious feats of memory by performers or reciters,[1] and the lack of positive direct evidence of a written *Estoire*, one is led to ask whether the so-called *Estoire* was not in fact an unwritten form of the story orally transmitted, a sort of vulgate form, enjoying a considerable measure of authority but tolerating very substantial variants and a certain amount of transposition and changes in the order of incidents.[2]

There might well be some gain from a methodological point of view if we abandoned the device of a genealogical tree, the branches of which exist only in virtue of *concordances* (more particularly in common error) and if we concentrated rather upon the differences and the idiosyncracies of individual versions. This means, in the case of Beroul, directing our attention to the elucidation and appreciation of those passages (single lines or whole divisions of the narrative) in which he differs from all other versions (with the possible exception of *Fb*),[3] whether these be taken singly or in groups. In that way one may hope to detect first-hand manifestations of the poet's personality which taken together would go a long way towards at least a provisional literary portrait of the

[1] Sir William Craigie, in his Taylorian Lecture of 1937 (*The Art of Poetry in Iceland*) cites the example of the preservation intact, among early Icelandic settlers in Canada, of a set of *rimur* running to 4000 lines, without the benefit of a written text or access to it for fifty years.

[2] The role of oral transmission in the propagation and in the creation of variant forms of the *chansons de geste* and in the multiplication of detailed textual variants has been much discussed of recent years, insisted upon by J. Rychner in his *La chanson de geste* (Geneva–Lille, 1955), but played down by M. Delbouille, notably in an important article contributed to *La Technique littéraire des chansons de geste* (Paris–Liège, 1959) (Proceedings of the Liège colloquium of 1957), and agreeing with the latter:—D. McMillan, 'A propos d'un travail de M. Delbouille sur *Les chansons de geste et le Livre*', *Cahiers de Civilisation médiévale* IV (1961), 47–54, and Madeleine Tyssens, 'Le jongleur et l'écrit', *Mélanges offerts à René Crozet* (Poitiers, 1966).

[3] *Fb* is regarded by Hoepffner as almost certainly based directly upon Beroul (see above, p. 61n), and this conclusion is accepted, among others, by F. Whitehead (in *Arthurian Literature*, p. 141). In view of this probability, a feature which is found only in *B* and *Fb* counts, for present purposes, as a feature distinguishing *B* from all other versions.

author and eventually to the placing of his work in the Tristan tradition as a whole.

By way of illustrating the desirability of maintaining a conservative attitude and of accepting an 'unvarnished' Beroul as he is presented to us in the sole surviving manuscript, one might select lines 1991–2000, a passage which is in several ways especially characteristic of Beroul. The scene of the discovery of the lovers by Mark as presented by the poet is concentrated entirely upon the reactions of the king: he insists that he be left as the sole witness; his first reaction is to raise his sword [a movement the poet is careful to describe as dictated by wrath]; but his strength fails him; the blow all but descended upon the lovers; had it done so and had he killed them, it would have been a grievous thing [this being in form a reflection of the poet's, but by implication attributed to the king as the consideration which stayed his arm]. Thereupon [and the return to the historic tense is here significant], when he observed that the lovers were lying apart, clothed and separated by Tristran's sword, he was sorely perplexed (*Ce que puet estre? . . . je ne sai que doie faire*), and the poet describes in great detail the thoughts which inspire Mark's subsequent actions (2005–54).[1]

Far from endorsing A. Henry's harsh verdict on this passage: 'Pauvre chose que ce texte! . . . C'est un affront à l'art d'écrire', I would regard this passage as typical of Beroul's style and manner, admirably employed here to convey with striking immediacy the agitated state of mind of the king as he finds the lovers: it would in fact be difficult to imagine a more telling way of doing so within the confines imposed by the octosyllabic couplet. Beroul's talent is essentially dramatic and his work requires to be judged as a performance in which the reading is enlivened by intonation and supplemented by

[1] See also the note to ll. 1991–2000 in the Commentary.

appropriate gestures and pregnant pauses. The requirements of formal grammar and of orderly, logical development are subordinated to vivid presentation. As M.
Henry himself rightly reminds us: 'Il n'y a pas de barrière
entre linguistique, critique des textes et esthétique
littéraire.' Of few works can it be said more truly than
of Beroul's romance that editing is an art rather than a
science: it is to be judged, not by standards of usage and
the application of logic, but by the closest possible
identification of the critic with the author's personality,
his intentions and his preoccupations.

To eliminate the superficial incoherences of Beroul's
narrative and substitute for his exclamatory and declama-
tory presentation a carefully co-ordinated psychological
analysis conceived on classical lines or in the conventional sophisticated manner of a Chrétien de Troyes is to
betray this most individual of authors. For, surely the
appeal which Beroul continues to make to the modern
reader is due in no small measure to the relative indifference he shows to the requirements of convention and the
dictates of fashion. He reveals himself as a well-informed
but non-conforming deviationist in grammar and style
no less than in his treatment of received narratives and
of the moral, legal and literary questions which exercised
the minds of his contemporaries, and it would be a dis-
service to him to seek to 'improve' and regularize his
text by introducing emendations and transpositions of
lines unless these can be shown to be strictly necessary.

VI. EDITORIAL PROCEDURE

The scribal imperfections of MS B.N. fr. 2171 are
numerous and I have attempted, in an article published
in the *Pope Miscellany* (1939), to identify, classify and
interpret them. I was led to conclude that the copyist,
a Norman, transcribed it in the latter half of the thirteenth
century, probably from a copy made by a Norman scribe

of the early thirteenth century. In that article and in the present commentary I have sought to justify the conservative treatment I have adopted. It implies that while the editor owes it to his prospective readers to eliminate from the text and record in the Variants all errors which a close study of the copyist's practice shows to be scribal, he should not be concerned to substitute for the reading of the MS what he thinks Beroul said or should have said, having regard to the testimony of other versions of the story and assuming a strict consistency both in the narrative and in the forms the poet employed.

Thus, at ll. 1326 and 3313 I have refrained from correcting *par soi* to *par foi* (with Muret, following G. Paris), although *par foi* is a very common formulaic expression repeatedly used by the poet and would suit the context, and in spite of some confusion of *s* and *f* in the MS. One cannot rule out the possibility that the poet deliberately made such departures from what our observation might indicate to have been authoritative or normal: in fact it might be held that it is just this sort of 'deviation' that might be expected of a poet of Beroul's stamp. It seemed preferable not to relegate such 'idiosyncrasies' to the variants, but rather to discuss them, where necessary, in the notes. Nor have I resorted to other primary versions for improvements, but chiefly for the help they might give in elucidating Beroul's text or correcting obvious (and chiefly scribal) errors. In other words, I have endeavoured to avoid, as far as possible, interposing conjectural emendations between the reader and the authentic text as it has come down to us. I have thus been led to restore progressively many readings formerly regarded (either by myself or by others) as demanding correction, and it is reassuring to find the editors of the latest CFMA edition[1] similarly motivated.

[1] It appears, from private information that 'L. M. Defourques' is a playful conflation of the names of the two scholars responsible for the revision: Lucien Foulet and Mario Roques.

In this matter of textual emendation the Grand Cham
of literature was not far off the mark when he declared:
'I have always suspected that the reading is right which
requires many words to prove it wrong, and the emendation wrong that cannot without so much labour appear
to be right.' The circumspect editor will know when to
resist the lure of the *lectio difficilior* and also the fear of
the *hapax legomenon* which an undiscriminating reliance
on parallelism might otherwise have relegated to the
variants, and he will heed the salutary warning of Joseph
Bédier: '... car enfin la facilité d'une conjecture n'est
nullement un gage de sa justesse'.

VII. SELECT BIBLIOGRAPHY[1]

Editions

Gottfrieds von Strassburg Werke, hrsg. durch Friedr.
Heinr. von der Hagen, Breslau, 1823, 2 vols. The Beroul
text appears in Vol. II, pp. 243–303.

Tristan. Recueil de ce qui reste des poèmes relatifs à
ses aventures ..., p.p. Francisque Michel, London and
Paris, 1835–8, 3 vols. The Beroul text appears in Vol. I,
pp. 1–212; Vol. II contains notes (pp. 161–92), glossary
(pp. 229–66), additions and corrections (pp. 303 ff.).

Le Roman de Tristan par Béroul et un anonyme, poème
du XIIe siècle, p.p. Ernest Muret, Paris, 1903 (Société
des Anciens Textes Français).   [Referred to as M⁰]
Béroul: *Le Roman de Tristan*, poème du XIIe siècle,

[1] ABBREVIATIONS.—*CCMe = Cahiers de Civilisation Médiévale—DL =
Deutsche Literaturzeitung—FS = French Studies—MA = Le Moyen Age—
MAe = Medium Aevum—MLR = Modern Language Review—N = Neophilo-
logus—PBB = Paul und Braunes Beiträge—R = Romania—RBPH = Revue
Belge de Philologie et d'Histoire—RF = Romanische Forschungen—RPh =
Romance Philology—ZDA = Zeitschrift für Deutsches Altertum und Deutsche
Literatur—ZFSL = Zeitschrift für Französische Sprache und Literatur—
ZRP = Zeitschrift für Romanische Philologie.*

édité par Ernest Muret, Paris, 1913 (Classiques français du moyen âge, 12). 2ᵉ édition revue, 1922. 3ᵉ édition revue, 1928. 4ᵉ édition revue par L. M. Defourques [= Lucien Foulet et Mario Roques], 1947. [Referred to as M¹, M², M³, M⁴ respectively.]

The Romance of Tristran by Beroul, a Poem of the twelfth century, edited by A. Ewert, Vol. I (Introduction, Text, Glossary, Index), Oxford, 1939. Reprinted 1946, 1953, 1958, 1963, 1967.

Béroul: *Le Roman de Tristan*, edited by C. Guerrieri Crocetti, Genova, 1947. (Coll. 'Romania'). (Said to reproduce the Muret text of 1928.)

Eilhart von Oberge, hrsg. von Franz Lichtenstein, Strassburg, 1877 (Quellen und Forschungen, XIX).

'Neue Funde aus dem 12. Jahrhundert: Ein Bruchstück der Urfassung von Eilharts *Tristrant*' von H. Degering, *PBB*, XLI (1916), 513. (461 lines = Lichtenstein edn., 7061 ff.)

Eilhart von Oberge, *Tristrant*, I, *Die alten Bruchstücke*, hrsg. von Kurt Wagner, Bonn and Leipzig, 1924 (Rheinische Beiträge und Hilfsbücher zur germanischen Philologie und Volkskunde, V).

Le Roman de Tristan par Thomas, poème du XIIe siècle, p.p. Joseph Bédier, Paris, 2 vols. Vol. I, 1902; Vol. II, 1905 (Société des Anciens Textes Français).

Les Fragments du Roman de Tristan, poème du XIIe siècle par Thomas, édités avec commentaire par Bartina H. Wind, Leiden, 1950. 2ᵉ édition, Geneva and Paris, 1960 (Textes Littéraires Français).

Gottfried von Strassburgs *Tristan und Isolde*, hrsg. von R. Bechstein, Leipzig, 1869, 1873, 1890, 1923⁴.

Gottfried von Strassburg, *Tristan und Isolde*, hrsg. von W. Golther, Stuttgart, 1890.

Gottfried von Strassburg, *Tristan*, hrsg. von K. Marold, Leipzig, 1906, 1920 (Teutonia 6).

Gottfried von Strassburg, *Tristan und Isolde*, hrsg. von Fr. Ranke, Berlin, 1930, 1949.

Die nordische und die englische Version der Tristan-Sage, hrsg. von E. Kölbing, Heilbronn, 1878–82, 2 vols.

Saga af Tristram ok Isond samt Möttuls Saga, ed. by G. Brynjulfsson, Copenhagen, 1878.

Sir Tristrem, ed. by G. P. McNeill, Edinburgh, 1886 (Scottish Text Society).

La Tavola Ritonda o l'istoria di Tristano, ed. by Filippo-Luigi Polidori, Bologna, 1864–5, 3 vols. (Coll. di opere inedite o rare).

Le roman en prose de Tristan, le roman de Palamède et la compilation de Rusticien de Pise, analyse critique d'après les manuscrits de Paris, Paris, 1891 (Bibliothèque de l'École des Hautes Études, Sciences philologiques et historiques, 82).

Le Roman de Tristan en prose, ed. by Renée L. Curtis, Vol. I, Munich, 1963.

La Grant Ystoire de Monsignor Tristan 'li Bret'. The first part of the Prose Romance of Tristan from Adv. MS 19.1.3. in the National Library of Scotland, ed. by F. C. Johnson, Edinburgh, 1942.

Les deux poèmes de la Folie Tristan, p.p. Joseph Bédier, Paris, 1903 (Société des Anciens Textes Français).

La Folie Tristan de Berne, p.p. Ernest Hoepffner, Paris, 1934. 2ᵉ édition revue, Strasbourg, 1949.

La Folie Tristan d'Oxford, p.p. Ernest Hoepffner, Paris, 1938.

'Tristan als Mönch', hrsg. von H. Paul, in *Sitzungsberichte der bairischen Akademie*, phil.-hist. Kl., 1895–6, III, 317 ff. and 687–92.

Le Lai du Chevrefoil by Marie de France. Recent editions of the *Lais* by A. Ewert (Oxford, 1944) and J. Rychner (Paris, 1966).

'Tristan Menestrel', p.p. J. L. Weston et J. Bédier, in R, XXXV (1907), 497 ff.

'Tristan Rossignol', in 'Le Donnei des amanz' (ll. 453–662 and 667–74), p.p. G. Paris, in R, XXV (1896), 497 ff.

L'Escoufle, roman d'aventures, p.p. H. Michelant et P.

Meyer, Paris, 1894 (Société des Anciens Textes Français).

Messire Thibaut: *Li romanz de la Poire*, hrsg. von Fr. Stehlich, Halle, 1881. (Cf. L. Sudre in R, XV (1886), 548–9).

Le Roman de Tristan et Iseut, traduit et restauré par Joseph Bédier; préface de Gaston Paris, Paris, [1900]. Often reprinted.

Studies[1]

J. Acher, 'Corrections au "Roman de *Tristan* par Béroul et un anonyme", p.p. M. E. Muret', *ZRP*, XXXIII (1909), 720 ff. Cf. M. Roques in R, XXXIX (1910), 409.

D. Beyerle, 'Der Liebestrank im Thomas-*Tristan*', *Romanistisches Jahrbuch*, XIV (1963), 78–86.

B. Blakey, 'On the text of Beroul's *Tristan*', *FS*, XXI (1967), 99–103.

L. Caulier, *Glossaire complet du roman de* Tristan *de Béroul* [typescript]. Mémoire de licence en philologie romane, Université de Liège, 1957–8.

H. H. Christmann, 'Sur un passage du *Tristan* de Beroul', R, LXXX (1959), 85–7. (Note on ll. 4221–5). Also *ZFSL*, LXXVI (1966), 243–5.

M. Delbouille, 'Le nom du nain *Frocin(e)*', *Mélanges István Frank*, Saarbrücken, 1957, pp. 191–203.

M. Delbouille, 'Non, Cercamon n'a pas connu Tristan', R, LXXXI (1960), 409–25; cf. R, LXXXVII (1966), 234–47.

M. Delbouille, 'Le premier roman de Tristan', *CCMe*, V (1962), 273–86 and 419–35.

Joan Evans, *Dress in Medieval France* (with 95 plates and 11 figures in the text), Oxford, 1952.

A. Ewert, 'On the text of Beroul's *Tristran*', *Studies in French Language and Mediæval Literature presented to Professor Mildred K. Pope*, Manchester, 1939, pp. 89–98.

[1] See also Vol. I, p. ix.

A. Fedrick, 'A Note on the *Folie Tristan de Berne* [ll. 191–213], *MAe*, XXXII (1963), 125–9.

A. Fedrick, 'The Love Potion in the French Prose *Tristan*', *RPh*, XXI (1967), 23–34.

L.-F. Flutre, *Table des noms propres figurant dans les romans français et provençaux du moyen âge actuellement publiés ou analysés*, Poitiers, 1962.

Ch. Foulon, 'Le conte des oreilles du roi Marc'h dans le *Tristan* de Béroul', *Bulletin philologique et historique 1951–2*, Paris, 1953.

J. Frappier, 'Sur deux paasages du *Tristan* de Béroul', [ll. 1909–11 and 3928–54], *R*, LXXXIII (1962), 251–8; and 'Note complémentaire sur l'expression "au chemin fors" dans le *Tristan* de Béroul', *R*, LXXXIV (1963), 77–9.

J. Frappier, 'Structure et sens du *Tristan*: version commune, version courtoise', *CCMe*, VI (1963), 255–80 and 441–54.

W. Golther, *Tristan und Isolde in den Dichtungen des Mittelalters und der neuen Zeit*, Leipzig, 1907.

W. Golther, *Tristan und Isolde in der französischen und deutschen Dichtung des Mittelalters und der Neuzeit*, Berlin and Leipzig, 1929.

W. Mary Hackett, 'Syntactical features common to *Girart de Roussillon* and Béroul's *Tristan*', *Medieval Miscellany presented to Eugène Vinaver*, Manchester, 1965, pp. 157–66.

Micheline Hanoset, 'Unité ou dualité du *Tristan* de Beroul', *MA*, LXVII (1961), 503–33.

V. J. Hayward, *The Dwarfs of Arthurian Romance and Celtic Tradition* (Columbia Univ. Diss. 1958), Leiden, 1959.

R. Heinzel, 'Gottfrieds von Strassburg *Tristan* und seine Quelle', *ZDA*, XIV (Neue Folge 2) (1869), 272–447.

B. Heller, 'L'épée symbole et gardienne de chasteté', *R*, XXXV (1907), 36–49 and XXXVI (1908), 162–3.

A. Henry, 'Du subjonctif d'imminence contrecarrée à un passage du *Tristan* de Béroul', *R*, LXXIII (1952),

392–407; and *Études de syntaxe expressive. Ancien français et français moderne*, Paris, 1960.

W. Hertz, *Tristan und Isolde* von Gottfried von Strassburg, neu bearbeitet und ergänzt, Stuttgart, 1877, 1894, 1901[3], 1911[6], 1912, 1921.

E. Hoepffner, 'Das Verhältnis der Berner *Folie Tristan* zu Berouls Tristandichtung', *ZRP*, XXXIX (1919), 62–82, 551–83, 672–99.

S. Hofer, 'Streitfragen zur altfranzösischen Literatur. I. Die Komposition des Tristanromans', *ZRP*, LXV (1949), 257–88.

S. Hofer, *Chrétien de Troyes*, Graz–Köln, 1954.

A. Holden, 'Note sur la langue de Béroul', *R*, LXXXIX (1968), 387–98.

J. Horrent, 'La Composition de la *Folie Tristan* de Berne', *RBPH*, XXV (1936–7), 21–38.

O. Jodogne, 'La Légende de Tristan et d'Iseut interprétée par Béroul', *Filološki pregled* (Belgrade), 1–2 (1964), 261–70.

P. Jonin, *Les personnages féminins dans les romans français de Tristan au XIIe siecle. Étude des influences contemporaines*, Gap, 1958.

P. Jonin, 'La Vengeance chez l'Iseut de Béroul et chez l'Iseut de Thomas', *N*, XXXIII (1949), 207–9.

P. Jonin, 'Le songe d'Iseut dans la forêt de Morrois', *MA*, LXIV (1958), 103–13.

J. Kelemina, *Geschichte der Tristansage nach den Dichtungen des Mittelalters*, Wien, 1923.

J. Knieschek, in *ZDA*, XXVIII, 261–358 [German translation of the Czech poetic version].

A. H. Krappe, 'Der Zwerg im *Tristan*', *RF*, XLV (1931), 95–9.

H. Küpper, *Bibliographie zur Tristansage*, Jena, 1941 (Deutsche Arbeiten der Univ. Köln).

F. Lecoy, 'Sur les vers 1461–2 du *Tristan* de Béroul', *R*, LXXX (1959), 82–5.

F. Lecoy, 'L'épisode du harpeur d'Irlande et la date

des *Tristan* de Béroul et de Thomas', R, LXXXVI (1965), 538–45.

P. Le Gentil, 'La légende de Tristan vue par Béroul et Thomas', *RPh*, VII (1953–4), 111–29.

P. Le Gentil, 'L'épisode du Morrois et la signification du *Tristan* de Béroul', *Studia . . . Spitzer*, Berne, 1958, 267–74.

M. D. Legge, 'The unerring bow', *MAe*, XXV (1956), 79–83.

M. D. Legge, *Anglo-Norman Literature and its Background*, Oxford, 1963.

R. Lejeune, 'Les "influences contemporaines" dans le roman français de *Tristan* au XIIe siècle', *MA* LXVI (1960), 143–62.

E. Loeseth, *Le Tristan et le Palamède des manuscrits français du British Museum*, Christiania, 1905.

E. Loeseth, *Le Tristan et le Palamède des manuscrits de Rome et de Florence*, Oslo, 1925.

R. S. Loomis, *Arthurian Tradition and Chrétien de Troyes*, New York, 1949.

R. S. Loomis, *Arthurian Literature in the Middle Ages*, A Collaborative History, edited by Roger Sherman Loomis, Oxford, 1959.

F. Lot, 'Godoïne', R, XXXV (1906), 605–7.

J. Loth, *Contributions à l'étude des romans de la Table Ronde*, Paris, 1912; and in *Rev. Celtique* XXXIV (1913), 365 ff., XXXVII (1917–9), 317 ff.

J. Loth, 'Les noms *Tristan* et *Iseut* en gallois', R, XIX, 455–8.

J. Loth, 'Dinas de Lidan. La voile blanche et la voile noire à l'île Molènes', *Rev. Celtique*, XXXVII (1917), No. 4.

J. Loth, 'L'épée de Tristan', *Bull. de l'Acad. des Inscriptions et Belles Lettres*, 1923, mars–avril.

W. Lutoslawski, 'Les *Folies de Tristan*', R, XV (1886), 511–33.

Malory. *The Works of Sir Thomas Malory*, ed. by E. Vinaver, Oxford, 1947, 3 vols.

J. Marx, 'La Naissance de l'amour de Tristan et Iseut dans les formes les plus anciennes de la légende', *RPh*, IX (1955), 167–73.

J. Marx, 'Observations sur un épisode de la légende de Tristan', *Mél. Cl. Brunel*, Paris, 1955, II, 265–73.

B. Mergell, *Tristan und Isolde. Ursprung und Entwicklung der Tristansage des Mittelalters*, Mainz, 1949.

W. Mettmann, Beroul/Thomas: *Der Tristanroman*. In Auswahl bearbeitet, Tübingen, 1962 (Rom. Übungstexte 45).

J. J. Meyer, *Isoldes Gottesurteil in seiner erotischen Bedeutung*, Berlin, 1914. (See also W. Golther's review in *DL*, March 14, 1914).

U. Mölk, *Beroul: Tristan und Isolde*. Text, Übersetzung, etc., Munich, 1962. [Extracts].

E. Muret, in *R*, XVI, 288–363 ('Eilhart d'Oberg et sa source française'); XVII, 603–9 (rev. of Golther, *Die Sage*...); XVIII, 175–80 (rev. of Novati); XXVII, 608–19 (rev. of Röttiger); *ZFSL*, XXXVII, 167 ff. (rev. of Golther, *Tristan und Isolde*, 1907).

E. S. Murrell, *Girart de Roussillon and the Tristan Poems*, Chesterfield, 1926.

H. Newstead, 'The Origin and Growth of the Tristan Legend', in R. S. Loomis, *Arthurian Literature* ..., 1959, pp. 122–33.

H. Newstead, 'The Tryst beneath the Tree, an episode in the Tristan Legend', *RPh*, IX (1956), 269–84.

H. Newstead, 'King Mark of Cornwall', *RPh*, XI (1958), 240–53.

S. G. Nichols, jr., 'Ethical Criticism and medieval literature', in *Medieval Secular Literature—Four Essays* (ed. W. Matthews), Berkeley and Los Angeles, 1965.

H. Nottaro, *Gottesurteile*, Bamberg, 1949 (Kleine allg. Schriften zur Philosophie ... Geschichtliche Reihe, Heft 4–8).

F. Novati, 'Un nuovo ed un vecchio frammento del Tristan di Tommaso', *Studj di filologia romanza*, II (1887), 369–515.

G. Paris, in R, VIII, 467 (rev. of Heinzel).

M. E. G. Parodi, ed. *Il Tristano Riccardiano*, Bologna, 1896 (Coll. di opere inedite o rare).

[M. K. Pope]. *Studies in French Language and Mediæval French Literature presented to Professor Mildred K. Pope*, Manchester, 1939.

M. K. Pope, 'A Note on the Dialect of Béroul's Tristan and a conjecture', *MLR*, VIII (1913), 189 ff.

M. K. Pope, *From Latin to Modern French*, Manchester, 1934. Revised reprint, 1952.

G. Raynaud de Lage, 'Faut-il attribuer à Béroul tout le *Tristan*?', *MA*, LXIV (1958), 249–70, and LXVII (1961), 167–8. (Cf. F. Lecoy, in R, LXXX, 88–9; M. Hanoset, in *MA*, LXVII, 503–33; M. Delbouille, in R, LXXXI, 503–33; and A. Vàrvaro *infra*).

G. Raynaud de Lage, 'Trois notes sur le *Tristan* de Beroul R, LXXXIII (1962), 522–6.

G. Raynaud de Lage, 'Du style de Béroul', R, LXXXV (1964), 518–30.

A. Regis, *Tristan als Mönch*, Strassburg, 1910.

T. B. W. Reid, 'On the interpretation of Béroul, *Tristan*, 4223–7', R, LXXXV (1964), 366–7.

T. B. W. Reid, 'The Tristan of Béroul: One author or two?', *MLR*, LX (1965), 352–8.

T. B. W. Reid, 'On the text of the *Tristan* of Béroul', *Vinaver Miscellany*, Manchester, 1965, pp. 263–88.

P. Rickard, *Britain in Medieval French Literature, 1100–1500*, Cambridge, 1956.

C. A. Robson, 'The technique of symmetrical composition in medieval narrative poetry', *Ewert Miscellany*, Oxford, 1961, pp. 26–75.

W. Röttiger, *Der heutige Stand der Tristanforschung*, Hamburg, 1897.

M. Roques, 'L'ancien français *enaines* et le vers 1678 du 'Tristan' de Béroul', R, LXIX (1946–7), 534.

G. Schoepperle, *Tristan and Isolt, a study of the sources*

of the romance, Frankfurt and London, 1913, 2 vols. New edition by R. S. Loomis, 1959.

A. Schultz, *Das höfische Leben zur Zeit der Minnesinger*, 2 vols., Leipzig, 2nd edn., 1889.

H. Stolte, 'Drachenkampf und Liebestrank', *Deutsche Vierteljahrsschrift für Literaturwissenschaft und Geistes-geschichte*, XVIII (1940), 250–61.

D. Stone, jr., 'Realism and the real Beroul', *L'Esprit Créateur*, V (1965), 4.

H. Suchier, *Les Voyelles toniques du vieux français* (transl. Ch. Guerlin de Guer), Paris, 1906.

L. Sudre, 'Les allusions à la légende de Tristan dans la littérature du moyen âge', *R*, XV (1887), 534–57.

F. J. Tanquerey, 'Notes sur le texte du roman de *Tristan* de Béroul', *R*, LVI (1930), 114–22.

F. J. Tanquerey, 'Giraut de Barri et le roman de *Tristan*', *MAe*, VI (1937), 1–20.

F. J. Tanquerey, 'Ancien français *por les membres trenchier*', *R*, LXIV (1938), 1–17.

T. Taylor, *St. Michael's Mount*, Cambridge, 1932.

J. M. Telfer, *A critical study of the episodic Tristan poems*, Oxford, 1950 (Unpublished thesis).

S. Thompson, *Motif-index of folk-literature*, Copenhagen 1955– (new edition), 6 vols.

J. van Dam, *Zur Vorgeschichte des höfischen Epos. Lamprecht, Eilhart, Veldeke*. Bonn and Leipzig, 1923.

J. van Dam, 'Tristanprobleme', *N*, XV (1930), 18–34, 88–105, 183–201.

A. Vàrvaro, *Il Roman de Tristan di Béroul*, Torino, 1963.

A. Vàrvaro, 'La teoria dell'archetipo tristaniano', *R*, LXXXVIII (1967), 13–58.

E. Vinaver, *Études sur le Tristan en prose*, Paris, 1925.

E. Vinaver, 'The love potion in the primitive *Tristan* romance', *Schoepperle Memorial Volume*, 1927, pp. 75–86.

E. Vinaver, 'The Prose *Tristan*' (pp. 339–47) and 'Sir Thomas Malory (pp. 541–52), in R. S. Loomis, *Arthurian Literature . . .*, Oxford, 1959.

E. Vinaver, 'Pour le commentaire du vers 1650 du *Tristan* de Béroul', *Studies in Medieval French presented to Alfred Ewert*, Oxford 1961, pp. 90–5.

[E. Vinaver]. *Medieval Miscellany presented to Eugène Vinaver*, Manchester, 1965.

Vollmöller, *Kritischer Jahresbericht über die Fortschritte der rom. Phil.*, I, 408 ff. and 426 ff.; III, 167 ff. (Freymond); IV, 396 ff. (Wechssler). [Tristan bibliography].

Warnecke, *Metrische und sprachliche Abhandlung über das dem Beroul zugeschriebene Tristan Fragment*, Göttingen, 1887.

F. Whitehead, 'Tristan and Isolt in the Forest of Morrois', *Pope Miscellany*, Manchester, 1939, pp. 393–400.

F. Whitehead, 'The Early Tristan Poems', in R. S. Loomis, *Arthurian Literature . . .*, Oxford, 1959, pp. 134–44.

G. Whitteridge, 'The Date of the *Tristan* of Béroul', *MAe*, XXVIII (1959), 167–79.

G. Whitteridge, 'The *Tristan* of Béroul', *Vinaver Miscellany*, Manchester, 1965, pp. 337–56.

F. M. Williams, 'Notes on the *Tristan* Romance', *Arthuriana*, II (1930), 36 ff.

H. F. Williams, 'Allusions à la légende de Tristan', *Bibliographical Bulletin of the International Arthurian Society*, XII (1960), 91–6.

B. H. Wind, 'Eléments courtois dans Béroul et dans Thomas', *RPh*, XIV (1960), 1–13.

B. H. Wind, 'Les Versions françaises du *Tristan* et les influences contemporaines', *N*, XLV (1961), 278–80.

A. Witte, 'Der Aufbau der ältesten Tristandichtungen', *ZDA*, LXX (1933), 161–95.

F. Wohlgemuth, *Riesen und Zwerge in der altfranzösischen erzählenden Dichtung*, Stuttgart, 1906.

B. Woledge, 'A rare word in Béroul: *traallier* "hunting-dog",' *FS*, X (1956), 154–9.

COMMENTARY

THE narrative contained in the Beroul fragment falls into six main divisions:

I. The Tryst and its consequences (2–580).
II. The Stratagem—the Lovers trapped (581–1270).
III. The Flight—the Woodland Scenes (1271–2132).
IV. Restitution—the Waning of the Potion and the return of Iseut to Mark (2133–3010).
V. Judgement—the Scenes at the Ford and the Oath (3010–4266).
VI. Revenge (4267–4485).

Of these six divisions the first four correspond in outline with the divisions I, J, K, established by Bédier in his reconstruction of the *Estoire*; the fifth combines certain common features (Judgement and Oath) with developments peculiar to Beroul (Scenes at the Ford); the sixth stands entirely apart from all other versions.

Each of these divisions has for convenience been broken down into sections having a unity or coherence of their own and thus lending themselves to comparative treatment. The notes to each section are preceded by a summary in which those elements which are peculiar to Beroul are enclosed in square brackets. To this are appended the substantial variants presented by other primary versions, the more particular variants being indicated in the notes. Much of the information under this head is already available in Bédier's edition of Thomas, but as my object has been the elucidation of the Beroul fragment, both selection and arrangement have been governed by different principles from his.

The reader should therefore not expect to find here all the evidence required for a classification of the Tristran poems, but he may hope to find the material relevant to the interpretation of the Beroul version and to at least a tentative assessment of the author's originality. As he was clearly a poet of talent exercising a selective procedure upon the material before him, it would seem essential to indicate, as far as possible, all the variant treatments of particular incidents or themes as they were known or might have been known to him. But this latter criterion is singularly difficult to apply objectively in his case, and it seemed desirable to go further and to include, for purely comparative purposes, at least some of the variant treatments which show how other poets, contemporary or later, handled the same matter.

I have adhered as far as possible to the sigla and abbreviations used by Bédier and commonly employed by other scholars:—

B = Beroul.

O = Eilhart von Oberge, ed. Lichtenstein.

R = Prose Romance extracts printed in Bédier, vol. II, pp. 321–95.

T = Thomas: *Roman de Tristan*, ed. Bédier.

G = Gottfried von Strassburg, ed. Bechstein.

S = *Tristrams Saga ok Ísondar*, ed. Kölbing.

E = *Sir Tristrem*, ed. Kölbing.

T.r. = *La Tavola ritonda*, ed. Polidori.

Fo = *La Folie Tristan d'Oxford*, ed. Hoepffner.

Fb = *La Folie Tristan de Berne*, ed. Hoepffner.

Bédier = *Le Roman de Tristan* par Thomas, p.p. Joseph Bédier, 2 vols. Paris, 1902.

Loeseth = *Le Roman en prose de Tristan* . . ., analyse critique d'après les manuscrits de Paris. Paris, 1890.

Escoufle = *L'Escoufle, roman d'aventures*, p.p. H. Michelant et P. Meyer, Paris, 1894.

Poire = Messire Thibaut, *Li Romanz de la Poire*, hg. von Fr. Stehlich. Halle, 1881.

M^0 = Muret's SATF edition of 1903.
M^1, M^2, M^3, M^4 = Muret's CFMA editions of
1913, 1922, 1928, 1947.[1]

References for O, G, Fb, Fo are to lines, for T, S, E to
chapters, for R to pages (in Bédier II), for T.r. to pages
(in Polidori).

The fragmentary text we possess of Beroul's poem
ends with the death of the last but one of the three hostile
barons. There is nothing to suggest that he left his work
unfinished: at least, the last folio of the MS bears the
catchwords for the following folio, now lost. It has been
conjectured that Beroul continued his narrative towards
a denouement similar to that of Eilhart, but this is far
from certain (see the note to l. 4485). It can, however,
be safely assumed that in the lost earlier portion of his
poem Beroul recounted the chief episodes of the story
of Tristan and Iseut as they appear in Bédier's reconstruction of the *Estoire*. The evidence of the *Folie Berne*,
while not conclusive, supports this assumption; for even
if it is not derived from Beroul, as Hoepffner concluded,
it is certainly based upon a version so close to Beroul
that its reference to the earlier course of the narrative
may be taken to reflect what was in Beroul. Moreover,

---

[1] The textual deviations of M^3 from the present edition were indicated
in Vol. I, and the misprints or misreadings it presented were listed in
Pope Misc., p. 93n.

In M^4 the manuscript reading has been restored in many instances,
particularly in respect of irregularities in declension (22, 225, 604, 874,
975, 1706, 1711, 1816, 1946, 2124, 2126, 2284, 2328, 2335-6, 2491, 2503,
2776, 2918, 3026, 3090, 3249, 3271-2, 3396, 3537-8, 4023, 4233, 4298,
4432, 4465), *lui* for *li* (657, 662, 2362, 2574, 2966, 3506, 3927, 4246, 4330,
4475), *li* for *lui* (523, 3960). M^4 also restores the MS reading in the
following lines:—194, 306, 312, 347, 422, 509, 820, 998, 1135, 1301-2,
1303, 1420, 1474, 1486, 1582, 1586, 1682, 1750, 1800, 1962, 2122, 2139,
2171, 2314, 2377, 2487, 2495, 2514, 2531-2, 2542, 2572, 2648, 2670, 2678,
2689, 2719, 2959, 2960, 3057, 3139, 3152, 3170, 3224, 3227, 3268, 3340,
3422, 3558, 3628, 3637, 3647, 3659, 3678, 3757, 3930, 3960, 3976, 4078,
4240, 4252, 4294, 4322, 4394, 4398. The remaining restorations are indicated in the following notes.

the latter refers to the Morholt battle (27–28, 49–53, 135–42, 848–59, 2038), the Voyage of Healing (53, 485), the Quest of Iseut and the Fight with the Dragon (485, 2558–60), the notch in Tristran's sword (2081, 2038?), and the potion committed to Brengain's charge (2208–9); see the notes to these lines. We may safely assume that the close parallelism between Beroul and Eilhart which marks the first two-thirds of our fragment applied also to the lost earlier portion. A rapid summary of Eilhart's first 3535 lines, as given in Lichtenstein's edition, has therefore been prefixed to the commentary and may serve as a substitute for the missing folios. This summary has been made slightly fuller for those incidents to which Beroul refers or which call for critical comment in this context. It will be seen that Eilhart did not include the incident 'La Harpe et la Rote' (cf. Bédier II, 244), in which Tristran wins back, with his *rote*, the Queen, who had been won by the Irish baron with his harp. The *Folie Berne* contains a passage which has been interpreted as referring to this incident and therefore implying its existence in Beroul (see below, p. 67 n).

A. *Birth and Youthful Exploits of Tristran*

Rivalin, king of Loonois, goes to the assistance of King Mark of Cornwall, who is at war with the king of Ireland; having helped him to victory, he receives the hand of Mark's sister Blancheflor. Rivalin returns to Loonois after the completion of his service with Mark. On the homeward voyage Blancheflor dies in the pains of childbirth and the child cut from her womb is called Tristran. In due course Rivalin entrusts his son to Governal, who instructs him in all knightly virtues and exercises, including the playing of the harp. (54–184)[1]

When he has reached a sufficient age, Tristran, acting

---

[1] Lines 1–53 constitute a sort of prologue in the course of which Eilhart inveighs against envious rivals and indicates the subject of his tale, which he will tell as he found it in the 'book'.

on Governal's advice, obtains his father's leave to go abroad. A ship is made ready and Tristran sails to Cornwall with eight squires, two noblemen and Governal. Without revealing his identity, he is received by King Mark, who commends him to his seneschal Dinas of Lidan. (185–350)

B. *The Morholt*

The redoubtable Morholt, whose sister was wife to the king of Ireland, having subjugated all neighbouring kingdoms to his master, except Cornwall, determines to conquer Mark and exact a tribute which had been withheld for more than fifteen years. He crosses with a large army and offers Mark the alternative of single combat between himself and a champion of equal birth or the payment of the tribute consisting of every third child born in Mark's realm during the fifteen years. (351–442)

Mark having summoned all his barons, Tristran persuades Governal to allow him to undertake the fight, and, on Governal's advice, Tristran asks Mark to knight him. This Mark does, having begged him in vain to wait a year. The barons, having been apprised by Mark of the Morholt's conditions, retire to deliberate; but none is prepared to challenge him. Tristran joins them and asks them to persuade Mark to allow him to undertake the fight, but stipulates that his name shall not be revealed until Mark has consented. However, the insistence of the Irish that Mark's champion must be of equal rank with theirs compels Tristran to reveal his identity. Mark, torn between joy and anguish, finally yields and informs the Morholt by messenger that in three days' time Tristran will meet him on an island. (443–741)

Tristran, having crossed alone to the island, casts the Morholt's boat adrift, saying that only one will be required to take off the victor. In the ensuing combat Tristran is wounded with a poisoned spear; but he cuts off the Morholt's hand in which he held the sword and, as he turns to flee, wounds him through the helmet, leaving a piece of his sword embedded in the Morholt's head. The mortally wounded Morholt is taken back to his land while Tristran is brought away amid general rejoicing. (742–943)

The followers of the Morholt send messengers to Iseut his niece, the daughter of the king of Ireland, requesting her to make all speed to meet them, for she was versed in the art of healing. She puts to sea, confident that she can heal the Morholt, but he is dead when she arrives. She finds in his wound the fragment of Tristran's sword and preserves it. They return to land. The Morholt is buried amid general mourning, and the king commands that any man coming to his realm from Cornwall shall be put to death. (944–1011)

C. *The Voyage of Healing*

Tristran's wound can only be healed by Iseut. It festers and gives off such a stench that none can bear to be near him. At Tristran's request, Mark has a hut built by the sea where Tristran lives alone, visited only by the king, Governal and Dinas. Despairing of recovery, he has himself placed in a boat with his harp and his sword and bids Governal take his place as heir to Loonois if he should not return within a year. (1012–47)

At length Tristran is cast ashore in Ireland. The king has him lodged, Tristran giving his name as Prô of Jemsetir and saying that he is a merchant and has also been a minstrel, and that he had been robbed and wounded by pirates. The king asks Iseut to heal him, which she does, but without his ever seeing her. (1048–1219)

There being a famine in the land, Tristran persuades the king to send him with ships to England to purchase food; and when he has done this, the vessels return to Ireland while Tristran takes ship to Cornwall and arrives at Tintagel one year after his departure. (1220–96)

D. The Quest of Iseut

King Mark, overjoyed at Tristran's return, wishes him to be a son to him and decides never to marry. This does not please his kinsmen ('nêste mâge'), who urge him to take a wife; they even say that the king's resolution was taken on Tristran's advice.

The barons, with Tristran, entreat the king to change his mind. He is vexed. Suddenly he observes two swallows struggling, and a fair long hair drops from their beaks. He informs the barons that he will marry the woman whose hair this is. The barons murmur and blame Tristran. (1357–1434)

Tristran offers to find the lady. The king has Dinas prepare a ship, and Tristran sets out with a hundred followers. A storm casts them upon the coast of Ireland. (1435–1504)

E. The Fight with the Dragon

Tristran, under threat of death, sends the king a golden cup and a message to say that he is a merchant come to trade and that his name is Tantris. While he waits for a reply, news is brought that a ravening dragon is ravaging the land: the man who slays it shall receive the king's daughter. Tristran sets forth and, after a fierce struggle, kills the dragon and cuts out its tongue. (1505–1685)

The false seneschal of the king of Ireland, who had fled from the dragon, believing Tristran to be dead, gives himself out as the slayer of the dragon and claims his reward. But Iseut will not believe him. Accompanied by Perinis and Brengain, she discovers Tristran and brings him back secretly to the town, where she tends him. (1686–1862)

Tristran recognizes Iseut as the one he is seeking. She discovers the notch in Tristran's sword and, finding that the fragment taken from the Morholt's head fits it, threatens him with punishment. Brengain persuades her to relent. Tristran is presented as the victor and his identity revealed to the king; the false seneschal is deprived of his office. (1863–2225)

Tristran informs the king that he wishes to take Iseut to Cornwall to be the wife of King Mark, he himself being too young to aspire to her hand. The king agrees, reflecting that Iseut might not be able to forget the wrong Tristran had done her by slaying her uncle. (2226–63)

F. *The Potion*

Iseut's mother entrusts a potion to Brengain, saying that none is to touch it save herself and that she is to give it to Iseut and her husband in their bridal bed, telling them to drink it entirely. Thus was the potion brewed: the man and the woman who should drink of it might not be separated for four years and must perforce love each other with all their senses as long as they lived, however much they might wish to desist; during the four years they might not be parted half a day: whichever did not see the other daily would fall ill. (If they did not speak to each other for a week they would die[1]). (2264–2309)

One day as they pause in a harbour, it being very hot, Tristran asks for a drink. A maid offers him the potion. He finds it good and offers it to Iseut. Immediately they feel the pangs of love. Their sufferings are such that Governal and Brengain, who has discovered that the potion has been taken, decide that Tristran and Iseut must be brought together if they are not to die. Tristran and Iseut give themselves up to love. When in sight of Mark's kingdom, they decide to ask Brengain to sleep the first night with the king. (2310–2797)

Mark receives Iseut with great honour at Tintagel. On the wedding night Brengain lay with Mark until midnight while Tristran lay with Iseut. This was not faithless on Tristran's part, for the fatal potion compelled

[1] This detail is in MS *H* (Heidelberg) only, not in *D* (Dresden).

him. Thus Tristran and Iseut bide for a whole year and
must see each other daily. (2798–2862)

G. *Brengain's Ordeal*

Iseut, fearing betrayal of her secret, pays two poor
knights sixty marks to kill Brengain and bring her liver[1]
back as proof. Brengain tells them that her only fault is
that Iseut's mother gave her and Iseut two shifts and
that, before they reached Mark, Iseut's was torn and
Brengain lent her hers, which had been kept intact, for
the nuptial night. The knights decide to spare her; they
kill a passing dog and one of them takes its liver to the
queen. Upon being told what Brengain had said, Iseut
repents and is told that she is not dead. Brengain and
Iseut are reconciled. (2863–3080)

H. *Tristran Banished from Court*

Tristran is calumniated by three wicked dukes and
four counts of the king's court.[2] They act from jealousy.
—Digression on the evil of envy and the value of virtue
(3096–3136).—Tristran's only fault was valour and
liberality and the favour shown him by the king. (3081–
3149)

The seven decide to destroy Tristran's position of
favour with the king. Four of the seven, with their
leader Andret, son of the king's sister and cousin of
Tristran, go to the king and, speaking in the name of all
seven, they lie to the king and seek in vain to turn him
against Tristran. Thereupon Mark retires and finds
Tristran and Iseut embracing and kissing before his bed.
He orders Tristran to leave the court. Tristran goes to
his lodging, intending to leave the land. (3150–3283)

I. *The Tryst*

Tristran and Iseut pine and sicken for each other.

[1] So MS *H*; 'her tongue' according to MS *D*.
[2] According to the older version: 'a duke and four counts' (ed. Lichtenstein, p. 16: Fragment VIII; and ed. Wagner, p. 18, l. 63).

Brengain goes to Tristran's lodging and tells him that Iseut would recover if she could have speech with him and if she were revenged on the hostile barons. Tristran sends word to Iseut that she is to come to the linden tree in her orchard when she sees floating down the stream which flows through her chamber a bough followed by a piece of wood (*spân*) marked with a five-pointed cross. Iseut revives at the news. (3284–3364)

Tristran pretends to be sick during the day, but at night he and Iseut meet. Their enemies are in doubt and Andret advises that they consult a dwarf versed in astrology. His familiar, Satanas, guides them to him. The dwarf declares that the lovers still meet and offers to prove it to the king. At his suggestion the king announces his intention to go hunting for seven days; but he returns from the wood with the dwarf mounted behind him. They hide in the linden tree; the moon shines as bright as day. The dwarf must surely have been helped into the tree by Satanas! (3365–3488)

Tristran comes and casts the bough and the piece of wood into the stream and then sees the shadow of Mark and the dwarf in the stream by the light of the moon. As Iseut approaches, he beckons behind him. Iseut: 'Why does he not rise and advance to meet me as is his wont?' Then she sees the beckoning and thinks: 'Something vexes him. Someone is spying upon us, I ween.' She becomes aware of the spies: their shadows are cast on the water by the moon. She showed her cleverness in that she did not turn her eyes in that (their?) direction and acted as though she was unaware. (l. 3535 = Beroul, l. 2).

I. THE TRYST AND ITS CONSEQUENCES (2–580)

O 3532–3791; *R* 349–53; *T* xxiii; *G* 14720–15050; *S* lv; *E* cxcii–cxcvii; *T.r.* 233–5; *Fo* 809–816.

The Tryst at the Fountain is one of the key situations in the tragic history of the lovers. Its significance is complex and its dramatic possibilities have been more completely realized and exploited by Beroul than by any other poet, and it therefore merits our particular attention. The lovers, caught in the toils of an irresistible passion—whether that be represented as the effect of the potion (Beroul, Eilhart) or not (Thomas)—are doomed to a course of deceit, equivocation, and even violence, in their inevitable struggle to avoid detection, to extricate themselves from compromising or dangerous situations, or to escape the rigours of retribution.

Following upon the initial deception, the first step, violent though abortive, had already been taken by Iseut, and it is not without significance that she is made solely responsible for the plan to eliminate Brengain, potentially the key witness against the lovers.

The Thomas version intercalates between Brengain's ordeal and the Tryst:—

(1) the incident of 'La Harpe et la Rote' (Bédier I, 168–75), which is purely episodic;[1]

---

[1] It relates how an Irish baron (called *Gandín* in *G*), coming to Mark's court, wins Iseut by means of his harp and how Tristran wins her back with his *rote*. In R (Loeseth, pp. 35–37) there is a similar incident, but there is no question of harp or *rote*, the enemy of Tristran is Palamedes, and the incident closes with a dour fight between the two. It has been held that a passage in *Fb* (378–91) refers to the 'Harpe et Rote' episode:—

> 'Po vos manbre de Gamarien
> Qui ne demandoit autre rien
> Fors vostre cors qu'il en mena.
> Qui fu ce qui vos delivra?'
> 'Certes, Tristans, li niés lo roi,
> Qui mout fu de riche conroi.' . . .
> 'Resanble je point a celui
> Qui sol, sanz aïe d'autrui,
> Vos secorut a cel besoin,
> A Guimarant copa lo poin?'

Gamarien (*Guimarant*) is a name that occurs nowhere else and, while it is true that the encounter is between the two protagonists alone (according to *T*), there is no mention elsewhere of Tristran having cut off his

(2) the intervention of the seneschal Mariadoc, who, prompted by a dream, spies upon Tristran and delates the lovers to Mark (Bédier I, 175–82: 'Mariadoc');

(3) Mark's testing of Iseut by his simulated departure, and Iseut's successful counter-ruse devised by Brengain (Bédier I, 182–91: 'Ruse contre Ruse').

These incidents are not of negligible entertainment value; they serve also to present more patently the state of doubt and perplexity to which Mark is reduced, and they underline the resourceful duplicity of Iseut and Brengain's role as the cunning go-between. They do not, however, motivate the separation of the lovers, which is a necessary preliminary to the Tryst, and they detract from the effectiveness of the latter.

In *T* the suspicions of Mark, momentarily allayed, are revived by the seneschal through the machinations of the dwarf to the point where he banishes Tristran from the court and the latter takes a lodging in the town (Bédier I, 191–2). In *O* the king, having refused to act on the denunciations of the hostile faction led by Andret, himself finds Tristran and Iseut embracing and kissing before his bed and orders Tristran to leave the court. The latter goes to his lodging, intending to leave the land (*O* 3238–85).

It may safely be assumed that Eilhart's description of the ensuing secret meetings of the lovers and of the plan to spy upon them existed in substantially the same form in the lost portion of Beroul.[1] Tristran's protestation (103–5) that he had summoned Iseut in vain and had

opponent's hand; in fact, *G*, who seems to have preserved the original account of *T*, states expressly that the Irish baron had no spear or shield but only his small harp. Hoepffner, however, considers that *Fb*, following Beroul, has perhaps preserved the original account and that l. 391 may be merely a variant of the severing of the Morholt's hand by Tristran (*Fb* edition, pp. 96–97).

[1] In *G*, the dwarf discovers their meetings at the fountain and tries to trick Tristran into betraying himself; he arouses Mark's suspicions and on the night in question summons Mark from the wood, whither the king had gone, ostensibly to hunt (from the castle according to *S*); both climb into the olive-tree. Tristran comes, casts the chips of wood into

been unable to speak to her is clearly intended to deceive the listening Mark.

When the lovers meet beneath the pine, it is implied in *B* that Tristran is not certain from Iseut's demeanour that she is aware of Mark's presence and it is only after she has spoken that he is reassured (97–98). But what of Iseut? Lines 3–4 make it clear that she was at least uncertain whether Tristran was aware of Mark's presence. It is therefore probably by design that the poet has given Iseut the long opening speech (no less than 76 lines), in the urgency of which it is possible to detect her agitation and anxiety lest Tristran should speak and betray them both, and it is significant that when he does speak (81–84) she interrupts him almost before he has begun. When, having himself been reassured, he blatantly asserts that, since his banishment from the court he has vainly sought to speak to Iseut, she can no longer remain in doubt, although she would seem to take the credit for having put Tristran on his guard, if we may judge by what she says to Brengain of their meeting (352).

the stream, and sees the shadows of both Mark and the dwarf upon the ground. Iseut, having retrieved the chips in the stream, approaches and sees three shadows; having noticed that Tristran does not advance to meet her as was his wont, concludes that he is aware of the danger (14587–719). She stands at a distance and speaks: 'I am surprised that you should summon me, Tristran . . .'—*S* gives such a mangled and fragmentary account of the whole Tryst incident (cap. lv) that Bédier's suggestion that a folio may have been missing in the French source of *S* is extremely probable.—In *E*'s summary and incoherent account Mark is in the tree, Tristran sees his shadow and at once upbraids Iseut by way of warning.—In *T.r.*, Mark is warned by an unnamed person and climbs into the pine-tree; Iseut comes and then Tristran. Both see a man's shadow; Iseut (*ch'era savia*) speaks first.—In *Fo*, Tristran *fou*, having referred to the seneschal's spying and delation (713–24) and to the cutting of the chips (*cospels*: 523–4), relates that the dwarf informed Mark, who got into the *espin* (corr. *pin*), that Tristran came and saw the shadow, that Iseut came and also saw it and drew back, whereupon Tristran made his request (795–810).

In *R*, Andret reveals the meetings to Mark, who gets into the *laurier*, armed with sword and bow and arrows to kill Tristran. Tristran comes and recognizes Mark by the light of the moon. Iseut comes and also recognizes him and speaks: 'What do you want of me? . . .'

O is even less explicit than *B*, but it is evident that Tristran's failure to rise and advance to meet her (which figures also in *G*) and the sign he makes with his hand (found in no other version) do no more than put Iseut on her guard and that Tristran cannot tell from her looks or actions that she also has detected the presence of Mark and the dwarf in the tree. We may therefore assume that in *B*, as in *O*, before she saw Mark's shadow (cf. 351), Iseut had been put on her guard by the demeanour of Tristran, but that Tristran's beckoning may well have been an independ nt and not altogether happy elaboration by Eilhart.

For analogues and possible sources of the Tryst scene, see: Hertz[3], Anm. 100; Schoepperle 212–3; and Helaine Newstead (in *RPh*, IX), who concludes that its ultimate origin is to be sought in Old Irish stories about Finn with later accretions from Oriental fabliau material through the medium of French treatments. The large number of extant pictorial representations bear witness to the special popularity of the Tryst scene; cf. R. S. Loomis and Laura Hibbard Loomis, *Arthurian Legends in Medieval Art*, New York, 1938, pp. 50–69 with corresponding plates; R. S. Loomis, *Illustrations of Medieval Romance on Tiles from Chertsey Abbey*, University of Illinois Studies in Language and Literature II, 2 (1916), with bibliography of Tristan illustrations, supplemented in RR VIII (1917), 196–209, in his article 'The Tristran and Perceval caskets', the carvings being held by Loomis to be based on Beroul rather than on Thomas (Golther); see also Margaret R. Scherer, *About the Round Table*, The Metropolitan Museum of Art, New York, 1945, and A. Del Monte, '*Desuz le pin*, postilla tristaniana', *Studi medievale in onore di Antonio de Stefano*, Palermo, 1956, 171–6.

(a) *Conversation of Tristran and Iseut* (2–234)

SUMMARY[1]

1–4   Iseut, apparently aware of Mark's presence, gives no sign but anticipates Tristran as she draws near.

5–8   I: 'You do wrong, Tristran, to summon me.' [She pretends to weep.]

9–15 *Illegible.*

16–25 I: 'Do not summon me again: I would not come. The king thinks I have loved you sinfully, but I swear that no man ever had my love save the one who had me as a virgin maid.

26–34 The felons, [for whom you fought the Morholt,] have persuaded the king of our love, but we are innocent.

35–43 Rather would I be burnt than bear any man love save my lord. Yet will he not believe me. How has my fortune fallen! Truly did Solomon say: "The thief rescued from the gallows will not cherish his rescuer."

45–48 *Illegible.*

50–55 [You suffered grievously from the wound you received in the fight with my uncle. I healed you: little wonder that you were well disposed to me!

56–59 They have persuaded the king that our love is guilty. May they never look upon God's countenance!]

60–68 Never summon me again: I would not dare to come. I tarry too long: the king would kill me if he knew.

69–80 [Following the teaching of my mother,] I cherished you because of your kinship with the king, and now I have lost his favour.'

---

[1] Details or developments enclosed in square brackets occur only in B or *Fb*.

81–84 T: 'The king does wrong to believe the false
          accusations of his men.'

85–92 I: 'Fie, Tristran, [my lord is courtly,] he has been
          misled. I tarry too long: I must be gone.'

93–96 T: 'Mercy, Iseut, as I cherish you.'

97–   [Tristran perceived that Iseut was forewarned:
100   their meeting will have a happy issue.]

101–   T: ['Since the royal chamber was forbidden me I
111   have summoned you on several occasions but
          could not have speech with you. Mercy on one
          who is mortally grieved by the king's ill-will
          and suspicion!]

112–   *Illegible*.
119

121–   [The Cornish felons triumph: they would not
130   have any of his kin near him: his marriage has
       cost me dear. Why is the king so foolish? I
       would rather be hanged than enjoy your love.

131   He will not even let me clear myself.

132–   These deceiving felons were speechless and
142   recreant when I defended his realm against the
       Morholt and drove him forth.]

143–   The king is to blame. [Tell him, lady, that I am
156   ready to undergo ordeal by fire, for I know
       that none of his court will accept combat.]

157–   Reconcile me with the king my friend. I wish
162   to leave his service [as I entered it].'

163–   I: 'You do wrong, Tristran, to ask me to inter-
178   cede. [I am alone in this land.] I would not
          dare.

179–   I should be glad if he forgave you his wrath.
183

184–   If the king knew of our meeting he would
196   have me burnt. In fear and trembling I depart.'

197   [Iseut turns away: Tristran recalls her.]

198–   T: 'Mercy, in Christ's name, lady: you alone can
203   help me against the king's hatred.

204   Have my pledged arms released for me.
205–   I will flee the land: others will be glad of my
216   service. The king will bitterly regret his accusa-
         tions [before the year is out].
217–   [Pay for my lodging for me.]'
218

219– I: 'How can you ask this of me, knowing the
230   king's suspicions: it would be too obvious if
         I were to dare to ask for your sureties to be
         released.
231–   [Know that it is not out of niggardliness that
232   I refuse.]'
233– Iseut departs and Tristran bids her a tearful fare-
234   well.

VARIANTS

O 3532–3609; *R* 349, 1–351, 13; *T* xxiii, 200–201; *G* 14720–14919; *S* lv, l. 13; *E* cxcii–cxcvi; *T.r.* 233, 1–235, 1; *Fo* 809–814.

R: Iseut asks what Tristran wants, voices her fear and protests her innocence in spite of what the evil tongues of Cornwall may say, while acknowledging that she cherishes Tristran as a valiant knight. Tristran protests his innocence and wishes to know if it is true that Mark is threatening him. Iseut is glad when she realizes that Tristran is aware of Mark's presence. She dissuades him from the project of departing for Logres.

G agrees in the main with those portions of the conversation which are not peculiar to *B*. Iseut says that she comes at Brengain's instigation, but her declared attitude is substantially as in *B*, she makes a similar ambiguous declaration (*B* 22–25) and their parting is similar. On the other hand Tristran makes no reference to pledges or liabilities, and instead of referring to the welcome he would receive elsewhere, he asks that Mark and Iseut keep up an appearance of good-will towards him for not more than eight days so that he may prepare for his departure and prevent the ill-disposed from suspecting the worst.—*T.r.* gives a shorter version of *G*'s account, but Iseut says explicitly that she would not come if summoned again and Tristran declares that, had he loved Iseut with a wicked love, he would not have given her to Mark but would have kept her for himself! Tristran is made to add incongruously that he wishes to return to Brittany to see his lady (*Isolda*) and asks Iseut to secure from Mark the cession to Governal of a part of the kingdom of Loonois. Tristran and Iseut part, sad that they had been unable to speak of more secret matters.—*S* may be ignored for the reason indicated above (p. 68 n): Tristran and Iseut, having seen the king's shadow, depart incontinently in the knowledge that they have been betrayed; Mark is perplexed but

F

abandons his anger against them.—In *E*, Tristran upbraids Iseut and threatens to depart to Wales; Iseut protests that she is being blamed on his account and makes the ambiguous declaration (*B* 22–25); Tristran asks her to settle his debts (?) she agrees to intercede; Mark considers them innocent and decides that Tristran shall remain at court: he hates the trouble-makers; Tristran is restored to favour.—In *Fo*, Tristran *fou* recalls how he asked Iseut to reconcile him with Mark or to have his pledges released so that he might leave the kingdom, and how they were saved and reconciled with Mark.

O presents a drastically modified account of the conversation. Instead of declaring that she will not answer any future summons from Tristran, Iseut says she is glad of Tristran's disfavour and, not content with insisting upon what she has suffered on his account, declares that she would be pleased if he were killed by Mark or failed to regain his favour; yet in ll. 3570–1 she says that she would be well content if, without her intervention, Mark forgave him. There is no trace of the ambiguous declaration (*B* 22–25), Mark is neither specifically blamed nor defended, apart from Tristran's passing protestation that Mark wrongs him, nor is there any tearful farewell.

We may take it that what is not enclosed in square brackets in the summary given above was available to Beroul either in his main source or through his knowledge of alternative versions. As for the details or motifs presented by one or other of the extant versions and not found in *B*, they would seem to have been introduced in those versions independently and subsequently. Thus, only according to *R* does Mark ascend the tree fully armed with intent to kill Tristran, and this is doubtless responsible for the fact that in *R* only does Tristran give as his reason for summoning Iseut his desire that she should verify the reports he has heard of Mark's intention to kill him: if they should be true, he wishes to leave Cornwall betimes for fear that he might in the event be responsible for Mark's death. Tristran's words fill Iseut with joy as they convince her that he is aware of Mark's presence, and it is possible that we have here a modification of what stood in *R*'s source (as in *B*,[1] where it is Tristran who is reassured by Iseut's words, she having already been at least partly reassured by Tristran's demeanour that he is aware).

[1] The other versions all lack this detail.

The indications of the destination of Tristran's proposed flight, if his departure should become necessary (R: Logres, E: Wales, T.r.: Brittany), are clearly independent additions, as are also Tristran's yielding to Iseut's request not to depart (in R), Tristran's request (in G) that Mark and Iseut should refrain for a space of eight days from giving any sign of Tristran's 'disgrace', and Iseut making Brengain responsible for her coming (also in G).

The most striking deviation is furnished by O,[1] where the exaggerated hostility to Tristran simulated by Iseut must be set down as an attempt by Eilhart to improve upon his source; the ineptitude of the attempt (in the light of what has preceded) being underlined by her admission that she would nevertheless be glad to see him restored to favour without her intervention. The contrast with the much greater subtlety displayed by Beroul in calculating the presumed effect of the conversation on the listening Mark is such that one is tempted to ask whether O has not had cognizance of and been influenced by the description of Iseut's feigned hostility in the episode 'Ruse contre Ruse' of the Thomas version (Bédier I, xxi).

Iseut's insistence on what she has suffered on Tristran's account (E, T.r., O) may well have figured in B in the now illegible lines 9–15 (see notes below).

By contrast with the other versions the conversation in B is a masterpiece of psychological penetration. It is true that, upon analysis, it is seen to involve a good deal of repetition. Twice Iseut declares in effect: 'You do wrong to summon me (6–7); do not do so again: I would not come' (18–19, 60–63); twice she threatens to leave (92, 196), etc.; but it will be seen that the context varies and that, while the repeated protestations of innocence

---

[1] It is difficult to believe, with Bédier (I, 199 n.) that G has here been influenced by O. In spite of differences in detail, the general tenor of the conversation shows a closer parallelism between G and B than between G and O or even O and B.

(22–25, 31–38, 67, etc.), complaints of Mark's unjust suspicions (20, 39, 80, 169, 223) and references to the fear he inspires in Iseut (68, 168, 184–5, 192) may be held to have a purely rhetorical effect, others have a more material relevance. Thus, the repeated references to the hostile faction and their machinations (26, 44, 56, 91, 121, 132, 144) serve no doubt to create in Mark's mind the conviction that the lovers are not animated by resentment against him personally and to sharpen his reaction against the 'traitors'; but they also prepare the reader or hearer for the important role they are to play in Beroul's narrative.

It will be seen that, in Beroul's work as a whole, repetition (with or without variations) is one of the characteristic features of the author's narrative technique, and this strengthens the conviction that his work was written to be read in public and not privately. It is in line with this intention that the poet should make extensive use of 'cross-references', presumably to help the hearer to retain the recollection of the narrative through successive instalments of a public reading. It will therefore be found that, while the interest of the audience is sometimes sharpened by indications of what is to come, references to past events are more common. Already in this first extant passage we are reminded of the Morholt episode (28, 50, 136), of the healing of Tristran by Iseut (53), and of the 'political' motivation of Mark's marriage (123–6). These are doubly effective in that they have, in the present context, the immediate purpose of reminding Mark of the services rendered him and of happier times in his relationship with Tristran.

Other additions and elaborations are equally effective: Iseut pretending to weep (8), her reference to being alone in a strange land (174),[1] and particularly, in their calculated effect on the listening king, her defence of Mark (85) and Tristran's reference to previous vain attempts to

[1] See the note to this line.

secure an interview with Iseut (103–5). The special importance attached by the poet to Tristran's claim to be heard and to be allowed to justify or clear himself, to make his *escondit*, is also foreshadowed (131), together with his more specific offer to undergo ordeal by fire in default of trial by combat, for which he proudly asserts that none will present himself (155–6). While his request to have his pledged weapons released occurs (though much less explicitly) in *O* also, no other version refers to payment for his lodgings (218) or to Iseut's supposed niggardliness (see note to 231).

But the individuality of Beroul is revealed no less clearly in the skill with which he has combined these diverse elements into a dramatic sequence. The whole of the opening speech is a clever exposition of Iseut's case, designed to give Tristran a lead, for Iseut is not sure that Tristran is aware of the king's presence in the tree and at the same time to make the deepest impression on Mark. There is here no denial (such as *O* shows) of her undeniable predisposition in Tristran's favour, but rather a recital of the reasons which justify her and incidentally should disarm Mark, interspersed with protestations of her innocence and culminating in her lamenting the fact that she has lost her husband's confidence and affection. And when Tristran appears too ready to blame Mark for his credulity, she flatters Mark's self-esteem by defending him and throwing all the blame on his barons. Taking his cue from Iseut, Tristran first of all echoes her protestations and then proceeds to produce very plausible reasons for having summoned her: his desire for reconciliation with the king, his demand for an *escondit*,—and when Iseut declines to intercede and in her mounting fear threatens to depart, he resigns himself to flight and asks for the release of his impounded weapons and the payment of his lodging. In refusing to undertake even this appeal for an honourable and equitable dismissal from Mark's court, Iseut completes the breaking down of the

king's defences, and we know that in the event her
embellished account of Tristran's requests and complaints (400–58) will be all the more effective for being
made, ostensibly at least, under duress.

The psychological consistency of Beroul's characters
is no less striking, in spite of the limitations imposed
upon him by tradition and respected by him. Here, as
elsewhere in his narrative, the characters are made to
reveal themselves without elaborate self-analysis. Not
only does the author refrain from describing their state
of mind, except in most sober and concise terms, but the
characters do not analyse their feelings in the sophisticated and 'methodical' manner of a Thomas, still less of
a Chrétien de Troyes. They (and we with them) are
concerned with their thoughts and feelings as proceeding
from action or motivating it, and not as interesting
passive states. And so the author, when he wishes to
comment upon the nature of their feelings, affects the
exclamatory style and thereby appeals to his hearers to
identify themselves with his own reflections or with the
action (4, 320, etc.). This direct appeal is carried into the
speeches of the characters themselves, and the exclamatory style manifests itself not only in the prevalence of
protestations (often in the form of 'rather would I . . .
than . . .'; e.g. 35, 128–30) and rhetorical questions, but in
the striking abundance and variety of formulae of
asseveration, oaths, invocations, appeals to God and the
saints, and imprecations directed at the 'traitors'.[1] The
author's syntax has not remained unaffected by this
penchant for the exclamatory. In particular, this opening
passage already furnishes examples of the concessive or
conditional clause being given an exclamatory turn (23,
58), a feature which would produce its full effect on the
hearer rather than the reader.

[1] In the first 232 lines alone, God is invoked in varying fashion no
less than 16 times; nor is the repeated use of *par* (*ma*) *foi* and the like to
be dismissed as mere padding.

The poet generally eschews moralizing reflections, whether in the heavy, rather matter-of-fact manner of Eilhart or the elaborate and sometimes casuistical style of Gottfried. Instead, he occasionally indulges in the more popular forms of sententiousness which affect the proverbial turn of speech, whether this be real or simulated reminiscence of clerkly learning (41–43).[1]

One may say therefore that from these opening lines there already emerges the figure of a writer showing an exceptional degree of independence and originality in the exploitation of a well-established and organized mass of 'traditional' material, placing observation of human nature above literary convention and basing his appeal upon the bare human facts of life rather than upon a particular fashion or creed, robust in the dramatic presentation of his tale no less than in the rhetorical quality of his style.

NOTES

2 There can be no doubt that this line corresponds to line 3535 in O ('als ob sie es nicht en wiste') and that the main clause upon which it depends must have indicated Iseut's circumspection in the face of danger, and one might conjecturally supply *Car bien se garde, en ceste place* (cf. O 3534: 'und rechte alsô gebârte'): 'For she took good care to give no sign of anything' (i.e. of having discovered Mark's presence).

5 *Tristran*. In our text the name always appears in this form, used as subject (1717) or object, except in ll. 1423 and 1637 where the nom. *Tristrans* is used correctly; other exceptions are attributable to scribal error: *Tristrans* 467, *Tristranz* 2960, and perhaps also *Tristrain* 407; see Introd., No. 35.—The name is of Celtic origin, being connected with the name (*Drest—Drostan*) borne by Pictish kings in the seventh–ninth centuries, transmitted

[1] Cf. also 75–78 (shared with O and G).

through Welsh (*Drystan*), Cornish (*Tröstan*), and possibly English (*Trystan*) to the French as *Tristan*.[1]—As early as Gottfried we find the name provided with an 'etymological' explanation: 'The child is to be christened *Tristan* in memory of the sad fate of his parents and the sad circumstances of his birth: for *triste* means sadness, and so he was named for the sad "adventure" of his parents. This tale of Tristan's sad birth, sad life and sad death will show how aptly he was named' (*G* 1989–2020). A similar explanation occurs in R (Loeseth, p. 16), but not in O or in E).[2] The fancied connection with *triste* (var. *tristre*[3]) would account for the hesitation between *Tristan* and *Tristran*.[4]

6 'You are so blameworthy in regard to me', i.e. 'you do me such great wrong'.

8 This detail is peculiar to B.

9–15 To judge from the words which can still be

---

[1] For bibliographical references, see Kelemina, p. 191.

[2] S is more explicit and further explains (cap. xvi) that *trist* means 'sad' and *hum* means 'man', but that the name was altered because *Tristam* is more agreeable to say than *Tristhum*! Bédier (I, 27, n. 1) inclined to the view that S here reproduces T and that G 2019–20 confirms this:

> Er was reht', alse er hiez, ein man
> und hiez reht', als er was, Tristan.

T.r. (p. 43) tells us that his mother named him *Tantri* (var. *Stanotri*), but that if the *Tri* were placed before *Tano*, it would be a fairer name and hence he would be called *Tritan* (cf. p. 241, where Tristan, disguised as a fool, tells the king that his name is *Tantri* and that if the *tri* is placed before the *tan*, he would be called *Tritan*!).

[3] The form *tristre* (due to the influence of words like *maistre, prestre* (?); cf. G. Paris, in *Rom.* XIX, 121) occurs in l. 346 (: *magistre*) and in other MSS of the thirteenht century, e.g. in the *Complainte Rustebeuf*, l. 36; according to Kölbing (p. 207) already at the beginning of the century. See Introd., No. 28.

[4] It would appear that the form without the second *r* is consistently used by Gottfried (anagram: *Tantris*) and by *Fb*, while *Fo* occasionally has *Tristran* (anag.: *Trantris*). O shows *Tristrant* (but in the older fragments sometimes *Tristant*) and *Tantris* for the anagram; E has *Tristrem* and *Trantris*; S has *Tristram* (but *Tristam* on p. 16, ll. 2–3) and *Trantris*. The Thomas fragments normally show *Tristran*, but occasionally *Tristan* and once *Tristrans*. The Prose romance MSS seem to hesitate between *Tristan* and *Tristram*.

deciphered and from other extant versions, these lines probably contained:—(*a*) a reference to what Iseut had suffered on Tristran's account (cf. *O*, *E*, *T.r.*; see above, pp. 73–74) and (*b*) a development of the thought contained in lines 6–7: 'Tristran, by summoning me you expose me to great danger: if the king knew of this our meeting, he would have me put to the sword, for he would suspect that I had come here with evil rather than good intent.' (Cf. particularly Bédier II, 349, ll. 3–6, and *T.r.* 232, 17–18). This is repeated with insistence in ll. 65–66, just as ll. 17–19 are re-echoed in ll. 60–63.

20 *folie*, here in the sense of 'wickedness', 'sinfulness' in reference to illicit love; so also in 1655, 4155; *folor* occurs once only and in this sense, which is also conveyed by the adverb *folement* (661, 2007). The meaning 'folly', 'stupidity' is found in 362, 2718. The adjective *fol* may similarly mean 'foolish', 'stupid', 'irrational' (127, 177, 273, 308, [413], 714; 311, 696; 2479, 2805, 4172), or 'wicked', 'sinful' (301, 496, 3042); cf. note to l. 34.

22 *Dex*, nom. for obl. (ind. obj.).

23 '(Who) may he place a scourge upon me if ever anyone had my love save he who had me as a virgin!' This ambiguous oath, of which we have a parallel in ll. 4205–8, is found in *G* (14769–70), *E* (st. cxciv), *T.r.* (233, 14–17). The fact that it does not occur in *O* has been attributed by Muret (*Rom.* XVI, 314–5) to Eilhart's reluctance (or that of his source) to retain such casuistical subtleties as the Ambiguous Oath (on both occasions) and the whole Judgement of God episode.

26 *Se* has here concessive force: 'even if', 'although'.

27–28 The references to the Morholt episode (27–28, 50–53, 135–42, 480, 848–57, 2081), with the doubtful exception of 2038, suggest that in the lost portion of *B* it was related substantially as in *O* (see above, pp. 61–62).[1]

---

[1] In *Fb* (77–83) Tristan *fou* recalls Iseut's healing of the wound received 'en Cornuaille Qant al Morholt fis la bataille En l'ile ou fui menez a nage

—The name has been variously interpreted as Germanic
(*môr* 'marsh' + *holt* 'monster') or Celtic (*mori-s(p)olto* 'he,
who cleaves the sea').[1] It is possible that it is a Celtic
name modified under the influence of French or Germanic names.[2] For a brief summary and bibliographical
indications, see Kelemina, p. 194 and pp. 203–5.

29 Here, as at ll. 83, 289, 429, 2859, the M⁰ reading
a croire (replaced in later editions by *acroire*) is hardly
possible, since it would imply an impersonal meaning:
fait a croire 'is to be believed', 'is credible'; cf. 1664.

34 'which would result in dishonour'; see note to l. 57.

35 *Mex . . . que* (37), 'Rather . . . than that'. See Introduction, p. 6.

35–43 These lines are almost certainly an addition by
Beroul and illustrate what has already been said (above,
p. 79) about his style and his taste for the pithy proverb
rather than elaborate sententiousness.

40 *De (si) haut si bas* is a well authenticated proverbial
expression (cf. Tobler, *Proverbe au Vilain*, pp. 75, 91, 163,
and M⁰, s.v. *bas*). Here, as in Chrétien de Troyes, *Lancelot* 6497 (see Foerster's note), it is connected with the
revolutions of the wheel of Fortune: 'How has my
fortune fallen!' Cf. l. 1697, and the more circumstantial
allusion to the wheel of fortune in Wace, *Brut* 1917–30
and 4665–8, and Marie de France, *Guigemar* 538–40.

42 This is said in reference to the ingratitude of the
hostile barons after Tristran's defeat of the Morholt. The
proverbial saying here attributed to Solomon had wide
currency in the Middle Ages; cf. Morawski 1048. Professor Reid (in *Vinaver Miscellany*, p. 280) calls attention
to the variant *ne amera qui lui reynt de f.* cited by Morawski,
and proposes to read *raient* (= ind. pr.3 of *raiembre* 're-
deem') for *traient* and to keep MS *nel*. This gives a much
more satisfactory reading: 'Nevermore will a thief

Por desfandre lo treüssaje Que cil devoient de la terre'. In ll. 399–400
it is specified that Tristran was wounded in the shoulder.
[1] J. Loth, *Contr.*, 29, n. 2.   [2] E. Muret, in *Rom.* XXVII, 612.

cherish him who rescues him from the gallows.' See also
M⁰, s.v. *Salemon*, and below, l. 1461.

45–48 The now illegible lines probably developed the
theme of the ingratitude of the barons (42–43) and their
jealousy of Tristran, thus leading up to the reference to
the fight with the Morholt being undertaken by Tristran
(50–53).

53 The poisoned wound received by Tristran in the
fight with the Morholt is healed by Iseut's mother
according to *G, E, S, Fo*; by Iseut herself in *Fb* (77), *R*
(MS 103; Loeseth, p. 21) and *O* (see above, p. 62). Note
that in *O* it is Iseut who sets out to heal the Morholt
(931–1050), being described as versed in the art of healing
(945); she alone, we are told, is capable of healing
Tristran's wound. See note to 27–28, 485. On a later
contradiction in *T*, see Hertz³, Anmerkung 140.

57 *vilaine*, here (and in 502) in the sense of 'blameworthy', 'wicked', and not (as in 900, 1266) 'uncourtly',
'uncouth'. The root meaning 'peasant', 'villein' is found in
3036. The class distinction is clearly brought out in 2378:
Cortois le virent et vilain. Similarly *vilanie* varies in meaning
from 'dishonour' in reference to illicit love and its consequences (34, 2230, 4165) to 'dishonour' in a more general
sense (3044) or 'disloyal conduct' (1090). Cf. note to l. 20.

58 Tanquerey (*Rom.* LXV, 122) would prefer to delete
the exclamation mark and interpret the subjunctive
without conjunction as concessive: 'Mourraient-ils, ils
ne seraient pas admis à voir la face de Dieu.' It is possible
to interpret the clause as concessive, but the inversion
and the parallel phrase in 841 suggest that in form it is
exclamatory: 'Let them come into the presence of God
and his kingdom! Never would they look upon his face.'
Muret (s.v. *Deu*) interprets l. 58 as an ironical formula of
asseveration ('So may they see God and his kingdom!'
sc. 'So help them God!') followed by a qualification
which makes the calumnies of the hostile barons appear
false ('but they will never look upon his face' sc. 'God

will not help them'). This explanation is inherently more probable and in conformity with Beroul's manner. Cf. also *Lancelot* 6611: 'Et se je Deu voie an la face'. As pointed out by Muret (s.v. *face*), the reference is to Jeremiah xviii, 17: *Dorsum et non faciem ostendam eis in die perditionis eorum.*

61 *mandez* is a subjunctive dependent on *gardez*.

67 'and it would be very unjustly done'.

67–68 Reid suggests (*Vinaver Misc.*, p. 276) that these lines may have been interverted by the scribe.

70 *pas* seems to be a scribal error resulting from the confusion of *s* and *r* and perhaps induced by the *ne* of l. 68. Muret had, in his first edition, justified *pas* as used 'dans une subordonnée affirmative dépendant d'une principale négative'; but in his later editions he adopted the emendation to *par*.

73–77 'I seem to remember in days gone by my mother cherished the kinsmen of my father, and she said that the wife would not (i.e. could not be said to) hold her husband dear who did not love his kinsmen.' The attribution of this or any similar saying to Iseut's mother is peculiar to Beroul. It is noteworthy that whereas O merely causes Iseut to say that she was kind to Tristran because he was Mark's nephew and gained him honour,[1] S (cap. liii) introduces a similar reflection at an earlier point (in the episode 'Ruse contre Ruse', Bédier I, 182–91): 'I showed you favour because I was commonly accused of hating your kinsman and best friend; for it is a well known saying that it is a bad trait in the character of women that they do not love the kinsmen of their husbands and do not wish to have them concerned in their words or actions.' Gottfried (13881–3) supports the attribution of S's version to their common source, Thomas.

74 *Amast*, subjunctive depending on a verb of opining

[1] O 3548–51:   Wen ich bin zu worte komen
von dir âne mîne scholt.
ich was dir dorch mînen hêren holt,
wen dû sîn nebe wêrist.

(*quidai*). The mood of *disoit* (75) indicates that logically the statement attributed to Iseut's mother is not a matter of opinion.

75–76 I assume that the poet wrote *la mollier*, the definite article being used with the demonstrative force which it still frequently had in O.F., and either that the scribe, taking the substantive in the generic sense (and therefore not requiring the article) misread *la* as *ia*, or that he simply allowed his eye to wander to the following line (cf. *Pope Misc.*, p. 96).—In l. 76 *son* may have been omitted by the scribe under the influence of the following word, likewise beginning with *s*-. M⁴ rightly notes that it is rare to find *ja* repeated in the same clause; it would be difficult to find a strictly parallel case: the example cited from the *Roland* (2429), even if it be accepted as a correct reading, is not really apposite.

78 While *diret* might be considered to be not altogether impossible, a scribal misreading of *diset* may be assumed in view of a number of similar cases (4146, etc.; cf. *Pope Misc.*, p. 94).

85–91 This specific defence of Mark by Iseut has no parallel in any other version of this scene and is a characteristic elaboration by Beroul (see above, p. 76).—In l. 90 Muret's later editions adopt Tobler's emendation (*Faire mal faire et . . .*), which expresses more clearly the thought of the author; but that is hardly a sufficient reason for rejecting the MS reading. The idea conveyed by the modal *faire* 'to cause to' is already implied in *desveier*, the following infinitives depending to some extent on *desveier* and serving to amplify it: *desveier* (*au point de*) *faire le mal*; cf. a similar looseness of construction in 165–6 and 1604–5. 'He would never have believed it of his own accord, that we both were of such a mind; but a man may be misled into doing evil and leaving the good undone: thus have they done with my lord.'

98 'He knew that she had become aware (of Mark's presence).' See note to l. 2.

101 *Iseut* or *Yseut* (for older *Iselt*, a Germanic name). The fact that the daughter of a king of Dublin bears a Germanic name was considered by Muret (*Rom.* XVII, 606) to be an historically authentic trait of local colour. Whether it in fact replaces an earlier Celtic *Essylt* (Loth) or not (Zimmer) must remain doubtful.—Note that in l. 1546 she is described as *a la crine bloie*; as this designation is used to distinguish the first from the second Iseut (*aux blanches mains*), it might seem to support the view that Iseut of the White Hands figured in the lost conclusion of Beroul's romance.

101–111 The reiterated appeals to Iseut's compassion, like the reference to repeated vain messages to Iseut, are peculiar to Beroul.

102 The emendation *en bone foi* was proposed and justified by Acher on the ground that the MS reading would constitute the only instance of the epithetic use of *bone foi* in the text. But this is hardly a cogent reason, particularly in the face of a similar use of *gente façon* in l. 2261 and *bele figure* in l. 1238.

104 *chanbre*, the private apartment of the king and queen, variously referred to as *la chanbre* (297, etc.) or as *ma chanbre* by the king or the queen (317) and once as *la chanbre painte* (549); occasionally the plural is used (2182, 3153). When used without the article in the phrase *chanbre(s) veer* (104, 175) it seems to imply not only that the *chanbre* itself is forbidden Tristran, but that he is banished from court. On the other hand, *sale* (1071, 1492, 2458, etc.) denotes the 'hall', 'great hall' which served for 'audiences' or meetings of the king's council (1865) and in which guests were received and fed and sometimes accommodated for the night. In l. 680 it seems to be implied that the king's suite slept in the *sale* (after the king had taken his evening meal) and that Tristran attended the king at his retirement (681) and shared the *chanbre* with the king and queen (694). Perinis slept at the feet of Tristran (764) and, on this occasion at least the

dwarf also was in the *chanbre*.[1] The three hostile barons apparently wait without (741) and accompany Mark and the dwarf on their return to the *chanbre* (771 and 805). Brengain's presence would seem to be excluded by the express statement in 762–5, but this need not perhaps be taken too literally.—For the 'Blades at the Bed' incident and the more primitive sleeping arrangements it involves (described by Eilhart, 5285 ff.), see Bédier II, 158–9 and the note to ll. 3546–7 below.

105 'Nor have I been able to speak to you since' (i.e. since the *chanbre* was forbidden me). Tristran is here suggesting (for the benefit of Mark) that they had not met previously. According to O, G, E, R (MS 757), the lovers had been able to meet on several occasions (eight times in eight days, according to G 14509), thanks to the device of the bough and the chips thrown into the stream; in B, Tristran's statement to the contrary is clearly intended to deceive the listening king. Muret's correction of *puis* to *plus* was therefore unnecessary and has been abandoned in M[4].

110 'Had thought ill of you concerning me.'—O.F. syntax allowed of this use of the indicative, which has the effect of presenting as a fact what is grammatically dependent on a verb of feeling (*j'ai tel duel*); or is *c'* (= *que*) causal?

111 'that there is nothing for it but that I die'.

119 The *losengiers*, 'deceitful flatterers', 'slanderers', 'intriguers', are stock figures of epic and romance. In courtly poetry they become the enemies of the courtly lovers and by deceitful flattery and slander seek to destroy their happiness (cf. 144).

120 I take *desor* as meaning 'from the presence of' rather than 'in spite of', which is the meaning attributed to it by Muret (cf. *sur mon pois* 4180). Translate: '[Would that] he did not believe a flattering deceiver (to the extent of) banishing me from his presence.'

---

[1] G (14254–6) tells us that the dwarf was a 'familiar' (*heimlich*) of the king and the *chanbre*.

126 The realization that, in the absence of a blood heir, Tristran would inherit Mark's kingdom was one of the chief causes of the hostility of the barons. In Thomas (*G* 5150–9; *E*, str. c) Mark had explicitly made Tristran his heir and renounced marriage after his knighting, and after the Voyage of Healing the barons insist that Mark marry (*G* 8354 ff.; *S*, cap. xxxiii; *E*, str. 123). In *O*, after the Voyage of Healing, Tristran, moved by the jealousy and calumnies of the barons, joins them in pressing Mark to marry (1337–63). *E* has obviously blundered in making Mark's followers swear, after the Morholt fight, that Tristran is to succeed Mark (str. ci).

130 *prendre drüerie* may refer to the acceptance (or exchange) of the love-token or it may mean, in the abstract, 'enter upon a relationship of lover'.

131 Tristran's claim to be allowed to defend or clear himself by an *escondit* (and in a lesser degree Iseut's) is consistently stressed by Beroul, who presents him as having acted under the influence of the potion and as therefore not being morally responsible, and in any case entitled to demand legally that he be not condemned untried and 'unheard'. The noun *escondit* (used in the plural on one occasion, l. 4176) denotes the defence against a charge (780, 2397, 3126) or, in a wider sense, the hearing of a case, whether it affects Tristran or Iseut (3043, 3238, 3223) or both (2227). It could take the form of a judiciary duel (155–6, 815–8, 2227–35, 2366–73, 2862, 3063–4, 3423), a sworn declaration (3233, 4159–66, etc.) or trial by ordeal (149–52); see note to 778–82.

The verb (*s'*)*escondire* is used in the same senses (except at l. 3915, where it has approximately the meaning of modern *éconduire* 'to demur'), but, as a transitive verb, is extended to apply to the espousal of Iseut's cause by Arthur and his knights if the hostile faction should return to the charge after her exculpation (3252).

To denote specifically a successful defence or acquittal our author uses (*s'*)*esligier* 'to clear, to justify oneself '(2855,

3419), (*s'*)*alegier* 'to alleviate, to clear of a charge' (2570, 3565), (*se*) *deraisnier* 'to make a successful defence' and the noun *deraisne* (see Glossary).

135 This may not be literally true (cf. the deliberations described in *O*; see above, p. 61), but it is a very apt description of the reluctance of the barons to engage in single combat with the Morholt, the only alternative to the payment of the tribute demanded by him (cf. *O* 533 ff.).

137 The impersonal (*il i*) *a* originally took the oblique case, but as the literal meaning of *avoir* faded it was equated with *être* and the nominative tended to replace the oblique; see above, p. 20. There are similar cases in 3426 and 4175. There is therefore no need to accept Tobler's emendation *Onc nen i out un sol d'eus tous.*—It is difficult to make anything of Tanquerey's suggestion that *sous* may be the past participle of *soldre* and not the adj. *sols* (< SOLUS).

139–40 Muret's normalizing corrections (abandoned in M[4]) are not absolutely necessary. The nominative *pensis* might well have been induced by a sort of ellipsis ('who was') and the oblique is by no means obligatory after the comparative *que*. Moreover, the poet did not always observe the case-distinctions (cf. 127, etc.).

146 *avoir pechié* might here mean 'be guilty', 'do wrong' (cf. l. 6), but preferably 'suffer damage', referring to the loss of Tristran's services: 'Does he think that he will not suffer for it: in truth that cannot fail to be.' Cf. *O* 3575–9:

> swie wênig daz mîn hêre clage,
> iedoch ne mag he den schadin
> nimmir mêr vorwinnen,
> ab ich mit unminnin
> uz sîme lande vare.

148 There is no compelling reason for breaking the couplet and taking this line with the following one, as suggested by Reid (*Vinaver Misc.*, p. 266), and punctuating as in M[4].

149 ff. Tristran offers to clear himself of the charge by

G

ordeal, for none would dare to enter the lists against him and submit to trial by combat.

158 'Has not pity possessed you (at the thought)?'

160 'Intercede in my favour (*or* reconcile me) with my kinsman.' (Cf. Marie de France, *Lanval* 20 and *Le Fresne* 367). *Mon* is hardly likely to be a mistake for *vostre* ('hold me as your lover').

161–2 Muret assumes a lacuna between these two lines; but allowing for the bold and often elliptical style of Beroul, it is possible to interpret them as signifying: 'I wish to return there (i.e. across the sea to his native land) in lordly fashion as when I crossed hither (i.e. to take service with Mark)', *com* being taken to apply to both clauses (sc. *comme quand* . . .). Tristran does not wish to return without his arms (which had been confiscated; cf. 204), but in lordly fashion (*a seignor*) as when he crossed from Loonois to Cornwall to take service with Mark.[1] In the corresponding lines in *O*,[2] Tristran merely asks to be allowed to live at Mark's court as theretofore, and two lines to this effect no doubt stood in *B*'s source but were deliberately altered by him. He reverts to the same idea again in ll. 238–48 (which are his invention) and both passages are to be connected with the special prominence given by Beroul to Tristran's request to have his arms restored and his lodging paid for. It is, however, possible that he was influenced by another passage preserved in *O* (in the same context as *B* 207–10) where Tristran says that if he were to return to his own land he would be as mighty a king as Mark himself.[3] It must

[1] The princely array in which Tristran set out for Cornwall is described in detail by Eilhart, ll. 234 ff.

[2] *O* 3539–41: daz mir mîn hêre sîne hulde gebe
        und mich aber lâze lebin,
        als ich eir was, in sîme hove.

[3] *O* 3585–7: swen ich zu lande kêre,
        sô bin ich ein koning hêre
        alsô rîche als he is.

That is to say, Tristran boasts that if he is banished and returns to Loonois he will take his rank as heir to his father Rivalin, king of Loonois.

be confessed that what Beroul has substituted does not
fit the context quite so well and that the couplet may be
held to bear the marks of improvisation; but this is
precisely what has happened in other passages where
Beroul has intervened to modify his source.—For the
use of *a* with the meaning 'in the manner of' or 'in the
capacity of', cf. 2308 and 2670.

166 The subject of *face* is clearly 'the king' and the
clause virtually depends on *mete a raison*: 'that I should
intercede in your favour with him to pardon you his
wrath'. *Et* might well be a mistake for *Que*.

170 'and am I the one to broach the subject?'

174 A similar reference to the fact that Iseut has no
kinsman to take up her cause in case of need is made by
her before her trial by ordeal in the Thomas versions (*S*,
cap. lvi; *G* 15498–15502). It does not occur in *O*.

181–3 Note that in *O* (3602–8) Iseut's reaction is to
declare herself content that Tristran should be out of
favour with the king (cf. 3544–5 and 3556–7) in view of
the harm done to her reputation by Tristran and to break
off the interview—a much less subtle treatment of a
situation, the possibilities of which are exploited to the
full by Beroul.

185 *Cel* neuter, object of *sai*, anticipating the dependent
clause.

186 Muret's reading (following Jeanroy), involving
the suppression of *la*, is unnecessary: *avroit* is impersonal
'there would not be'.

187 M⁴: 'Entre *Vois m'en* et *ne p.* mot incertain.'

193–4 For the identical rhyme see Introd., p. 5.

197 This action, here effectively introduced, is absent
from the other versions.

204 In *O*, Tristran's request refers to the releasing of
pledges ('daz her ... lîze mir lôsen mîn pfant' 3598–9)
without specifying what they are, and the request comes
after his boast that he will not lack recognition if he goes
elsewhere (*B* 207–10, *O* 3580–95), that is at the point

where in *B* (218) Tristran asks Iseut to pay for his lodging. In *O* there is no reference to the pledging or confiscating of his arms at the time of his banishment from the court. In *Fo* (811–4)[1] all that is reported of the lovers' conversation is that Tristran asked Iseut to reconcile him with the king or that he should have his pledges released and be allowed to leave the kingdom. There can be no doubt that this detail figured in Thomas, but *E* alone of the derivatives refers to it, and in terms which are not clear (str. cxcv): *Of sake he make me fre.*[2]

207–10 The general sense is clear: Tristran claims that his prowess is such that he will have no difficulty in finding a new liege-lord (cf. *O* 3580 ff. and see above, note to 161–2). Muret corrects *fol* to *sol* (208) and with this correction one might translate: 'I know that I have such great prowess that in whatever land I so much as set foot, I know there is no court in all the world where the ruler would not accept my fealty, if I present myself there.'[3] This involves two awkward repetitions (*bien sai* and *tote terre . . . u munde*), *adoise* as 1 pres. subj. (with analogical *-e*) and an unattested use of *adeser* in the sense of 'set foot', 'land' (?).—Two alternative explanations suggest themselves: either 207–8 and 209–10 are variant redactions which have both been taken up into the text, the first being defective, or there is an omission between lines 208 and 209 resulting in the corruption of the end of 208. The testimony of *O*, while not decisive, would tend to support this latter explanation: to ll. 206–10 there

---

[1] Ke vus al rai m'acordissez,
   Si vus fare le puussez,
   U il mes guages aquitast
   E del regne aler me lessast.

[2] Kölbing, in the note to this line (2138), conjectures that it means 'debts' but confesses that the meaning is unattested. As the usual meaning is 'guilt', 'inculpation', it would seem that the author of *E* had in mind the desire of Tristran to be cleared of the charges against him, one consequence of which would be the release of any sureties held by Mark.

[3] Caulier favours *sol* and translates: '. . . que, par toute terre où seulement je pose le pied . . .'.

correspond no less than 22 lines in *O* (3574-95)—an unusual situation. In *O*, Tristran says in effect: 'I must depart, however little the king may regret it; but he will not make good the loss if I depart in enmity (cf. *B* 211-6); yet I am not dismayed and shall find a place where I am rewarded better, honoured and cherished. The king does not reflect that if I return to my land I am as mighty a king as he, and if I must bide elsewhere I shall not be cast out but treated better and provided with an hundred knights and mounts for them.' Cf. note to 161-2.

210 Rhymes such as *cort : avot* are quite permissible (see p. 16) and the correction *anort*, suggested tentatively by Muret, seems unnecessary.

211 The conditional clause postulates the thing denied (cf. note to 58-9): 'I never had anything belonging to king Mark and even if I did, my uncle would wish before the year is out that he had never harboured such a thought, even at the price of his own weight in gold.' These lines would seem to be a recasting, in the bold exclamatory style typical of Beroul, of the thought rendered in a more prosaic manner by Eilhart in ll. 3575-9. In l. 213 *se* is dative (lit. 'thought to himself').

212 Cf. *Fb* 281: *Par lo mien chief, qui ja fu bloi.*

215 'for a quantity of gold equal to his size'. For this locution see M⁰, s.v. *grant*. It is derived from ancient juridical practices and formulae involving the assessment of the fine or reparation in terms of an amount of gold or silver or some other commodity calculated according to the size or weight of the offended party.

218 'Discharge my obligations to my host (i.e. pay for my lodging)' (cf. 444). Eilhart at this point in his narrative (3284-5) merely says: 'mit sorgin quam her gegân vor sîne herbergen.' In *E*, Tristran is 'in the town', and we are left to assume the same by *G*. Beroul would seem to have followed an account similar to that in *S* (cap. liv),[1] where we are told that Tristran is parted from Iseut and

[1] Attributed by Bédier to Thomas also.

lives in *a* town overlooked by the castle, and there he prepares a sumptuous lodging for himself.

221 'You are bent upon achieving my ruin.'

224 Muret's correction of *a voir* to *savoir* is based upon such examples as 2718 (*Ou soit savoir ou soit folie*); but, although such a scribal error is quite explicable, there is no need to suppose absolute uniformity or parallelism: *a voir* 'truthful', 'genuine', 'serious' may stand as the opposite of *enfance* 'childish notion', 'folly', 'fond fancy'.

225 *li sire* nom. for obl.

228 *face*, 1st pers. or 3rd pers.? 'If he hears a word of the request to have your pledges released.' Cf. note to 166.

231 The MS reading does not make sense, and Muret's emendation seems indicated.—Iseut's insistence that she declines to meet Tristran's obligations out of fear and not out of niggardliness or for mercenary reasons would seem to imply a suggestion of some such trait in her character. That this is not inconsistent with Beroul's conception of her would seem to be indicated (in ll. 3311–2) by her request (made through Perinis) that Tristran (disguised as a leper) should keep for her the money he collects as alms from the knights at the crossing of the ford. A similar trait appears in *T.r.* (p. 234), where Iseut rejects Tristran's request on behalf of Governal (see above, p. 73), saying: 'E certo, io non mi moverei saviamente, e voi non mi donereste buono consiglio, a volere io tôrre a mio marito, cioè a me medesma, per donare a Governale . . . io già non consiglierei il mio signore ch'egli togliesse a sè per dare altrui.'

(b) Monologue of Tristran (235–257)

SUMMARY

235–
248 Tristran laments: ['Never did I think to flee thus bereft, with no companion save Governal. Un-

armed in a foreign land, I shall not dare to speak
of knightly deeds.

249– I must suffer fortune's spite. How little my uncle
254 knew me to suspect me!']

255– *Illegible.*
257

VARIANTS

O 3610–13

O: Tristran merely calls God to witness that Mark does him an injustice: he goes to his lodging.[1]

Tristran's monologue serves above all to give point to
his request that Iseut should help him to secure the
release of his arms and to pay for his lodging. He is not
merely concerned to return in the knightly fashion in
which he left his native land to take service with Mark;
for, as we are reminded by the semi-proverbial *Hom nu
n'a nul leu de parler* (248), to be left without arms[2] and
without resources meant loss of caste and standing. It is
not surprising that the poet, who insists repeatedly on
Tristran's legitimate claims, should have given Tristran's
lament this added content and substance.

NOTES

238–9 Inattention or ignorance would account for the
scribe's misreading of *eurol* as *eutol*; the substitution of
sainte for *perte* was perhaps induced partly by the presence
of *saint* in the preceding line. The name (*Evrol*) would
come naturally to the mind of a Norman author: St.
Ebrulfus was born at Bayeux, his cult was widespread in
Normandy and inspired the twelfth-century *Vie de St.*

[1] *Fb* might be considered to show at most a distant recollection of this
monologue in certain parts of Tristran's lament (54–113), notably in ll. 54–
55 and 94–95.
[2] This is well brought out by Caulier's gloss: *desatorné* 'armé in-
suffisamment'.

Evroul (ed F. Danne in *Rom. Forschungen* XXXII, 748 ff.).

242 *Governal*, tutor and companion of Tristran. The original form was undoubtedly *Gorvenal* (*Kurvenal* in *O*), a Celtic name (perhaps for *Gor-wenwal*; cf. Loth, p. 103). The metathesis may have been partly induced by association with O.Fr. *governer*.

243 The exclamatory use of *de* (often after interjections of distress or pity) may derive from the meaning 'concerning' 'in regard to' (cf. Engl. 'alas for'). Cf. *Vie de saint Alexis* 476: *O chiers amis, de ta jovente bele*.

244 'Little does one esteem him.' Cf. *Fo* 37–38 (in quite a different context): *Mais de povre hom ki a pé vait N'en est tenu gueres de plait*; and *Fb* 94–95.

248 'The bare (i.e. unarmed) man has no occasion to speak' or 'It is not for an unarmed man to raise his voice (when men speak of feats of arms).' The line has a proverbial ring, but I can find no analogous proverb.

254 *Savoir* would here seem to mean 'have a savour', 'be pleasing to one's taste': 'Little would it be to my taste.' The word should have been given a separate entry in the Glossary.

255–7 These lines, now illegible, must have contained an indication of Tristran's departure; cf. *O* 3614.

(c) *Reaction of Mark* (258–319)

SUMMARY

258–264	Mark weeps with pity at what he has seen and heard while in the tree. Great is his hatred of the dwarf of Tintagel.
265–284	[M: 'I have been deceived by the dwarf who lied to me about Tristran and made me ascend the tree. I shall have him hanged for it. He shall pay for my wrath and for the hatred my wife bears me. I shall have him burnt. At my hands he shall suffer a worse fate than

Segoçon, mutilated by Constantine of Rome,
with whose wife he had been found.'

285– Tristran having departed, Mark descends from
297   the tree; he will believe his wife and disbelieve
       his deceiving barons. He will not refrain from
       putting the dwarf to the sword. Tristran and Iseut
       shall have the freedom of his royal chamber.

298– M: 'This meeting has given me proof of their
319   innocence. I repent of my credulity. Tristran
          shall be reconciled and have the freedom of
          my chamber. His flight is remitted.']

VARIANTS

O 3614–35; *T* xxiii, 201; *G* 14920–14945; *S* lv, 14–16; *E* cxcvi; *T.r.* 235,
1–12

O: As Tristran leaves the orchard, Mark draws his sword and would
have killed the dwarf, but the latter drops from the tree and flees. Mark
is glad of what he has heard but regrets that the dwarf has escaped:
Satanas had helped him to escape!—Mark returns to the wood, wondering
whether Tristran will consent to remain.

G: Mark, saddened by what he has heard, curses the trouble-makers,
scolds Melot the dwarf; they both ride back to the hunt.—*T.r.*: Mark
descends from the tree, convinced of the lovers' innocence, and retires
to his chamber to rest.—For *S*, *E*, *Fo*, see above (p. 69 n).

In *R*, we are merely told that Tristran returns to his lodging, rejoicing
in the knowledge that Mark will now disbelieve the 'traitors' and guard
the queen less closely. (Yet he will carry the queen off and leave Cornwall
with her, if the occasion should arise.) Nothing is said of Mark's movements until he appears before Iseut (see p. 109).[1]

NOTES

261–3 'With the pity which assailed his heart he would
not have refrained at any price from weeping.'

263 The incongruous *nistra* can only be explained as
an inept transliteration of *ml't a* of the scribe's model.
M[4]: *mout a.*

270 This threat of hanging does not prevent Mark
from promising Frocin death by fire a few lines further

[1] Both Mark and the dwarf had climbed into the tree in *O* and *G*;
Mark alone in *B*, *R*, *E*, *Fo*, *T.r.*; Mark waits under a tree in *S*.

on (276) and the poet from foretelling his death by the sword (293). Such variations have an effectiveness of their own, reflecting the state of mind of Mark; although they do not all take the form of predictions, they should put the critic on his guard against drawing unwarranted conclusions from discrepancies and contradictions which the poet may have allowed to stand in his narrative. In this instance, it is true, the poet fulfils (1347) his own prediction.—It is possible that the scribe may have substituted *porqoi* for the poet's *porqoil* (= *porqoi le*), but the pron. object is sometimes omitted in such cases.

277–84 A. Tobler (in *Jahrbuch für rom. und engl. Spr. und Lit.* XIII (1874), 104–8) cites two other O.Fr. versions of this story, which evidently had wide currency in the Middle Ages: in the Paris MS of *Auberi* the dwarf is called Seguçun, but in *Le Blasme des Fames* he is not named. Constantine (Costantin) is merely mentioned along with Solomon and Samson as a victim of marital infidelity in Guiot de Provins's *Bible*, l. 2130.

284 That the scribe should have misinterpreted *El li mesfist* (Tobler's emendation (p. 742), adopted by Muret but abandoned in M⁴) as *En lié mesfist* is quite possible, but the MS reading might be interpreted: 'He did wrong in respect of her (i.e. by laying violent hands on her) and later regretted it' as against the emended 'She wronged him and later wept for it'. The fable has it that he killed his wife with a sword and had the dwarf trampled to death by his horse. (The quotation should be closed at the end of this line.)

289 *Que* may be for *qui* (cf. 540, 758, 1956) or it may be the causal conjunction 'because', 'for'. In the following line the second *que* is a conjunction introducing a noun-clause: '(of) which he knows that it is not true'.

292–4 For the uncertainty in which Beroul leaves us about the dwarf's movements, see below, p. 101 n and note. He meets his death, in effect, by Mark's sword, though from a different motive (1347).

298 *enfin* 'finally', 'for good and all'.

299 'If it (i.e. the accusation) were true'.

303 *entrebaisier* is described in the Glossary as *v.n.*, but strictly speaking it is a reflexive verb with the reflexive pronoun omitted as it frequently is after *voir* and other modal verbs.

304–5 As at l. 147, I see no reason for breaking the couplet, as suggested by Reid, and punctuating as in M⁴.

306 For *cro*, variant of *crui* (l. 273), cf. Fouché, *Le Verbe français*, pp. 313–4.—*outrage*: the same term is applied to Tristran's offence in *Fb* 10–11.

309 *ainz . . . Que* (311), conj. 'before': 'before I formed this foolish expectation'.

312 *Buen* is here used adverbially (with a meaning similar to that of *buer*) 'happily', 'fortunately'; see other examples in Tobler-Lommatzsch I, col. 1049. Translate: 'Happily (i.e. with good augury) did they see this evening approach' or 'This evening was auspicious for them'.

317 *a ma chanbre*. Here and in a number of other instances *a* is used with the meaning 'in' when *an* might be considered normal. It is of course possible that the scribe omitted the titulus (or that he failed to correct the omission in his model), but I have refrained from emendation except in one or two cases which are duly noted in the Variants.

318 The scribe adds the 'correct' flexional *s* and spoils the rhyme.

318–9 'Now is his flight abandoned which he was intending to make on the morrow.' But l. 319 may be considered suspect (see the note to 320–38).

(d) The Dwarf forewarned (320–338)

SUMMARY

320–
329
The dwarf, versed in astrology, consults the stars.

330–   Bent upon deceiving him who will yet kill him,
338   the dwarf flees [towards Wales]. Mark seeks him
       in vain.

The versions other than *B* tell us no more about the dwarf at this point than what is indicated under (*c*). His ability to read in the stars is however indicated at an earlier point in *O* (3391–5), where Andret advises that he be consulted: 'for he can read in the stars whatever has happened and whatever may happen'. The dwarf sees in the stars (3406–7) that Tristran and Iseut still meet, offers to furnish proof of this to Mark and makes arrangements to spy upon the lovers at their tryst.—*G*, at the corresponding point in his narrative, (14245–53) tells us that the dwarf 'could read of secret things in the stars, so it is averred;[1] I will not profess anything about him except what I find in the book: I find in the true history nothing except that he was knowing, cunning and ready of tongue, and he was in the confidence of the king and the womenfolk (the queen?)'—*S* and *E* do not introduce the dwarf until later and make no mention of his ability to read in the stars.—He does not appear at all in *T.r.*, nor in *R*.

Bédier (I, 197) has furnished convincing reasons for assuming that *G* here reproduces *T* and that the latter, finding in his source a version similar to Eilhart's, had 'rationalized' the incident and the role of the dwarf by eliminating his astrological gifts.

We may reasonably infer that *B*'s source introduced the dwarf in the same way as *O* and the source of *T*, and that *B* either indicated summarily (as *O* does) the dwarf's powers at his first appearance and then elaborated upon them in the later context, or transferred the indication of his powers completely to the later context.[2] At first sight it may seem that there is no reason why the dwarf should consult the stars or why his astrological powers should even be mentioned at this juncture, immediately after Mark's soliloquy. But Beroul's elaboration may have been induced by another modification introduced by him.

[1] und kunde ein teil, alsô man giht,
umbe verhólné geschiht
an dem dèstirne nahtes sehen. (14245–7)

[2] Compare a similar and much more important 'elaboration' in connection with the love-potion (*B* 2133–46).

In *O* and *G*, both the king and the dwarf hide in the tree, and even if we allow (with Bédier) that *G* has here been influenced by *O*, and that in *T* the king was alone, it may be assumed that in *B*'s source both hid in the tree and that the dwarf escaped as in *O*—a faintly absurd denouement to an incongruous situation which may well have prompted Beroul to eliminate the dwarf from the scene of the tryst. The dwarf has therefore no means of knowing the result of the plot and has in fact no reason to assume that it has miscarried, and his flight from Mark's wrath would remain unmotivated if his powers of divination were not brought into play to enlighten him. Beroul would appear to have done this by transposing the description of his powers from a place where it was more appropriate, if not essential, and adapting it to this new context. That the operation was not very adroitly performed and that the suture marks are still discernible is shown in the notes.[1]

NOTES

320 *Frocin*. On three occasions the poet uses the variant form *Frocine* for purposes of rhyme (470, 1328, 1349). Twice the dwarf is described as being 'of Tintagel' 264, 880). In *O*, he is named once only (in the scene of

[1] In *T.r.*, the dwarf does not appear, in *S* and *E* the king is alone, in *Fo* only the king is mentioned. It is just possible that *Fo* may have suppressed any mention of the dwarf as quite unessential to his purpose and that *S* and *E* (whose accounts are in any case fragmentary) may in fact have eliminated him independently from the scene.

In *B*, it is clear from Iseut's words (349–51) and from Mark's reactions and words (265–80, 292–4, 469–74) that the dwarf is not a witness of the tryst, but that he had told Mark of the lovers' meeting (471) and that the king hid in the tree at his instigation. The dwarf's astrological powers are used by Beroul (321–4) to tie up one loose end, but he leaves another: the dwarf's flight in the direction of Wales (336; cf. 385–6); but he is nevertheless immediately available (639) when the hostile barons advise that he be consulted. *O* shows a bungling attempt to tie up this second loose end (see below, p. 156).

In *G* (14929–36), the dwarf is let off with a chiding from Mark and both ride back to the hunt (*mit jâmer und mit leide!*).

the trapping of the lovers: l. 3931) and there only in one MS as *Aquitayn*. In Gottfried and his continuators he is called *Melôt petit von Aquitân*, and he probably bore this name in Thomas.[1] He bears no name in the other versions and is absent from R and *Fb*.

The name has been regarded as a diminutive of *Freoc*, a name found in the *Cartulaire de Redon* in documents of the years 834–66 (see Bédier, II, 118 n.), *-in* being a diminutive suffix and (according to G. Schoepperle, 242) the commonest ending for the names of dwarfs in both Celtic and Romance languages. But M. Delbouille, in the article mentioned in the Bibliography, makes out a strong case for regarding the name as originally the common noun *frocin(e)* 'être humain de petite taille, et peut-être un avorton, un nain'. For the role of the dwarf in the literature of the time, see the Bibliography under: Hayward, Krappe, Wohlgemuth.

320–38 The abrupt introduction of the dwarf at this point has been discussed in a general note to this passage (p. 100). Various internal features support the conclusion there reached that these lines are largely an interpolation. The exclamatory *Oiez* itself suggests that the author has felt it necessary to 'introduce' this digression. He proceeds to state that the dwarf was out of doors scanning the sky; but why and where, we are left to infer from what follows. He then describes the dwarf's astrological powers and adds that he was 'intent upon deceiving him who would kill him'. It is not clear what deception is referred to and why it should be mentioned between the indication of his powers and his use of them on this occasion.[2] Finally there is the linking of *asente* and *enfle*,

[1] But see Bédier, I, 191; also II, Index, s.v. *Melot*.

[2] Lines 329–30 would on the other hand be more appropriate in the context in which the indication of the dwarf's powers occurs in O (see above, p. 100), and they have probably been transferred together with that indication to their present context by Beroul. They could hardly, in any case, refer to the betrayal of Mark's secret which was the immediate provocation (1306–46).

which do no more than assonate. One is tempted to conclude that Beroul had before him roughly the account preserved by *O*, that he interpolated lines 319–31 inclusive, and linked them imperfectly with the following lines 332–38, the line which originally rhymed with 332 having been discarded. One may further conjecture that line 332 (which hardly describes the emotion uppermost in the dwarf at what he sees) originally applied to the king and that 332 has been altered from the mere indication of Mark's threats. Lines 335–6 would remain (with the indication 'vers Gales' added) as the relic of the original description of the dwarf's escape from the tree and from Mark's vengeance.

322 *Orïent* = *Orion*. *Lucifer*, the name given to the planet Venus when it appears above the eastern horizon before sunrise and sometimes when it appears above the western horizon after sunset.

325 'He knew what was to be' 'He could foretell the future'.

326 'When he heard of the birth of a child he detailed all the points of his life.'

329–30 'He took great pains to deceive him who was to kill him' (lit. 'deprive him of his soul').—Muret rightly rejected Heinzel's suggestion that *cel* refers to Tristran, pointing out that, in spite of an indication to the contrary in *L'Escoufle* 616, there is no suggestion in any extant Tristran romance that Tristran killed the dwarf.—It is possible that the scribe inadvertently substituted the plural *ceus* for *cel*; but *ceus* (referring to Tristran and Iseut or to Mark, Tristran and Iseut, or even to the barons[1]) may be a relic of the earlier version in which these lines stood at the same point as in *O* (see above, p. 100), the plural being allowed to stand after the adaptation of the second line to the new context. One might go on to conjecture that l. 330 originally read: *Qui de l'ame le feront soivre.*

---

[1] Note that in *O* (3796–9) Andret complains that the dwarf had deceived him and he wishes to kill him.

331 'He observes the conjunction of the stars.' Cf. *O* 3406–7: *der vâlant dô begunde/daz gesterne schauwin.*

332 The heightening of colour and the puffing out of the cheeks are the conventional signs of anger; cf. 335, 1068, 1895, and 3055. The linking of *asente* : *enfle* may, as suggested above (p. 100), result from an imperfect adaptation of the passage to its new context.

333–4 'He well knows that the king threatens him and will not refrain from killing him.'

336 According to *O*, the dwarf escapes the king's sword by dropping from the tree and fleeing (3615–25). Later he is found in a wood by Dinas and restored to the king's favour (3772–91). In *G*, the king and the dwarf return to their hunting without more ado (see above, p. 101 n). In *B*, although the dwarf cannot be found by Mark (337 and 385), he appears from ll. 635–9 not to have strayed far from court; *vers Gales* would therefore seem to be little more than a cheville for the sake of the rhyme.

338 *s'en* (for scribal *si en*) finds support in 397, 2584, 3683.

(e) Iseut confides in Brengain (339–380)

SUMMARY

339–343	Iseut enters her chamber. [Brengain, observing her distress (asks the reason?).
345–369	I: 'We have been betrayed. I saw Mark's shadow in the water. By God's grace I spoke first and reproved Tristran, saying that I would not intercede nor come again at his call.] Mark learnt nothing of my case and I was saved.'
370–380	[B: 'God, who favours all those who are good and loyal, has saved you from fateful indiscretion.']

VARIANTS

R 351, 14–34

R: Iseut returns to her chamber and reports the adventure to Brengain. At the latter's request Iseut relates how she and Tristran, having become aware of the king's presence, successfully disguised their actions and words. She foretells the discomfiture of Andret and the rehabilitation of Tristran. Iseut and Brengain rejoice.

It would seem from the text (MS 757)[1] that R has abbreviated Iseut's account, presumably because it was repetitive.

In *B*, on the other hand, the scene has been dramatized and elaborated in characteristic fashion, notably by the addition of Brengain's response (371–80).

NOTES

340 *Brengain* is a Celtic name, probably Welsh (Old Welsh *Bran-wen*; Loth, p. 104); cf. Golther, in *ZRP* XII, 352; and *ZFSL* XXII, 5; Hertz[3], p. 527, Anm. 76; G. Paris, in *Rom.* XVIII, 323. The name appears in various forms. *B*: *Brengain* consistently; *O*: *Brangêne*; *G*: *Brangaene*; *S*: *Bringvet*; *E*: *Brengwain, Bringwain*; *T.r.*: *Brandina, Banguina*; *Fb*: *Brengain* (: *main*), *Brangien*; *Fo*: *Brengain* (: *main*); *R*: *Brangien, -ein, -ain, -em*; *T* fragments (Wind): *Brengvein, -ven, -ien, Brigvain*.

345 *magistre*. Similarly Tristran addresses Governal as *maistre* (979, etc.), and Brengain's role, like his, combines the functions of a confidante and friend and companion with those of a retainer or servant (4417–9).

349 *Marc* (the nominative form *Mars* occurs once only, and in rhyme, at l. 1969) is to be identified historically with the sixth-century king of Cornwall named in the ninth-century *Vita Sancti Pauli Aureliani* (AA. SS. mens. mart., Vol. II, p. 114a) as Marcus, 'quem alio nomine

---

[1] 'Et nos avint, la Dieu(s) merci, que nos nos aperceümes de lui, si chanjames maintenant nostre afere et noz paroles,' et li conte en quel maniere et en quel guise. 'Nos en partismes . . .' (Bédier, II, 351).

H

Quonomorium vocant'; cf. Hertz[3], Anm. 7; F. Gourvil, 'Le nom propre *Marc'h* 'cheval', ses dérivés et composés dans l'anthroponymie brittonique', *Ogam* VII (1955), 59 ff.; Helaine Newstead, 'King Mark of Cornwall', *RPh* XI (1958), 240–53; Rachel Bromwich, 'The character of the early Welsh tradition', *Studies in Early British History*, ed. N. K. Chadwick, Cambridge, 1954, p. 122; P. Rickard, pp. 93–94. In our text his chief residences are Lancien and Tintagel, the latter mentioned explicitly as such in l. 3150, and by implication in l. 1040. At one point (2232) Durham appears as part of Mark's kingdom, but according to l. 4264 it is in Arthur's. According to Thomas, Mark ruled over England as well as Cornwall, with residences at Tintagel and London. There is no suggestion in Beroul that Mark owes allegiance to Arthur; although he is prepared to receive reproof and advice from him (4141–69), they are not proffered condescendingly 4257–9). The prestige of Arthur and the knights of the Round Table is taken for granted and it is enough for Beroul that their participation should add a certain solemnity to the exculpation of Iseut and glamour to the jousting and entertainment which mark the occasion.

350 The emendation is of doubtful necessity as *estoit* may be a mere graphy for *estait* (cf. *voit* for *vait* 1271). A scribal error, resulting from the similarity of *a* and *o* and from the influence of *estoit* of the preceding line, is quite conceivable. Cf. *estoit* for *estot* 973, 2200(?). The *perron* is a detail (cf. 235) not mentioned in other versions.

352 Note the suggestion that Iseut, far from having been warned by Tristran of Mark's presence (see above, p. 69), was herself afraid that Tristran was not aware of it.

357 The indicative (*mandot*) would suggest that *que* is causal or virtually so.

360 Whatever the precise meaning of *error* in l. 2217, it is difficult to justify here the alternative interpretation

suggested by Tobler: 'he was distraught'. It is true that other versions insist upon Mark's state of doubt and perplexity, but the context and Iseut's own words at the tryst make it clear that she could only have meant: 'who, very wrongfully, was mistaken concerning his (Tristran's) relations with me'.

364 The scribe, apparently forgetting who is the interlocutor, misreads *au roi* as *a toi*.

366 The correction to *complainz* is obvious; cf. 355.

369 Cf. l. 100; also Hoepffner's note to *Fb* 401.

372 and 377–80 God is identified by Brengain with the cause of the lovers because they are *buen et loial*. As to the precise concepts covered by these two adjectives the poet is less explicit than Gottfried or even Eilhart. It is clear, however, that he means to present the lovers as acting under the influence of the potion and therefore not morally responsible. Cf. 755–6.

375 *Que* consecutive, or possibly causal? 'So that (*or* Since) the king has seen nothing upon which a good construction cannot be put.'

(f) *Tristran and Governal* (381–386)

SUMMARY

381– [Governal receives with relief Tristran's account
384 of the tryst.
385– Mark cannot find his dwarf: so much the worse
386 for Tristran!]

There is no trace of this in any other version. Lines 381–4 (imperfectly transmitted by the scribe) are clearly an addition by *B*. This digression, following upon the elaboration of the scene between Iseut and Brengain, prompts the poet to provide yet another of his 'renvois' or 'cross-references': lines 385–6 repeat lines 337–8, and this linking-up prepares the re-entry of the king.

NOTES

382–3 That the scribe should have misinterpreted *cōt'*
as *Got'* is palaeographically probable, and the form of
Governal may similarly have induced, at least partly, the
erroneous *son oncle*—The subject of *ot* is of course
'Governal'.

386 'So much the worse for Tristran', *ert* being either
imperfect or future.

(g) *Mark and Iseut* (387–505)

SUMMARY

387– Mark enters the royal chamber. [Iseut fearfully
390   enquires: 'What ails you that you come thus
      alone?']
391– M: 'I come to hear the truth from you.'
394
395– [I: I swear to speak truly.'
398
399   M: 'Have you seen my nephew since?'
400– I: 'Saving your doubt and false suspicion, I saw
446   Tristran at his bidding beneath the pine. I
          would gladly serve him and reconcile him with
          you, were it not for the felons, the deceitful
          flatterers; but I told him to be gone, that I
          would not speak to you nor pay for his lodging
          or aught else.
447–   This I swear: gladly would I pay for him, but
458   I dare not because of your gossiping house-
          hold. Wrongfully do you drive him forth. He
          is bereft, but God will befriend him, to what-
          ever land he goes.']
459– Mark consoles Iseut, [promises her and Tristran
474   the freedom of his chamber and disowns his

Cornish barons. He tells her of the dwarf's treachery.

475   I: 'Were you then in the pine-tree?']

476– M: 'Yes, [and heard all: how Tristran told you of
492   the fight he waged for me, and you related the
pain he suffered from the dragon, of which
you healed him. Ah! the pity of it, when you
refused to have his sureties released!'

493– I: 'Now you have proof that we are not given
505   over to wicked love. Had you not seen, you
would not have believed.' M: 'Nor would I.']

VARIANTS

O 3636–3701; R 351, 34–36; G 14946–15032

In R, the king comes in due course (*au chief de piece*) to Iseut's chamber. Iseut, hearing him approach, lies down and pretends to sleep. The king gets up early the next morning to go to Mass.

In *G*, Mark leaves the hunt on the following morning and seeks out Iseut and asks her how she has whiled away the time. She replies jestingly: with harp and lyre in womanly fashion. Pressed by Mark for news of Tristran, she says that he has petitioned, through Brengain, for milder treatment from both Mark and Iseut for a space of eight days so that he may leave the court and the land with honour; she tells Mark the rest of Tristran's requests as they were made to her at the fountain, Mark confesses himself repentant and convinced of Tristran's innocence, and promises lasting forgiveness.—In *S, E, T.r.,* there is nothing to correspond.

O presents a version showing changes consequential, in part at least, upon those introduced into the scene at the fountain: early next morning Mark returns to the town and asks Iseut what she had said to Tristran that night. I: 'I have not seen him for twelve days and hate him.' M: 'I was in the tree and saw all; help me to keep him at my court.' Iseut refuses but, upon Mark's having promised to make amends, suggests that Brengain might be persuaded, although with difficulty, to intercede with Tristran.

NOTES

387 ff. It is noteworthy that Mark only half answers Iseut's questioning (389–90). His desire to speak to her alone upon a private matter might explain his going

about unaccompanied, an unusual proceeding for a king (cf., in another context, ll. 1926–42); but Iseut's 'dont venez vos?' remains unanswered. It is clear that *B* proceeded from an account similar to that of *G* and *O*, in which the king, having left the hunt (accompanied only by the dwarf) to spy upon the lovers, returns to the hunt and leaves it again on the following morning to seek out Iseut. (*G* specifies that Mark orders his huntsmen to continue with the chase and departs alone.) All of this has been allowed to drop and we are merely told that Mark seeks his dwarf in vain. It is in the movements of the lovers that Beroul is particularly interested and these he has treated in much greater detail and elaborated far beyond the meagre details given, even by *R*.

399 *puis* 'since'. One might interpret: 'since I last saw you'; cf. *O*'s specific *des nachtes* (3641). But it is more likely that the poet intended: 'since Tristran's banishment' (cf. 105).

400 Tobler shows that the correct reading must be *desno* (not *desvo* as in M[0]); cf. *Yvain* 3912 and *Lancelot* 2142 ('La verité m'an desnoez').

404 *sor*] *soz*; cf. 415. Beroul is almost alone in making the tree a pine. Cf. Hertz[3], Anm. 99.

407–8 See p. 14.

412 'I have told you the truth and yet you do not believe me.'

413 Omission probably induced by the form of the preceding word (*parole*).

417–8 The scribe having misread *li dui* (under the influence of the preceding line) omitted *non*. 'He said nothing but that I should pay him honour of a not too niggardly kind.' Alternatively one might conjecture a lacuna after l. 418 and a defective l. 419.

422 The scribe writes *iert* for *ert*, but the confusion of the two forms (cf. 701, 1112 and 466, 294 and 386) makes it impossible to tell whether he meant the future or the imperfect: either tense fits the context.

425 *ç'oi dire*—a mere *cheville*—'methinks'.

439 *mentirez*. Muret's emendation to *m'en creirez* pre-supposes a highly probable scribal misreading; cf. *nen-terra* for *mencrerra* (468) and other similar cases cited in *Pope Misc.*, p. 91 and passim. It would also seem to find support in ll. 401 and 412. On the other hand, the MS reading might be interpreted: 'You will not be in any way mistaken (if you accept my statement that) there was nothing more.' This would involve a very slight extension of the attested meanings of *mentir* (cf. Godefroy, V, 244): 'speak falsely' > 'report incorrectly'.

442 'Tristran is leaving because of the strife and dis-cord.'

452 'Not even four whole sovereigns was I prepared to place in his wallet because of (for fear of) your scandal-mongering retinue.' Cf. Muret, s.v. *besanz*: 'monnaie byzantine en or, qui valait, à la fin du xii⁰ siècle, en Normandie, sept sous d'angevins'. 'Sovereigns' is conse-quently a free rendering, the real value being considerably less.—It is interesting to note that in *G* (16642–3), on the later occasion of the lovers' flight to the forest, it is from Iseut's private treasure that Tristran takes twenty marks of gold for their sustenance; this detail, though not found elsewhere, was considered by Bédier (I, 232–3) to have been derived by Gottfried from Thomas.

456–8 'Very wrongfully do you drive him forth. Wherever he goes, God will be a true friend to him' (or more literally: 'he will not go unto that land where God will not be a true friend to him').

460 i.e. the words spoken by Tristran and Iseut be-neath the pine.

468 The scribe probably misread an abbreviation in his source (*nencᵉrra*).

470 *9me* misread as *Dame*, the scribe mistaking indirect for direct speech.

475 This effective trait, peculiar to Beroul, is charac-teristic of the author's manner and may be said to under-

line the comparative ineptness of Eilhart's handling of this scene (3650–60).

477 'No word was ever uttered there but that I heard it, great or small.'

483–6 There is here apparently a confusion (not necessarily scribal only) between two incidents: (1) the healing of the wound inflicted by the Morholt (see note to 53); (2) the healing of the infection from the dragon's tongue which Tristran had hidden upon his person (cf. p. 63)— by Iseut's mother in *G*, *S*, *E*, *Fo*, while Iseut merely assists, by Iseut herself in R (MS 103), *O*, *Fb*[1]. The second incident is not referred to by either Tristran or Iseut, though it may have been mentioned by Tristran in ll. 112–6, which are no longer legible. It might therefore be better to place a comma after *traire* and delete the comma after *serpent* rather than to punctuate as in the text and thus to attribute to the poet the mistake of describing the effects of the infection from the dragon's tongue as having been suffered at sea. Line 485 would thus be loosely linked with 483, and it hardly seems necessary to assume, with Acher, a lacuna between 484 and 485.

The emendation *plaie* for *serpent* (the latter restored in M[4]) removes the ambiguity and produces a smoother though not necessarily more authentic narrative; and it is just possible that in l. 483 the emendation *vos* (for *li*) is a similar 'improvement' of doubtful validity: it assumes that the scribe substituted *li* for *vos* partly under the influence of the *li* in the following line, partly through a misunderstanding of the context; but it is not certain that the poet necessarily made Mark's recollection of 'who said what' perfect or attached quite the same importance to consistency as the modern critic, and there remains the possibility referred to above that Tristran did in fact

---

[1] *Fb*, 404–6: Del velin del cruiel sarpent
　　　　　　—Panduz soie, se je en mant—
　　　　　　Me gareïstes sanz mehain.

refer to his healing by Iseut in the lines 112–6. Cf. Hertz[3], pp. 522–3.

489 The direct object pronoun (*les*) is implied with *li*.

490 Jeanroy's suggested emendation to *aboter* is ill-founded. The meaning 'approach' is well attested, as is also the meaning 'have intercourse with'; see examples in Tobler-Lommatzsch I, col. 54.

498 'But rather (*or* instead) you did not see . . .'.

500 Gaston Paris's emendation is plausible, but *mespreïst* (restored in M[4]) 'was guilty of unseemly conduct' is quite acceptable.

504 The MS reading seems to be *creissiez* (analogical scribal form or careless copying), but possibly an indistinct *creusiez*, the vellum being damaged by damp at this point.

(*h*) *Mark and Brengain* (505–526)

SUMMARY

505–511 M: 'Brengain, bid Tristran come to me.'

512–524 [B: 'He hates me mortally; but under your protection I go: reconcile me with him.'—Hear the deceitful wench!—'I go; make peace between us.'

525–526 M: 'That will be my care; go, bring him hither.']

VARIANTS

O 3702–41

O: Brengain is persuaded with difficulty to ask Tristran to remain, saying that she cannot trust him; she consents only after Mark has offered to have Tristran's bed in the royal chamber and to allow him to be with the queen at all times.

NOTES

510 'Say that I command . . .'

511–4 Cf. the scheming of Brengain with Iseut and the latter's simulated hatred for Tristran in Gottfried, cap. XXI.

512 *Si* here has the force of an emphatic 'and'.

516 *Bien tost* may here (as in 711) mean 'perchance'; *que* is consecutive: 'on your account (*or* for your sake) he will perchance refrain from laying hands on me.'

519–22 Once again the poet apostrophizes his hearers in order to underline a development which, we may safely assume, is his own elaboration of a bare indication in his source such as is preserved in O (see above, p. 109).

521 *esscient*, with expunctuation mark under the second *s* (?).

(i) Brengain and Tristran (527–550)

SUMMARY

527–   [Mark and Iseut laugh as Brengain skips lightly
534   from the room. Tristran had heard all; he em-
       braces Brengain and is joyful at the thought of
       being with Iseut again.

535–   B: 'The king has forgiven all. Come, but do not
546   yield too easily when he bids you forgive me.']

547–   Tristran and Brengain repair to the royal chamber.
550

VARIANTS

O 3742–6

O: Brengain goes to Tristran's lodging and has no difficulty in per-
suading Tristran (*mit liste sie ez zu samene treip*).

NOTES

529–35 Raynaud de Lage (in *Rom.* LXXXIII, 522–6) considers that these lines are an interpolation in *B*.

533 Lacuna. The scribe has left a line blank at the foot of the column. He may have noticed, on reaching the end of the column, that his source lacked a line, or having marked off in his source the number of lines for his column, he may then have omitted a line by accident.

543–6 'Pretend that you require entreating. Do not come readily. If the king intercedes on my behalf, pretend to view it with an ill grace.'

549 *painte*, i.e. adorned with mural paintings. Cf. Schultz, *Höfisches Leben* I, 102, and the elaborate description of the *chanbre peinte* in Marie de France, *Guigemar* 233–4.

(j) Tristran restored to favour (551–572)

SUMMARY

551–554	M:	['Tristran, forgive Brengain and I forgive you.'
555–566	T:	'You take your defence lightly: you have accused me so unjustly. Henceforth take better counsel and bear us no ill-will.'
567–571	M:	'I promise.'] Tristran is pardoned and has the freedom of the chamber.

VARIANTS

O 3747–91; R 352, 25–353 end; T xxiii, 201; G 15033–50; E cxcvii–cxcviii; T.r. 235, 13–24; Fo 815–6

In R, Mark, returning from Mass (see above, p. 109) upbraids Andret, saying that if he were not a kinsman, he would chastise him (*je vous feïsse du corps honnir*), and banishes him from court (*mon ostel*). He summons Tristran, declares his remorse and promises reparation; Tristran accepts reconciliation on condition that he is to be immune in future. Tristran may now speak to the queen when he wishes and is in command, to the chagrin of the traitors. Tristran and Iseut are completely happy: *il clamassent bien a Dieu quite son paradis pour mener tout adès tel vie.'*

In G, Tristran is summoned and restored to favour, Iseut being confided to his care. The lovers resume a life of bliss: but it was to be of short duration.—*E* says more briefly that joy and happiness revived, Iseut has her way and Tristran is high marshal; for three years they have their pleasure in secret: so cunning were they that none could destroy their love.—In *T.r.*, Mark banishes Federumgotto (= Andret) from his kingdom and grants Tristran's request for Governal (see above, p. 69).—For *S* and *Fo*, see above, p. 69.

O: The king grants Tristran the freedom of his chamber and commands all to obey him. Tristran orders Governal to carry his bed to the royal chamber.—Here *O* relates that one day Dinas comes upon the dwarf in the wood and offers to regain the king's favour for him: had he known what was to come, he would rather have had him hanged!

NOTES

552–67 These lines are peculiar to Beroul. The offhand manner in which Mark offers Tristran reconciliation may be taken to excuse the tone of the latter's response which, by its almost insolent tenor, contrasts with his normal attitude to his uncle in Beroul and also with the mild reproaches he addresses to Mark on this occasion in R (see above, p. 115).

556–61 'Lightly do you defend yourself as regards me [i.e. 'you do not take seriously the wrong you have done me'], you who have brought this upon me whereat my heart weeps within me, such great wrong, such wickedness! I should have been damned and she disgraced (sc. if you had given effect to your intention). Never did we harbour such thoughts, God knows.'—Note that the poet does not follow up the reconciliation with Brengain as foreshadowed in 543–6 and that Tristran's speech would follow more naturally on the *O* version, which speaks only in general terms of the supposed enmity between Tristran and Brengain and not at all of a reconciliation between them.—Tanquerey's suggested interversion of lines 559 and 560 is interesting but unnecessary. To replace the comma after l. 558, as Reid suggests, by a full stop would obscure a characteristic feature of Beroul's style.

(k) *The lovers' anxiety* (573–580)

SUMMARY

573– [Alas, how difficult is the course of true love, and
580   who can conceal it!]

There are analogous developments or reflections at
various points in *G* (e.g. 16407 ff.), and the nearest
equivalent at this point in any version is furnished by *G*,
where in ll. 15049–50 (see above, p. 116) it is indicated
that the lovers' joy is short-lived.

The passage in *B* has little immediate relevance unless
the story continues as in *G*, where these signs and tokens
rouse Mark's suspicions without the intervention of the
barons. It may be yet another of the elaborations introduced by Beroul to mark a fresh departure in his narrative, the intervention of the three hostile barons; the
elaboration or interpolation being joined imperfectly to
the main narrative.

NOTES

576 *cline* may be for *cligne* 'winks', and not 'bows' as
the Glossary has it; cf. l. 3854 and Gottfried, particularly
ll. 16488–16504. 'Often one bows (or winks) to the other,
they meet and converse secretly and openly. Not every-
where can they find leisure (to meet and speak); many a
rendez-vous must they arrange.'

II. THE STRATAGEM—THE LOVERS TRAPPED (581–1270)

O 3792–4327; *R* 356, 17–360, 22; *T* xxiv; *G* 15051–15270; *S* lv, 17–
    50; *E* cxcviii–ccii; *T.r.* 235, 24–236, 28; *Fo* 725–754

The scene involves the conflation of two popular
motifs. The ruse of the flour spread between the beds is

encountered in various forms in folk-tales and in literature: according to S. Hofer (ZRP, LXV, 278) it goes
back to the biblical story of Daniel and the priests of
Baal (cf. Kelemina, p. 61). Tristran's counter-ruse is
defeated by the second motif, the evidence of the blood
on the floor and in the queen's bed, it being necessary
that the condemnation of the lovers and the flight to the
forest should ensue. And yet, in Beroul's hands the evidence is equivocal and leaves a lingering uncertainty in
Mark's mind which no doubt contributes to his subsequent repining and tergiversation.

(a) Plot of the hostile barons (581–648)

SUMMARY

581– 612	[Three] hostile barons, having seen the adulterous association of Tristran and Iseut, conspire to have him banished and proceed to inform Mark, [who hears them with bowed head:
613– 626	'King, banish Tristran or we renounce our fealty.'
627– 634	M: 'Counsel me faithfully: I am not proud.'— 'Summon the dwarf and follow his advice.'
635– 648	The dwarf comes: hear now what villainy he plots, God's curse upon him!]

VARIANTS

O 3792–3820; *R* 356, 17–21; *T* xxiv; *G* 15051–15120; *E* cxcviii–cxcix;
T.r. 235, 24–236, 6;

R: Sandret (= Andret), having learnt from a *damoiselle* that the lovers
meet, summons the hostile faction and proceeds with fifty knights to the
tower in which Iseut has been confined.

G inveighs against envy and hypocrisy, personified by the seneschal
(Marjodo) and the dwarf (Melot), who revive Mark's suspicions and
inspire him to devise a new stratagem.—In *E*, the seneschal (Mariadok)
spies on the lovers, advises Mark to undergo a blood-letting together

with Tristran and Iseut, and foretells that he will find their bed covered with blood.—In *T.r.* Mark's suspicions are aroused by a report and by his observing Iseut. He places three beds in a room and proposes a blood-letting, to which Tristran assents.—For *S* and *Fo*, see above, p. 69.

In *O*, the hostile faction (*die bôsin nîdêre*) soon resume their envious intrigue. The dwarf, threatened with death by Andret, offers to prove Tristran's guilt. The king agrees to subject the lovers to another test and threatens the dwarf with burning if Tristran should be proved innocent.

The manner in which the hostile barons are here introduced by *B* suggests that this is their first appearance as a group. One might urge against this that Beroul frequently introduces a new stage in his narrative by such a reference back, in this instance a 'formal re-introduction' of three of the principal actors. But such recapitulatory introductions are sometimes induced by a displacement of episodes or features undertaken by Beroul, and if one seeks a parallel for the following lines (583–634), it is only partly to be found at the corresponding point in other versions and is furnished much more fully by the passage which precedes Tristran's banishment from the court (*O* 3150–3249). It is therefore possible that Beroul in fact transferred the greater part of this earlier passage (together with the first explicit mention of the *three* hostile barons) to its present position, where it serves to lead up to the trapping of the lovers.

The fact is that in the text as we have it, the enemies of Tristran are at first referred to in general terms: it is not until l. 581 that they appear as a group of three, and a trio they remain in spite of the death of one of their number at the hands of Governal (cf. note to ll. 1656 ff.). It is only at ll. 3138–9 that we are told their names in anticipation of their role and their fate as individuals (3462 ff.). We cannot tell whether, in the earlier lost portion of *B* the hostile faction appeared as a group of three or other specified number, or were named; but it would seem not.

In *O* too, the hostile faction is not particularized until ll. 3086–95 (before the banishment of Tristran from the court), where it is described as consisting of three dukes and four counts with Antrêt at their head, but in the fragmentary older version the faction consists of one duke and four counts. In fact, Eilhart is thoroughly confused and inconsistent, and his confusion probably arose (as suggested by Muret and, following him, by G. Schoepperle) from the fact that he found in his source mention of three hostile barons, and when Andret was included, four: hence his three dukes and four counts. It would appear, then, that B and O presuppose a common source (perhaps the γ version postulated by Bédier), in which the number of hostile barons was three with Andret as a fourth, the one of the highest rank and a sort of leader.[1] Beroul reproduces γ, but he makes Andret a secondary figure, perhaps partly because he did not feel at home with the role of Andret, a cousin of Tristran and guardian of the queen, and at the same time Tristran's chief enemy (see note to l. 2869). The three barons become principal actors in the drama with a different role and a different fate from those of his source, an essential ingredient in the unfolding of the plot. They intervene and precipitate crises and fulfil what one might call a catalystic function. They rouse the author's indignation and incur his repeated imprecations. He cannot resist the temptation to have one of their number despatched by Governal (1694 ff.), particularly as the situation (Governal in ambush awaiting Husdent) might be held (as suggested by Röttiger, p. 23) to have virtually invited such an interpolation. Coming to the 'prophecy' (2754 ff.), he follows slavishly and inattentively the source he had before him, not realizing that he had (possibly in an earlier session of the public recital of his tale) accounted for one of the barons.

[1] In R, Andret (*varr.* Audret, Sandret) plays the leading role as an implacable enemy of Tristran and at need commands a varying number of confederates or followers. In T, the hostile element is summed up in the person of Mariadoc, 'premier seneschal du roi', the traitorous enemy of Tristran, who takes him for a friend.

NOTES

587 This threat is in fact given effect on a later occasion (3143–7).

601–2 'Whether he love or hate us, we desire that he should banish his nephew.'

604 *Li* (nom.) for *Le*.

612 *sovent erre* 'he walks up and down (distracted?)' rather than 'he is in perplexity'; *sovent* being used here in the sense of 'repeatedly', 'back and forth' in reference to the 'repetitiveness' of his action. Similarly in l. 3928 (cf. J. Frappier in *Rom.* LXXXIII, 256).

621–2 'We will not maintain our loyalty to you nor keep the peace with you.'

625 A *jeu parti* is a dilemma or problem posed in such a way as to require a choice between two alternatives (cf. the lyric genre of the same name). The barons declare in effect that they will without delay present Mark with an ultimatum requiring him to make a choice, a vivid way of saying that they are in fact doing so.

631–2 Cf. 2529–30. 633–4 Mark's perplexity is not enlarged upon to the same extent as in other versions (particularly *G*), but the complexity of his motives is indicated by this reference to his reluctance to lose the service of his barons and his readiness to swallow his pride if need be.

636 'He is versed in many an art.' Latin, as the vehicle of learning, came to be regarded as the key to knowledge, occult no less than 'scientific'; cf. the analogous development of *grammaire—grimoire*.

640 'And he came very quickly; a curse upon him, hunchback that he is'—rather than, as Tobler suggests (with a different punctuation): 'He—cursed be he—has come very quickly (for a hunchback!).'

642 'The king tells him (Frocin) what is in his mind' (or 'what he has to say').

647–8 'Who ever imagined such villainy as this dwarf

perpetrated (whom may God curse!)?'—G. Paris's emendation to *porpensast* (cf. 678) has been abandoned in Muret's later editions.

(b) *Frocin's stratagem* (649–692)

SUMMARY

649–670	F:	'Order Tristran to take a message to Arthur [at Carduel] in the morning. He will wish to see Iseut this night. Leave the rest to me, but conceal the errand from Tristran until evening.'
671–678		Mark agrees. [Frocin buys flour of a baker and hides it in his bosom.
679–681		Tristran attends Mark at his 'coucher'.]
682–692	M:	'Take this letter to Arthur [and remain but one day with him.']—T: 'I will set out early.'—M: 'Do so, before the night is out.'

VARIANTS

O 3821–3892

In *O*, the dwarf says in effect: 'Tell Tristran he is to ride abroad on an errand not later than early to-morrow morning and that he is to be absent seven nights. I shall spread flour between their beds: if he does not go to Iseut during the night, then have my head cut off. I shall lie hidden under Iseut's bed and will call you when I hear Tristran go there, and do you have men posted at the door to take Tristran, for he is powerful; and tell Andret and his companions to have three of their number guard the door from within and the other four from without.' Mark orders these things to be done and when night falls tells Tristran of the errand, adding that it is to Arthur (*Artûse deme herren*: *Britanja ist niht verre*) and that he will tell him the message at daybreak. Tristran is distressed but agrees; Mark thanks him.

There is no trace of such an errand in any version other than *B* and *O*.

NOTES

649 For the poet's use of the forms *Artur* and *Artus*, see Introd., Nos. 28 and 36.

650 *Carduel* = Carlisle, one of the residences of King Arthur; in the latter part his residence is at *Cuerlion* (3368) or at *Isneldone* (3373); see the notes to these lines.

651 The metre demands *qu'il aut* or *qu'alle*, but the latter is not found elsewhere in the text in the third person.

652 The correction is obvious (cf. 686), but not so the explanation of the scribe's *deus*.

657 and 662 *lui* for *li*.

658 Muret's emendation *Pour ceu que* certainly produces a smoother reading, but this would be the only instance in the text of *ceu* (= *ço*); *que* is causal.

663–4 'If he comes there (or 'to her') without my knowing it and without your seeing it (or 'him'), then kill me.' Muret's emendation *n'i* for *i* seems unnecessary and has been rejected in M⁴. The equivalent lines in *O* (3842–5) read:

> sêge he denne nicht die vrawen mîn
> in desir nacht vor dem tage,
> sô heizet mir mîn houbet abe
> mit einem dilen stôzen morgen.

663–6 There is nothing in *O* to correspond with these lines. Line 666 taken by itself refers to the lovers: 'they will be proven guilty without (the need of) a judicial oath', i.e. there will be no need to lay a sworn information or charge against them (cf. the procedure leading to the trial by ordeal in the Thomas versions). This would seem to be the meaning of *soirement*, and not that of 'evidence on oath' suggested by Muret's glossary.

Line 665 is suspect. If we supply *il* at the beginning of the line and eliminate the hiatus (*homë*) we might interpret: 'Otherwise (i.e. if Tristran comes to Iseut and *is* discovered) he and all his men will be found guilty . . .', the implication being that the condemnation of his followers (and sureties?) is to be involved in that of Tristran. But this can hardly have been meant by the poet, unless we connect it with Tristran's earlier reference to the anticipated loss of his followers with the exception of Governal (241 ff.).—G. Paris's rather bold emendation (adopted by Muret) to *Et tuit ti home outreement* ('and all your men without exception') links l. 665 with l. 664; but it must seem odd that the dwarf should wish all the king's men to take part in punishing him; or does he intend that all the king's men should be associated with the witnessing (*tu nu voiz*)? For the semantic development of *autrement—outrement*, see J. Orr, 'Autre, outre . . . et foutre', *RLiR*, IX (1933), 52–83.

667 'King, now let me see to it and prognosticate at my pleasure, and do thou conceal his errand until the hour of retiring': the dwarf does not intend that Tristran should have time to arrange a rendez-vous with Iseut before the evening and plan a counter-ruse.

669 Tanquerey's suggested emendation (*si* for *se*) is unnecessary: *se* is often used for *si* (< SIC), particularly if the following word contains an *i*; cf. *Aucassin et Nicolete*, ed. Roques, p. xvii.

675–7 This detail is peculiar to Beroul and may be considered a characteristic, picturesque addition.

680 *sale*; see note to l. 104.

681 Jeanroy proposed the emendation *touchier* (for *couchier*): 'Marc se lève et va réveiller Tristran en lui touchant l'épaule.' But the MS reading is perfectly satisfactory: Tristran as chamberlain to the king attends him when he retires and occupies the same room, his bed being near the king's; it is in fact a primitive and rudimentary *coucher du roi*.

688 Why this injunction to Tristran to remain only one day at Arthur's court? Can it be that it is induced by the poet's recollection of the potion whose effect does not allow Tristan and Iseut to be separated for more than a day and night? This would be inept as it does not allow for the time taken by the journey there and back, for which Eilhart allows seven days (l. 3879). We have here perhaps a mere picturesque addition, though not neces-

sarily made by *B* since *O* also seems to envisage a prompt return.

690 *respondre de* 'answer for', 'promise to do'; *lui* (= *le mesage*) is here the accented direct object.

(*c*) *The lovers trapped* (693–826)

SUMMARY

693– 700	Tristran resolves to speak to Iseut when Mark is asleep. [His bed was the length of a lance from the king's.]
701– 706	Frocin spreads the flour between the two beds.
707– 715	Tristran observes Frocin and perceives his plan.
716– 720	[Tristran had been wounded by a boar the day before and his wound was unbound.]
722– 726	Mark leaves the darkened chamber accompanied by Frocin.
727– 735	Tristran leaps across, his wound opens and the blood flows down upon the royal bed.
736– 740	Frocin sees them: ['Now, king, if you do not catch them, have me hanged.']
741– 749	The three felons were there. Tristran, hearing the king approach, leaps back; [the blood drips upon the flour.]
750– 756	[Would that the queen had removed the bedclothes! But yet it pleased God to save them!
757– 765	Mark and Frocin find Tristran, who pretends to sleep and snores loudly. Only Perinis is with him, who sleeps at his feet, and the Queen in her bed.]
766– 770	Mark sees the blood in the bed and the trace of the leap upon the flour.
771– 777	[The three barons seize Tristran, with threats and insults.

778– M: 'You are proven guilty. Be assured, Tristran,
782   that to-morrow you die.']
783– [T: 'Pity, sire!'—The barons: 'Take your revenge,
786   sire.'
787– T: 'Out of regard for you, fair uncle, I submit to
804   your pleasure. Have pity on the queen. I am
          ready to meet in combat any of your knights
          who would accuse me of sinfully loving the
          queen.']
805– The three barons bind Tristran and Iseut.
808
809– [Had Tristran known that he would not be allowed
826   to justify himself, he would have killed all three of
          them despite the king. Ah! why did he not? It
          would have been better so!]

VARIANTS

O 3893–3975; *R* 356, 21–357, 5 and 354, 1–355, 6; *T* xxiv; *G* 15121–
15270; *S* lv, 17–41; *E* cc–ccii; *T.r.* 236, 6–28; *Fo* 739–754

R: Sandret and his companions, warned by a *damoiselle,* light torches
and find Tristran in the queen's bed; they bind him hand and foot. (In
R, the motif of the blood in the bed is utilized in quite a different and
much earlier incident, before the marriage of Mark and Iseut (see above,
p. 68): Tristran lies with the lady (wife of Segurades) and bleeds from
the wound which had been inflicted on him by Mark. A dwarf in the
service of the lady warns them of the coming of Segurades. Tristran
departs for Tinthanel. The lady explains that her nose had bled all night;
but threatened with her husband's sword, she confesses that the blood
is Tristran's. Segurades overtakes him, unhorses him and wounds him
(cf. Loeseth, p. 25).)

G: Mark, on the advice of the seneschal and the dwarf, undergoes a
blood-letting together with Tristran and Iseut, and on the second night
retires to his chamber with Iseut, there being present also Tristran, the
dwarf, Brengain and a maiden. Early in the morning Mark and the dwarf
go to matins, the dwarf having spread flour upon the floor. Brengain
observes this and warns Tristran. Tristran in desperation leaps across,
but his vein bursts, blood covers the bed and flows down. Having leapt
back he lies in his bed till daybreak. Mark returns. Iseut attributes the
blood in her bed to a burst vein. Mark, finding blood in Tristran's bed
also, leaves the room, speechless and perplexed by the conflicting evidence
and in doubt. He consults his barons.—In *S* the blood-letting follows
immediately upon the abortive tryst (see above, p. 69). The king devises

the stratagem at the suggestion of the dwarf. The action proceeds as in *G*, except that Iseut says her hand has bled.—*E*'s account is very fragmentary: the blood-letting apparently takes place in the royal chamber, which is then swept clean and sprinkled with flour by the dwarf; the distance between the beds is thirty feet (as we are told three times). Mark, who for all we are told, was present throughout, sees the blood and tells Brengain (!) that Tristran has broken the truce. Tristran leaves the land.—In *T.r.*, after the blood-letting, Mark Tristran and Iseut sleep in their own three beds, the king gets up and, having spread flour on the floor, tells Tristran he is going to matins. Returning, he finds blood in the beds of Tristran and Iseut: he is filled with suspicion. (There is no mention of Brengain or any other person.)—In *Fo*, Tristran *fou* recalls how the dwarf spread the flour between the beds, how, having observed this, he leapt and in doing so burst [the vein in] his arm and stained Iseut's bed with blood and his own when he leaptback; how Mark, returning, discovered the blood and how Tristran was banished for love of Iseut.

In *O*, the dwarf's instructions having been carried out, Tristran, 'with little foresight but compelled by the potion', leaps across to Iseut's bed, the wound (of which *O* has made no previous mention) breaks open and covers Iseut with blood. The dwarf cries: 'Now you can take Tristran.' Mark calls those on guard. Tristran could not leap back to his bed: his foot touches the floor. On Mark's orders the barons bind Tristran's hands behind his back like a thief's. Mark threatens to destroy their love so utterly that men shall speak of it to the end of the world. He asks his followers to propose a dire death: Andret proposes that Tristran be broken upon the wheel and Iseut burnt at the stake.[1]

There are various points of resemblance between this episode and the scene in Chrétien's *Lancelot* (4651 ff.) where Lancelot, having injured his hand when forcing his way through the barred window, joins the queen and stains her bed with blood. The more striking resemblances of detail are indicated in the notes. See also Hertz[3], pp. 542-3.

It has been shown (Schoepperle, p. 221) that the dwarf's stratagem is but one of many devices used in popular tales to catch the master-thief who usually escapes by a counter-ruse. Here too we have a tentative counter-ruse, but as Tristan must be caught, he is made to bleed from a wound, and in *O* his foot also touches the ground (see note to l. 770).

[1] Muret (*Rom.* XVI, 327) considered that in the original Eilhart version (as implied by the Czech translation) Mark prepared the same death for both lovers, i.e. burning.

695 No such specific indication is given in any other version except *E* (see above, p. 127).

697–8 The extra line in the MS may have resulted from the incorporation of a variant reading from the scribe's model. On the other hand, it is possible that originally there were four consecutive lines with the same rhyme (as in 725–8) and that a line has been omitted; in which case one might read conjecturally:

> En son cuer dist qu'il i iroit
>
> . . . .
> A la roïne parleroit
> A (*or* Ainz) l'ajorner, se il pooit.

701 According to *O* (3847) the dwarf is under Iseut's bed and the king sleeps in the room!

707 In *G* and *S* it is Brengain who observes the dwarf and warns Tristran (see above, p. 126).—*Besuchier*, a rare word, represented by only one other example in Tobler-Lommatzsch, is a dialectal form of O.F. *besocher*. J. Derocquigny (*Rom.* XXXIV, 458) cites the Boulogne form *bésuquer* 's'occuper à des riens, faire peu d'ouvrage' (from Haigneré, *Le patois boulonnais, vocabulaire*), but this meaning hardly fits our context, which demands an intermediate meaning in the development 'to dig' 'to turn over and over' 'to poke about' 'to fuss' 'to waste time over trifles'. Cf. also the note in M^0 and M^4, s.v. *besuchier*, and A. Thomas, in *Rom.* XXV, 441.

711 The conditional after *bien tost* has the effect of presenting the statement as conjectural.

715 Ironical: 'He'll duly see if I go there!'

720 *par son pechié*. Muret: 'Formule impliquant la croyance qu'un malheur est la conséquence d'un péché.'

725–8 Four consecutive lines rhyming together, a common feature in Norman and Anglo-Norman works.

728 *fist*; cf. note to 270.

729 *esme* 'estimates the distance' or simply 'reflects',

'considers' (cf. *G*'s description of Tristran's perplexity, ll. 15171–92).

731–4 Cf. *Lancelot* 4662–4:

> Mes del sanc qui jus an degote
> Ne des plaies nule ne sant
> Cil que a autre chose antant.

748 'It goes badly', 'Alas!'; cf. 606.

750 ff. A characteristic intervention by the poet; cf. 825–6.

750–4 Cf. *Lancelot* 4758–61:

> De ses dras ne se gardoit mie
> Que il fussent tachié de sanc,
> Ainz cuidoit qu'il fussent mout blanc
> Et mout bel et mout avenant.

755 *Deus* (restored in M[4]) is probably a mistake for the oblique *Deu* (cf. 22), but it is possible to take *Deus* as a nominative and *out* as the equivalent of *fist*. The interpretation *d'eus* might serve, were it not that *li* (756) obviously requires *Deus* or *Deu*. Cf. 377: *Granz miracles vos a fait Dex*, and (in another context) Fb 203: *Mout faisoit Deus ce qu'il voloit*; Fo 881: *Mais Deus aveit uvré pur vus*. The poet leaves us in no doubt: God is on the side of the lovers, for they were not killed although discovered. Such reflections are developed at great length by Gottfried, e.g. in ll. 15548 ff.; cf. also the extraordinary 'casuistry' of ll. 15737 ff. (Bédier I, 212).

759–61 This characteristic detail is not found elsewhere.

764 *Pirinis* (usually *Perinis* in *B*), *Perenîs* (*Peronîs*) in *O*, *Paranîs* in *G*, *Perinis* in *R*. He is Iseut's valet in *B*, her chamberlain in *O*; he accompanied Iseut from Ireland. The name is Breton according to Bédier (II, 122, n. 1); according to Loth it is of doubtful origin (p. 107), or either Cornish or Breton (pp. 99, 103).

766 'On the floor the blood, still warm, showed.'

767–8 Cf. *Lancelot* 4766–7:

> Veillant la trueve et les dras voit
> De fres sanc tachiez et gotez.

770 In *B* it is not clear whether the reference is here to
the trace left by the blood (cf. 748–9 and 766) or from the
contact of his foot with the floor (cf. *O*, where Tristran's
foot touches the floor as he leaps back to his bed). On
either interpretation the MS reading is acceptable and the
emendation *sanc* (for *saut*), though palaeographically
plausible, has rightly been rejected in M³ and M⁴.

771–2 A lacuna was assumed by Muret (but no longer
in M⁴) because *chanbre* and *prenent* cannot possibly rhyme.
The correction tentatively suggested in the variants
assumes that the corruption resulted from a misreading
of *pensent* as *par ire* (cf. *O* 3950–3). The rhyme *chanbre* :
prendre is imperfect, but not more so than *asente* : *enfle*
(331); see above, p. 31.

774 I take *roïne* not as governed by *por*, but as the
object of the verb (and therefore parallel with *l'* in the
preceding line), and l. 775 as referring to the queen,
with an abrupt return to Tristran in 776–7. The correction
le . . . le (abandoned in M⁴) is unnecessary.

778–82 Cf. *Lancelot* 4774–5:

> Et dist: 'Dame, or ai je trovees
> Teus ansaingnes con je voloie!

and 4805–9:

> 'Par mon chief', fet Meleaganz,
> 'Quanque vos dites est neanz.
> N'i a mestier parole fainte,
> Que provee estes et atainte;
> Et bien sera li voirs provez.'

The evidence of the customaries and other texts
adduced by Jonin in his thorough examination of the
'Procès d'Iseut' (*op. cit.*, pp. 59–108) would suggest that
while the apprehension of the lovers in *flagrante delicto*
entitles Mark to exercise summary judgement and invalidates any claim Tristran might otherwise have had to

demand an *escondit*, it does not absolve the king from submitting the case for formal judgement before punishment is carried out, as Dinas reminds him (1096–1100).

780 *pois* 'pea', here used (like *mie*, etc.) as a negative complementary particle. Wrongly identified in the Glossary with *pois* 'weight'.

788 From its use with *mal* (cf. 410) and other adjectives (*périlleux*, etc.), *saut* developed, by contamination, the meaning 'hazardous leap', 'dangerous pass', 'doom'; cf. the expressions *faire le saut, franchir le saut*, etc. (examples in Godefroy X). The emendation *mau* (for *mon*), though palaeographically plausible, is therefore unnecessary.

788–93 'Well do I know that I have come to my doom; were it not for fear of angering you, this judgement (*or* affair) would be dearly bought. Never, by their eyes, would they have thought to touch me with their hands. But I bear you no ill-will (*or* I am not guilty towards you).'

789 For *acorocier*, see Godefroy I, 79.

790 *plez*, here probably used, not in the sense of 'judgement', but with the more generalized meaning 'affair', 'matter'.

791 Jeanroy proposed *sor* for *por*, no doubt having in mind such cases as *sor lor eulz* (1032); but *por* is perfectly satisfactory and has been restored by M⁴.

794 'Whether it turn out well or ill.'

798 *encliner* sometimes takes the direct object, though more commonly the indirect object (cf. 3158) of the person (bowed to); see examples in Godefroy. Hence *l'* = *le* or *li*.

799–803 Miss Hackett has called attention (in *Vinaver Miscellany*, 157–66) to the striking resemblance between these lines and ll. 4670–76 of *Girart de Roussillon*, and to other similar instances. Cf. note to l. 131 above. Jonin (p. 65) quotes J. Guilmain, *Le procès civil . . .*, to the effect that the 'duel judiciaire' was 'le trait caractéristique de la procédure dans les cours seigneuriales'.

808 *est torné* is impersonal (cf. 794): 'Hatred wins the day.'

810 *nul = ne le* (cf. 59, etc.), *le* being the object of *escondire*, the impersonal *leüst* being used absolutely or generically without a dative denoting the person: 'that there would be no leave (or facility) to defend himself'.

812 *que* 'than that'; cf. 37.

814 *Que* might be interpreted as causal (with comma after *fiot*).

819 In the MS reading, *se* is redundant, unless one were to interpret *soi* (820) as a graphy for *ç'oi* used parenthetically (cf. *ç'oi dire* 425).

820 *par nul desroi* would be normal (cf. 2574), but *por* frequently alternates with *par* in such uses (cf. 157, 231, etc.).

822 *qui* might be interpreted as *qu'i*.

825–6 Once again a characteristic intervention by the poet.

826 *venist*, impersonal: 'A much better judgement would have resulted' or 'things would have had a far better issue' (cf. note to 790).

(d) *Distress of the townsfolk* (827–861)

SUMMARY

827–832 Distress of all the citizens:

833–859 ['Alas, Tristran! alas, Iseut! Death to the dwarf! Alas, Tristran, that you should die thus!] When the Morholt came hither for our children, you alone of all our barons offered combat and killed the Morholt, who wounded you mortally with a javelin. We should not condone your death!'

860–861 [The citizens rush to the palace amid a general clamour.]

VARIANTS

R 358, 4–8

R: (Mark, having handed Tristran over for punishment as indicated under (e) and (j) below—retires to his chamber, laments and deplores what he is doing to Tristran and Iseut, and curses the evil counsellors: *mieux voulsist qu'il l'eüst* (i.e. Iseut) *que les meseaulx*). The people, seeing Tristran led forth to die, say: 'If the king remembered the anguish you suffered when you fought the Morholt for the freedom of Cornwall, he would honour you instead of killing you.'

NOTES

831 ff. While the identification of the people with the cause of the lovers is not confined to Beroul (cf. R), in no other version do we find the same repeated insistence on the popular sympathy with them. The populace is used very effectively by the poet not only to play a chorus-like role but to reinforce Tristran's demand for legal judgement of his case.

839 *ton cors* may here be a mere periphrasis for *te*.

841–3 'May he never look God in the face (cf. ll. 58–59) who finds the dwarf, wherever it be, and does not strike him with a sword.'

846 The scribe's error may have been induced by the form of the future (in *-oiz*), perhaps unfamiliar to him as an obsolescent feature; see Introd., No. 45.

848 ff. Cf. Eilhart's account summarized above, p. 61. For the tribute demanded by the Morholt and G's protest (5967 ff.) against those who say that he demanded a tribute of children, see Bédier I, 76–77; II, 83. According to E, in the fourth year the tribute is 300 noble youths.

850 The loss of the final *t* of *tos[t]* is induced by the fact that the following word begins with *t*.

856–7 For the confusion of *tu* and *vos*, see Kr. Nyrop, *Grammaire historique* V, pp. 232–3. It was particularly common in Norman and Anglo-Norman.

857 '... of which you were like to die', i.e. 'were

doomed to die (had you not been miraculously healed by Iseut)'.

(e) Preparations for the lovers' punishment (862–908)

SUMMARY

862–   [Mark, consumed with wrath, has the pyre pre-
872   pared.]
873–   All [the Cornishmen] are summoned and all show
880   their grief save the dwarf of Tintagel.
881–   [Mark expresses his resolve to have Tristran and
894   Iseut burnt and refuses the request for a trial.]
895–   He sends for Tristran, who is to be burnt first.
898
899–   [Tristran is brought forth bound, in tears.
902
903–   I: 'Alas, that you are bound, Tristran! If by my
908   death you were saved, it would please me:
             revenge would yet be taken.']

VARIANTS

O 3976–3994, 3995–4097; R 357, 6–23

R: On the morrow Sandret hands Tristran and Iseut over to the king, who threatens vengeance: *Ja mais ne puisse je porter couronne, se je n'en pren vengeance.* Tristran's four companions tell Governal and they decide to ambush themselves 'near the place where criminals are put to death' and to rescue Tristran. Tristran and Iseut having been brought before Mark, he denounces and threatens Tristran. He causes the pyre to be prepared on the sea-shore.

O: Mark, impatient for the day of punishment, issues a ban summoning all in the land to come to the judgement, but the criers refuse to tell them what it is for. On the appointed day Mark goes to the pyre.—None dares intercede save Dinas, who appeals to the king's honour, offering to make reparation for Tristran and refusing to witness the death of the lovers, but in vain. Dinas rides sorrowfully away and meets Tristran being led by a crowd; he weeps, swears fidelity, cuts Tristran's bonds and bids his captors not to bind him again. The captors are moved to sorrow by Dinas's tears and lamentations. (Cf. the intervention of Dinas on behalf of Iseut in *B* 1083–1140.)

In the versions derived from *T*, there follows upon the detection of Tristran and Iseut: the declaration of her innocence by Iseut before the assembled barons, the ambiguous oath and the ordeal by fire ('le fer rouge'), Tristran's flight to Wales, his acquisition of Petit-Crû, Mark's revived suspicions and the banishment of Tristran and Iseut from the court (Thomas, ch. xxiv–xxv, ed. Bédier I, pp. 205–32).

NOTES

864 *mot* used as in *ne sonner mot, sans mot sonner*.

865 The emendation of *Qui li* to *Qu'il li* (or *Que li* as in Muret) is perhaps hardly necessary: for a similar use of the relative, see l. 23.

866 ff. Cf. *Fb* 447 ff.

867–70 Once again it would seem that an unsatisfactory text has resulted from the incorporation of alternative variant readings (867–8 *Li rois . . .* and 869–70 *Li rois . . .*) from the scribe's model. Quite apart from *quiert* (for *querre*), the imperfect rhyme (*sarmenz : tenant*) and the obscurity of l. 869, it is strange to find the king intervening in the actual construction of the pyre. There is nothing of the kind in *O* and *R*, where the king merely commands a fire to be made. In these circumstances l. 869 may well be an unintelligent scribal makeshift. Two interpretations suggest themselves: (1) the king in his impatience to see the lovers punished, himself takes part, armed with a pruning hook or shears, to cut branches, or (2) to punctuate and interpret as in M⁴: *Li rois, tranchanz, demaintenant . . .* 'The king, peremptorily, straightway . . .'. See the examples given in Godefroy VIII and X, s.v. *tranchant*. The word division in the MS is *demain tenant*.

For striking resemblance of the character and behaviour of the king in *Dolopathos* to those of Mark, see Jessie Crosland, '*Dolopathos* and the *Seven Sages of Rome*', *Med. Aev.* XXV (1956), pp. 6–7: King Dolopathos shifts the responsibility for his son's fate to advisers and magnates of the realm, commands a fire to be made and himself brings forward faggots to the pyre.

871–2 '. . . and heap them up with blackthorn and hawthorn pulled up by the roots'.

874 *Li* for *Les*. 'They cried the king's proclamation throughout the kingdom (to the effect) that all should go to the court.' For the *cri* as a normal proceeding in such cases, see Jonin, p. 71.

876 'They all come hurrying as quickly as they can.'

878 *tibois* may be a scribal error (or a variant?) for *tabois* 'noise', of which Tanquerey cites examples from the *Chanson des Saisnes* I, 60 and *God. Bouill.* 181.

880 Nowhere else (except at l. 264) is the dwarf described as 'of Tintagel'.

884–94 This development is peculiar to Beroul.

887 *puis* 'afterwards', i.e. after judgement.

891 'Even at the price of being disowned (by God), I would not refrain from burning them in the pyre'; or '. . . of being deprived of my heritage (i.e. my kingdom)'. For this construction, see Tanquerey, in *Rom.* LXIV (1938), 1–17; and for the rare use of the infinitive with pronoun subject (as at ll. 1927 and 3565), see W. M. Hackett, in *Vinaver Miscellany*, p. 158.

893 This line might be taken as exclamatory, i.e. postulating a condition with an implied threat, the same thought being repeated imperatively in 894. Alternatively, as suggested in M⁴, l. 893 might be linked with 892: 'quoi qu'on puisse m'en dire maintenant ou plus tard.'

906 *Qui* 'whoever', 'if anyone': 'If one were to kill me, provided you were safe it would be a great joy, fair friend: vengeance would yet be taken.'

(f) Tristran's leap (909–964)

SUMMARY

909–
914   [Hear now how merciful is God!]

915–   Tristran and his guards pass a chapel set upon a

941   cliff. He asks to be allowed to enter and pray. His
guards consent [and remove his bonds].

941–   Tristran enters and leaps from a window in the
952   apse to a large rock in the face of the cliff.

953–   The [Cornish] still call this rock 'Le Saut Tristran'.
954

955–   [While the service continues and the guards wait
964   without, Tristran escapes along the strand.]

VARIANTS

O 4098–4143; *R* 358, 9–32 and 359, 27–360, 9; *Fb* 445–6

R: Tristran, passing before the church, disarms one of his captors, puts the remainder to flight, enters the church and approaches the window: *la mer avoit bien quarante toises de parfont.* Tristran, attacked by Sandret and twenty knights, kills one and leaps through one of the windows into the sea. His captors think he is drowned. *Ce sault doit bien estre appellé le Sault Tristran.* Cf. Loeseth, p. 42.

O: the captors grant Tristran's request after one of them has pointed out that there is but one door and beyond there is the sea. Tristran locks the door from within, squeezes through a window and leaps into the sea. He swims to land, runs along the shore, looking behind him to see if he is pursued.

In *Fb*, Tristran *fou* reminds Iseut of *lo Saut de la chapele, Qant a ardoir fustes jugiee.*

NOTES

909 *Oez . . . de . . .* 'Hear now about . . .' Cf. similar instances of *oïr de* 'hear about' at ll. 320, 1306, 2134, 2200, 2319–20.

911 *vieat = veut.*

916 It is possible that the MS reading (*sor*) is the scribe's misreading of *ē sor* (= *est sor*); cf. *Pope Misc.*, p. 91.

918 'Overlooking the sea, facing north.'

921 'There was nothing beyond save the cliff.'

922 *aaise* is clearly a scribal error, induced perhaps by the copyist's unfamiliarity with the word to be transcribed. I have emended tentatively to *atoise* 'slate',

'slaty': 'This cliff was of solid slaty stone'; for this rare form (= mod. *ardoise*), see *Percevalroman* (ed. Hilka), l. 1774 note. Muret's emendation to *alise* assumes also scribal substitution of the variant *faloise* for *falise*; cf. *terre alisse* 'terre compacte, peu fertile' in *Doon de la Roche*, l. 3722. Caulier adopts *adoise*.

925 *dube* 'apse'? Conjectural meaning; cf. M⁰, s.v. *dube*. Or *l'adube*?

938 M⁴ restores the MS reading and tentatively suggests emendation: *En es l'ore a vos revendrai.*

947 Absolute construction: 'before the eyes of such an assembly'; cf. 2548. See C. W. Aspland, 'The so-called absolute construction in Old French', *AUMLA*, No. 30 (1968), 151–68.

949 *u mileu* 'in the middle', 'half-way down the rock'. Beroul's account is not clear. One is reduced to conjecture that Tristran first leapt from the chapel to a flat stone half-way down the cliff, the impact being broken by his cloak billowing out, parachute-like, under the wind, and that from this stone he leapt to the soft sand of the sea-shore. It is the flat stone (*pierre lee*) and not the whole cliff (*roche*), it would seem, that is called *le Saut Tristran*.

951 'The wind catches his clothes, preventing him from falling all of a heap (i.e. breaking his fall)'.

954 *Le Saut Tristran*, identified by J. Loth (pp. 76–78) with Chapel Point in Goran, some distance to the south of Lancien, Tristran's leap is said to have been repeated in 1485 by Henri de Bodrugan and the place is still called Bodrigan's Leap or Jump.

It is possible that the episode would signify, in the minds of Beroul's public, that God intervened by a miracle and that it was therefore a sign of Tristran's innocence. G. Schoepperle pointed out (pp. 284–5) that such extraordinary leaps are a common trait in stories of Irish heroes. In Wace, *Brut* 1161–87, where Corineüs hurls the giant Goëmagog to his death over the cliff, we are told that the place is named after the giant: it appears as *Saltus Goemagog* in Geoffrey of Monmouth's *Historia*, ch. 21.

955–8 The narrative is once again disjointed. The poet takes his audience back and forth from the chapel to Tristran and to his captors, adding the detail of the soft sand to explain the fact that Tristran was uninjured: Tristran leaps to his feet; in the meantime all the (*toz* for *tuit*) worshippers continue their orisons while the captors wait outside the chapel, but in vain.

961 *La riviere*, accusative of direction: 'along the shore'; *granz sauz*, accusative of manner: 'in great leaps'.

962 Poetic licence or a reminiscence of a version in which the pyre is built upon the sea-shore (cf. R 357, 23).

963–4 'He is not minded to turn back and runs as quickly as he can.'

(g) *Governal and Tristran meet and lie in ambush* (965–1044)

SUMMARY

965–	Governal, [in fear of his life,] had left the city
978	bearing Tristran's sword. Their joy on meeting.
979–	T: 'Master, I have escaped, but what is life to me
988	when Iseut is being burnt?'
989–	[G: 'Let us hide in yonder thicket. We may hear
999	news of Iseut. May you never mount a steed again if you do not avenge her!
1000–	Never shall I lie in any human habitation until
1007	the three felon barons are killed; nor shall I ever have joy if you die before vengeance is taken.'
1008–	T: 'I am an encumbrance to you, for I have not
1012	my sword.'—G: 'You have, for I have brought it.'—T: It is well; now I fear nothing save God.'
1013–	G: 'And a strong light halberk I have for your
1022	service under my tunic.'—T: 'Give it me: if I

arrive betimes at the pyre I would rather be
cut to pieces than not kill those who hold her.'

1023– G: 'Be not hasty: a better opportunity may pre-
1039   sent itself. All the citizens are subject to the
king, and at the king's behest there are those
who might betray you if the hue and cry were
raised against you.'

1040– Had not Governal forbidden it, nothing would
1044   have restrained Tristran.]

VARIANTS

O 4144–4202; R 357, 11–18 and 359, 1–26

In R, Governal and Tristran's four companions had gone into ambush
(see above, p. 134) with the object of rescuing Tristran. They are sought
out by a *damoiselle* when Iseut has been handed over to the lepers (see
below, p. 149), and Governal proceeds to take Iseut from them and
brings her to the ambush. She reports that she saw Tristran enter the
chapel (*une vielle eglise*). Governal and two of the companions go to the
chapel; they find Tristran sitting, sword in hand, on a rock in the sea.
He swims to land and together they rejoin Iseut: thus Tristran and Iseut
escaped death!

In O, Governal, riding from the town and bringing Tristran's horse
and sword, meets him; he fears they may be pursued. Tristran prefers
revenge and death with Iseut to flight. He hides in a thicket near the
place of execution.

NOTES

973–4 *estoit* : *aportoit* for *estot* (impf. ind. 3 of *ester*) :
aportot; cf. 350 and 2200.

975 *Tristran* (oblique for nominative).

977 *il* = Governal.

978 *il* = Tristran.

982–5 'Since I have not Iseut, it avails me nothing,
wretch that I am, the leap which I made but now. What
did it portend that I did not kill myself? It might yet be
a matter of regret to me.'

M[4] restores the MS reading and in a note (p. 143) aptly
justifies the disjointed nature of the narrative, but interprets l. 985 differently.

994 Corr. *trespassent*?

996 The scribe apparently misread *an cele* (= *sele*) as *ancele* (it is so written in the MS) and was thereby led to read *ne montez* as *n'encontrez*.

997–8 *briment* to be taken in close connection with *enprés*: 'quickly thereafter', 'without delay'.

1003 *quoi* referring to persons, loosely: 'through whose agency'.

1008 *anoie*, 3rd pers. (impersonal) rather than 1st. pers. with analogical *-e*.

1009 *point de*—*de* being due to the fact that *point* still retained some of its original substantival force, or by analogy with partitive uses (*pas de*, etc.)?

1012 *imais*, reduction of *huimais*? Cf. *aprisme* for *apruisme* (l. 3).

1018–22 Cf. *O* 4188–95.

1020 *rez* for *ré* (obl.). For the rhyme see Introd., Nos. 7 and 39. M[4] restores the MS reading and suggests a possible emendation to *desmenbré* : *ré*, citing ll. 66 and 1710 in support.

1026–8 'You will not then encounter the difficulty which you might now have. I see nothing that you can do.'

1030 Muret[3] adopted Acher's emendation *Avocques* in preference to his own original emendation in M[0]: *Avoc lui*. Tanquerey proposed *Avoé*, which he interpreted as a graphy for *avoié* (cf. *ro* for *roi*, etc.), pple. of *avoier* 'direct', 'instruct'. The interpretation 'retainers' is supported by ll. 1036–8, which I take to mean that the citizens and other townspeople, being bound by their allegiance to Mark, will obey him in spite of their sympathy with Tristran.

1035–8 Muret's emendation *qu'autrui* (MS *que toi*) is supported by considerations of rhyme and of sense. It is interesting to find a similar phrase in *T.r.* (p. 234): 'non è nato colui che ama più altrui che sè', and in *S*, in another context (Cap. LVI): 'There are many in our land who accuse Tristan and yet would not dare to justify the charge against him.' In l. 1036 M[4] adopts *Se l'en*. Tanquerey's conjectural *Se loi levout sor toi le roi* is inherently unconvincing and does not fit the context. Governal merely states as a hypothetical case what might now be expected to happen: 'Each is more concerned for himself than for you (Muret: 'for others'). If the hue and cry were raised against you, there are those who would gladly save you (i.e. help you to escape the ban) and yet would not even dare to contemplate it.'[1] For the rhyme *toi* : *hui*, see above, p. 31.

1040–4 'Never, for all those of Tintagel—even if he were to be cut to pieces so that no one piece clung to its neighbour—would he refrain from going there, had not his master forbidden him.'

1040 This reference to Tintagel implies that it is a residence of King Mark, as it is in other versions. A more precise indication is furnished by l. 3150. It would appear that, like Arthur (cf. Rickard, p. 101), Mark disposed of more than one royal residence and resided now at Tintagel, now at Lancïen (see note to l. 2359). Tintagel represents a relatively late addition to the legend under the influence of Arthurian romance. In *Fo* (ll. 133–4) Tintagel is described as a *chastel faez* which disappears twice a year, once in summer and once in winter: this is based upon Thomas who follows Wace. See Bédier I, 6–8 and II, 118–9; Hertz[3], Anm. 6, and for the form of the name: J. Loth, *Contrib.*, pp. 73 and 93 n.

1041 For the rhyme, see note to 1020 and Introd., No. 7.

(h) Iseut and Mark hear of Tristran's escape (1045–1082)

SUMMARY

1045– [Iseut, informed of Tristran's escape, exclaims:

---

[1] For the penalties incurred in real life by those who failed to heed the *cri* or *ban*, see Jonin, pp. 73–76.

1050 'Thanks be to God, now I care not if I be killed or bound or unbound.'

1051– So tightly were her wrists bound that the blood
1054 issued forth from all her fingers.

1055– I: 'What care I, now that Tristran has escaped.
1064 The dwarf and the felons shall have their deserts.']

1065– Mark, enraged at Tristran's escape, has Iseut
1071 brought forth.

1072– [The citizens lament: 'Little profit will they have
1082 who by their slander brought this grief upon the land, curse them!']

VARIANTS

O 4203–4255

O: The captors, weary of waiting, break open the chapel door and find Tristran gone. The news is brought to Mark, who offers great rewards for his capture, but all seek him in vain. Andret was glad of this: he *vorchte, he nême im ein pant* (4242). Mark, enraged, orders Iseut to be burnt forthwith.

NOTES

1051–4 In having Tristran and Iseut bound, Mark is acting in conformity with legal provisions of the time. On the other hand the burning of a woman taken in adultery was not recognized as a regular punishment (cf. Jonin, pp. 67–70), nor was Tristran's offence a capital crime. But Beroul would seem to be less concerned with legal conformity and consistency than with credibility, and it could hardly have imposed a serious strain upon the credulity of his audience to see Iseut condemned to a fate which was not inappropriate in an earlier age, the age of King Arthur; for, as G. Schoepperle pointed out, in medieval romance the punishment threatened and in some cases inflicted is burning at the stake (p. 446, n. 1) and from a number of Old Irish texts it appears that the punishment of the adulterous woman was usually burning (pp. 463–5). See also Loomis, *Arthurian Tradition*, ch. LIV ('The Rescue of Lunete from the Pyre', *Yvain* 4313–575).

1053 *Qu'* consecutive, to be linked with *si* (1051), l. 1054 being in its turn a consecutive clause depending on l. 1053.

1054 *est*, Eastern dialectal form for *ist*.

1055 The context, and particularly l. 1059, indicates a lacuna at this point. Supply (with G. Paris): 'if ever I [complain of my fate . . .]'. Reid questions the lacuna and proposes emendation of *mes jor* to *m'esplor* 'burst into tears', to which B. Blakey (in *French Studies* XXI, 99) prefers, as an emendation, *m'escor*, 'a recognized form of *s'acorer*, "to grieve" '. Professor B. Woledge has suggested to me that *mes proisier* (1059) might be read as one word *mesproisier*, and this is what in fact the scribe wrote.

1062 *qui* for *cui* (obl.): 'by whose counsel'.

1074 *A laidor ert* ' 'twas shamefully done'.

1075 *Qui* exclamatory: 'Who then had heard . . .!', 'You should have heard . . .!'.

1079 '. . . through whom this scandal has been spread abroad. Truly in a small purse will they be able to put their reward! May they suffer vile mutilation!' For *novele* 'scandal', cf. *mesnie noveliere* 454.

(i) Dinas intercedes (1083–1140)

SUMMARY

1083– Iseut is brought to the pyre. [Dinas, lord of Dinan,
1087   falls at the king's feet:

1088– D: 'Sire, by my loyal service as your seneschal,
1100   have mercy on the queen. It is not meet that you should burn her without judgement for a misdeed she does not avow.

1101– Tristran has escaped and will attack your

1118   barons. Had a king of seven lands killed a mere squire of mine all seven would be thrown into the balance before my vengeance was satisfied: think then what he must feel for such a noble lady brought by him from a foreign land!

1119–1120   Surrender her to me in the name of my services to you.'

1121–1123   The three barons are speechless with fear.]

1124–1128   Mark swears Iseut shall be burnt.

1129–1140   [Dinas will have no part in this: 'I go to Dinan; not for all the wealth in the world would I see her burnt.' He departs in sorrow.]

VARIANTS

In O, there is an intervention by Dinas, but at an earlier stage (3995 ff.) and in favour of Tristran (see above, p. 134).

Dinas, seneschal of King Mark is the most consistently attractive figure in Beroul's romance. He appears as such in O, where we first encounter him when he is entrusted with the youthful Tristran (328 ff.), and again when, together with Governal, he tends the wounded Tristran (1085 ff.), intercedes for him (3995 ff.) and continues to act as friend and go-between for the lovers until Tristran's departure for his native land (8552). Beroul alone causes him to intervene at the present juncture: he protests against the injustice of punishing Iseut without a formal judgement on her case and warns the king of the reprisals to be expected from Tristran. Particularly striking is the proud but dignified reminder to Mark of his faithful and incorruptible discharge of his duties as seneschal which Beroul puts into his mouth: 'You will not find a single person in all this kingdom, poor orphan

or old woman, who because of my office of seneschal
(which I have held all my life), had given me so much as
a farthing': i.e. he has not used his office to extort money
from the poor and helpless.

Broadly the same picture emerges, in spite of disparate
accretions, in the Prose Romance (Bédier II, 325; Loeseth,
§§ 86, 176, 270 ff., 545). *Fb* introduces him as the friend
and protector of Tristran (33–42).

Beroul describes him as 'sire de Dinan' (1085, 1133,
2847); but *Dinan* occurs in no other version, and in *O* his
castle (*veste* or *borg*) is always *Lîtân*. *Lidan* is mentioned
twice in *B*: at l. 3562 we are told that when Perinis had
given an account of his errand, of Arthur and of Tristran,
'they lay that night at Lidan'; but it is not clear who
'they' are, since Tristran is still in hiding, together with
Governal, in Orri's 'celier' (3577–8), and Iseut is with
Mark. Assuming that *Lidan* is to be equated with *O's*
Lîtân, one might suppose that the account which survives
in other versions, for example in *O*, of Tristran and
Kehenis finding shelter at Lîtân (6272) and of Tristran and
Kurvenal being sheltered by Tînas (7445 ff.), coupled
with the meeting of the lovers 'chiés Dinas' referred to
by Beroul (4301), resulted in this residual mention of
Lidan. The other mention of *Lidan* occurs at l. 2232
('There is no knight in all this kingdom, from Lidan to
Durham'): any significance it might have is diminished
when we note that, while here Durham is placed in
Mark's kingdom, at ll. 4263–5 it is unequivocally in
Arthur's (as distinct from Mark's kingdom of Cornwall).
Lidan is mentioned in *B* and *O* only.

The identification of Dinan with Devon and of Lidan
with Lidford in Devonshire, tentatively advanced in M[0],
is not at all convincing and has been abandoned in later
editions. J. Loth (*Contrib.*, 90–91) agrees with F. Lot
(*Rom.* XXIV, 339) in holding that originally Dinas cannot
have been a man's name: it signifies 'fortress' or 'fortified
town' and is in fact a very common place-name in

Cornwall. Loth concludes: 'Si ce personnage était ori-
ginaire de Dinas que la source distinguait en l'appelant
lidan large, ample, ou y résidait, on devait dire couram-
ment *Dinan Dinas Lidan*', in which *Dinan* is the personal
name, *Dinas* the place of origin or residence, and *Lidan*
the adjective (cf. the Cornish place-names *Great and Little
Dinas* cited by Loth). Accepting this conjecture as
reasonable, we may conclude that *O*'s *Tînas* of *Lîtân*
represents one interpretation and *B*'s *Dinas de Lidan*
another with (*de*) *Lidan* as a residual alternative, while
other versions in which the personage appears content
themselves with *Dinas*.

The scribe's *Dinan* at l. 3483 is an obvious blunder and
might be held to support the suggestion that by a similar
error *Andrez* (or *Audrez*) was substituted for *Dinas* at l.
2870; but see the note to this line.

NOTES

1106–8 Taking *vilonast* as a subjunctive in the second
of two conditional clauses and *ert* as a future used to
express the result in a more vivid way (than by the past
subjunctive or the conditional), one might translate: 'But
if he got your barons in his power or assaulted them,
your land will yet be laid waste (or left lordless?) in
consequence.' But these lines are suspect, and M^4 notes
that 'l'enclise de la conjonction *ne* et du pronom personnel
est insolite'. Reid takes l. 1107 as a rhetorical question.

1110–8 Interpreting *ses* in l. 1113 as *se* (for *si* < SIC) +
les), one might translate: 'Whoever had killed or committed to the flames, on my account, even so much as a
squire, even if such an one were king of seven countries,
yet would he have to throw them all into the scales
before my vengeance would be satisfied. Do you not
think then that he will feel aggrieved concerning such
a noble lady whom he brought hither from a distant
realm, if she is destroyed? Great discord will yet result

from it.' Cf. l. 2179: *poise moi de la roïne* 'it grieves me for (lit. 'concerning') the queen'; and l. 2404. Miss Hackett (in *Vinaver Misc.*, p. 160) points to a similar passage in *Girart de Roussillon*, 5749–50, but her interpretation of the syntax differs from mine in respect of the use of *de* after impersonal *peser*, as it does also at lines 2179–80.

1116 Muret has pointed out that in Geoffrey of Monmouth's *Historia regum Britanniae*, vol. VIII, ch. xi, Ireland is designated *longinquum regnum*.

1119–20 '. . . by my deserts, in that I have served you all my life.'

1121 *sort*, ind. pr. 3 of *sordre*: 'through whom this affair arises'.

(j) The leper scene (1141–1270)

SUMMARY

1141– [Iseut, brought to the pyre, excites the compassion
1154 of the crowd.]

1155– [Ivein] the leper asks that Iseut be handed over to
1179 him and his [hundred] companions.

1180– Mark wishes to be assured of her punishment.
1216 [Ivein] the leper describes the life Iseut will lead among the lepers.

1217– [In spite of Iseut's protest,] Mark hands her over.
1234 [Ivein] the leper and his companions lead Iseut out of the city past Tristran's ambush.

1235– G: 'What now, Tristran, behold your lover.'
1236

1237– T: 'These fellows shall pay dearly if they do not
1244 set you free, Iseut.']

1245– Tristran, mounted upon his steed, breaks from the
1249 thicket [and calls upon Ivein to release Iseut].

1250– [The lepers struggle and utter threats, but Tristran
1258 did not wish to do them violence.

1259– Governal strikes Ivein and takes Iseut by the right
1264 hand.
1265– The 'contor' say that they drowned(?) Ivein, but
1270 they are not courtly and do not know the 'estoire'.
'Berox' remembers it better: Tristran was too
courtly to slay such people.]

VARIANTS

O 4256–4327; R 357, 23–31 and 358, 32–37 and 360, 9–22; *Fb* 447–459

R: The king being about to have the lovers burnt, the men of Cornwall propose that Iseut would suffer a more condign punishment if she were handed over to the lepers. The king agrees and hands Tristran over to ten 'pautonniers' and Iseut to ten 'autres garchons'.—Later Sandret and his companions, having concluded that Tristran is drowned, proceed to 'a leper-house'; Iseut implores Sandret to kill her or lend her his sword that she may kill herself rather than hand her over to the lepers. Sandret refuses; the lepers take Iseut away by force, Iseut is then rescued by Governal in the manner indicated above (p. 40).

O: A leprous duke comes hurrying up and proposes a more shameful death than burning: 'Give her to me and I will take her to my lepers for their pleasure: if she does not die a shameful death you may have me, my nephew and all my lepers hanged or beaten to death.' Mark hands Iseut over, which many in the land counted for his shame; the leper places her on his horse before him and rides off past the ambush. Governal recognizes her from afar and tells Tristran, who laments the dishonour done to Iseut, and as the leper approaches, spurs towards him in anger and cleaves him, the upper half falling with Iseut to the ground. (MS. H only: 'They lay about them among the lepers: methinks they left few alive, perhaps none' (?).)

In *Fb*, the lepers are described as quarrelling and struggling over the possession of Iseut and giving the preference to one of their number, while Tristran and Governal lie in ambush:

> Mult me deüssiez bien conoistre,
> Car je formant les fis la croistre;
> Ainz par moi n'en fu un desdit,
> Mes Governal, cui Deus aït!
> Lor dona teus cous des bastons
> Ou s'apooient des moignons. (454–9).

The leper scene is developed more fully in *B* than in any other version, and with a stark realism which shows a close familiarity with the symptoms of leprosy and with the conditions in which lepers lived (for which see, for example, Schultz I, 527–9, and P. Rémy, 'La lèpre, thème littéraire au moyen âge' *MA*, LII (1946), 204). There is no mention of a lazar-house in *B*, such as we find in *R*. It appears from the thorough examination to which P. Jonin subjected this scene in his chapter on 'Iseut et les lépreux' (pp. 109–38) that Ivein and his companions may have been accommodated, not in a lazar-house, but in a leper-village of the type which existed at the beginning of the twelfth century and in the preceding centuries. This would explain the comparative freedom with which Beroul allows Ivein and his companions to move about and behave. The accurate realism with which Beroul presents the characters and the drama of this scene contrasts significantly with the looseness of the setting. The pyre would seem to be sited between the gates of the city and the leper-village (cf. l. 1209), and yet it appears to be near the sea (cf. l. 1230), in which direction Ivein leads Iseut while his companions go off in the direction of the thicket where Tristran and Governal lie in ambush: but it is Ivein whom they challenge and, on the other hand, Tristran is described (961–2) as hearing the fire as he flees along the sea-shore, and the chapel from which Tristran makes his leap overlooks the sea and is presumably on the way from the city to the pyre, this being the route taken by Tristran and his captors (915–7). These inconsistencies and loose ends would seem to be due to Beroul's preservation of certain details from his sources and his failure to assimilate them to the more elaborate narrative he has contrived. The whole scene may serve to illustrate once more Beroul's absorption in his characters and in the observation of life, and his comparative indifference to details of plot or coherence of narrative.

NOTES

1144 *le roi*, objective genitive: 'they curse the betrayers of the king'.

1146–50 The resemblance of this description of Iseut to that of Camille in *Eneas* 4009–11 has been pointed out by S. Hofer (*Streitfragen*, p. 271) and to that of Argie and Deiphile in *Thèbes* 961–2 by P. Jonin (p. 166). Beroul may have been influenced by one or both of his predecessors, but it is more than likely that all three authors reproduce a model description picked up in the schools or from the arts of poetry and rhetoric of the time.

1148 *menu cosue* 'finely embroidered' or 'sewn with small stitches'. As *cosue* can only agree with *dame*, the second meaning seems required, in reference to the practice indicated by Muret (s.v. *cosue*), viz. that, in the twelfth and thirteenth centuries, certain parts of the costume might require to be sewn on each time it was worn: 'The lady was garbed in a close fitting tunic of dark silk, sewn with thread of gold in small stitches.' If the correction to *vestu* : *cosu* (so M[1]) be accepted, *fil* would mean the net overgarment often worn as an added adornment (cf. Schultz, *Das höfische Leben* I, 257).

1149–50 'Her hair reached to her feet and was tressed in gold net.' Cf. Schultz, *op. cit.*, I, 239.

1155 *Lancïen*; see 2359 n.

1156 The chief of the lepers is not named in other versions, though it is possible that his name figured in the original of *Fb* (cf. Hoepffner's note to l. 450).

1157 and 1162 *desfait* 'infirm' or 'deformed' (see examples in Tobler-Lommatzsch).

1161–2 Corr. *laits* : *desfaits* (?).

1162 The adjective *boçu(z)* bears its normal meaning when applied to the dwarf Frocin (320, 640, 724) and clearly also, to judge from the context, in 3624. But it can also mean 'covered with scrofulous tumours or swellings'; cf. the gloss cited by Godefroy (s.v. *boçu*): STRUMOSUS, *bochu*, and the example quoted by Tobler-Lommatzsch from *Wistasse le Moine*, ll. 1418–9 (not 261): 'Les dois avoit trestous croçus Et ses visages ert boçus.' This is the meaning the word probably bears in this line

(1162) and in l. 3922, and there is therefore no need to emend to *bocié* (which alternates with *bocelé*: *bociez son vis* 3306, *bocelé son vis* 3626.

1163 *tartarie* 'clapper' (in the shape of a bowl), used by lepers to give warning of their approach or when begging alms (cf. Schultz I, 528). The *tartarie* and the *baston* were, according to Jonin (114–5), regular and compulsory items in the leper's equipment.

1164 *serie*. It is difficult to see how this adjective could have developed from 'still', 'quiet' the meaning 'hoarse' which Jonin would attribute to it on the ground that hoarseness is one of the specifically recorded symptoms of leprosy. One must agree with him, however, that the gloss 'doux' is clearly inappropriate, and this would apply also to 'soft'. It is possible that *seri* is used by the poet to describe a voice that, owing to the constriction of the throat and the nasal quality observed in the speech of lepers, is 'grêle', thin, high-pitched and lacking in resonance.

A lacuna after this line is no longer assumed in M[4].

1167 *Granz est* 'it is a grievous matter'; cf. the use of *en grande* in *Fb* 154, 271, 387.

1171–2 'This fire will subside, in these embers the punishment will remain' (i.e. the punishment will not outlast the fire itself). Acher sought to justify the scribal *prise* (with the correction of *en* to *o*).

1174–8 'But if you would believe me [you would give her such a punishment that she would . . .] and that she would rather die and that she would live without reputation, and that none would hear tell of it but would think the more highly of you for it.' B. Blakey (in *French Studies* XXI, 99) would postulate a corruption rather than a lacuna, emend *Et que* (1175) to *Qu'ele* and intervert 1173 and 1174.

1185–9 The somewhat involved construction of these lines becomes clear if 1189 is read as following logically upon 1186: 'Never was such a manner (of punishment) described, so painful and so fierce, but that he would have my regard forever who could straightway select the worst.' Cf., in another context, *O* 3968–70:

> daz sie im râtin woldin,
> welchin tôd daz her in tête
> den man sêre ze laster hête.

See Miss Hackett's interesting and perceptive discussion (in *Vinaver Misc.*, p. 161) of the syntax of this passage and of an analogous passage in *Girart de Roussillon*.

1193–4 'Give us Iseut, and she will be our common property; a worse end did never any lady have.' *Commune* might here be a substantive with a meaning similar to that in 2329, 3773; cf. also 4163.

1202 *solier* = *solarium* 'balcony', 'loft', 'top-room'; cf. Schultz, *op. cit.*, I, 117.

1205 *escouellier* (so M⁴) for *escuëllier*, rather than for *connillier* (proposed tentatively in M⁰).

1208 *de pieces, de quartiers*, the partitive being induced by the neuter *que* (= *ce que*): 'ce qu'on nous envoie de pièces et de morceaux . . .'.

1209 *hus* (= *huis*) confused by the scribe with *hues* (<ŏPUS): hence *a ces hues* for the more usual *a cel hues* 'for this purpose', i.e. for our sustenance. There can be little doubt that *hus* is what the poet wrote. Lepers commonly congregated (for the purpose of begging alms) or found accommodation in lazar-houses or leper-villages outside the city-gates: see note above. M⁴: *a ces hus*.

1212 *si*, adv. of degree. Cf. 2702. Restored in M⁴.

1218 'Nor did he move for some time.'

1220 For the word-order, cf. Gaimar 3900: *Prist la par la main*; but *prist* may be a scribal error for *pris : pris l(i) a la main* (?)

1222 *i* here probably signifies 'to him'; cf. 517.

1223 *li* = *la li*, the direct pronoun object being understood.

1224–6 Cf. *Fb* 448–51:

L

Mout s'antraloient desrainnant
Et mout duremant estrivant
Li qeus d'aux vos avroit el bois.
A l'un en donerent lo chois.

1226-7 *Qui* generic: 'All are filled with pity, all those
who heard the wailing and the crying.' For *tote genz*, cf.
994.

1238 *bele figure*; for this 'personifying' use of an abstract noun, cf. 102.

1244 'There are those among them whom I shall
cause to suffer.'

1248 *qu'* concessive: 'lest . . .'.

1251-2 'Now to your crutches! Now it will appear
who is one of us (i.e. who is on our side).'

1255-8 'All shake their crutches at him: some threaten,
others struggle. Tristran did not wish to touch them in
any way, bash their heads or maltreat them.' Cf. 1269-70.

1259-70 This passage has been held to prove that
Beroul could not have been the source of Eilhart, who
relates (4318-21) that the chief of the lepers was killed
by Tristran; but only in one MS (*H*) is it added that a
general slaughter of the lepers ensues (4322-7); both
MSS relate that one leper survived to bring the news to
Mark (4331-5). The contention is that, had Beroul been
Eilhart's source, the latter, true to his usual procedure,
would have taken this hint by Beroul and brought Tristran's conduct into line with the courtly code of behaviour. Bédier considered that in the common source (γ) of
B and *O*, Yvain was in fact killed by Tristran, but that
B modified this account 'par un scrupule de courtoisie'.
This view seems to me to be supported by the fact that,
according to *B*, no such scruple inhibited Tristran from
threatening to kill Yvain (1247-9)—unless we are to
dismiss this as an idle threat—and it is only at l. 1257
that the deviation from γ appears to have suggested
itself to Beroul. The way in which he adapts this to his
narrative is singularly inept: ll. 1257-8 show Tristran's

'courtliness' restraining him from so much as offering violence to the lepers, yet 1269–70 make it appear that it is the actual slaying of a leper that would have branded Tristran as 'uncourtly', and at 1265–6 Beroul is concerned to exculpate both Tristran and Governal, although Governal at least showed no hesitation in belabouring Yvain (1259–62).[1]

The terms in which *B* refers to *l'estoire*, of which he claims to have preserved a truer recollection than certain *conteurs*, suggest that he is referring to a commonly accepted, though not necessarily the original account; nor need he be taken to refer to a specific written source, were it not that at ll. 1789–90 he states explicitly that he has read it. About its nature we can only speculate: we are merely entitled to say that, whatever the language in which it was written, it was a text which by its age or in virtue of some other quality, was held by Beroul to authenticate what he advanced. See the Introduction, pp. 39–44.

1265 *contor*. There can be no doubt that this is for older *contëor*; while hesitation may have existed in ordinary speech at the time when the poet wrote, he probably treated it as trisyllabic and elided *que* (*qu'Yvain*).

1266 *nïer* (<NECARE). The restriction of meaning to death by drowning is almost universal in the Romance languages from the beginning, and *nïer* (*neier*) can at this time only mean 'to drown'. As there is not the slightest suggestion in any version that Yvain (or any of the lepers) suffered or was even threatened with such a death, *nier* may be a scribal error for *tuer*. Such a misreading is, palaeographically, highly probable: cf. note to 263, and other similar instances discussed in *Pope Miscellany*, pp. 92–93. The correction to *tuer* was tentatively proposed by G. Paris. Michel's edition (I, p. 62) reads: *tuer*.

[1] In *Fb*, Governal is described as having struck the lepers with their crutches: see the passage quoted above, p. 149, and Hoepffner's note to l. 456.

1268 *memoire* 'memory' could be either *m.* or *f.* in Old French.

Berox, nominative form of a name of Germanic origin (*Berulf*). There is extant a version of the *Purgatoire de Saint Patrice*[1] written in W. France or England in the first half of the thirteenth century by a poet who at the end calls himself *Beroz*, but the language and style are too unlike those of our author to justify any suggestion that the two might be one.

1270 *gent de tes lois.* Jonin (p. 118) is inclined to regard this as a rendering of the expression *homines de lege*, 'parfois employée, nous dit L. F. Plateau, pour désigner ces malades, "ceux auxquels est appliquée la loi de Moïse prescrivant la séparation des lépreux" '.

III. THE FLIGHT—THE WOODLAND SCENES (1271–2132)

O 4328–4723; *R* 360, 22–365, 4; *T* xxvi–xxviii; *G* 16683–17662; *S* lxiv–lxvi; *E* ccxxiv–ccxxxiii; *T.r.* 245, 5–247, 4; *Fo* 859–892; *Fb* 184–5, 194–207, 460–3, 485–92.

The flight to the forest and the lovers' woodland life are common to all the versions of the Tristran story and are among the two or three most popular scenes of the romance (cf. Bédier I, 234). In *T* and its derivatives the life of Tristran and Iseut in the forest is an idyllic existence embellished with magical castles and marvellous grottoes, and Bédier has shown irrefutably that these versions have either completely transformed or grossly mangled and emasculated the *Estoire* account, while *O*, *B* (and *Fb*) have preserved it with minor variations. This account has many close parallels in Celtic literature, in particular the Old Irish Elopement Tales (*Aitheda*), of which the story of *Diarmaid and Grainne*[2] is a striking example (cf. G.

[1] Particulars in J. Vising, *Anglo-Norman Language and Literature*, London, 1923, p. 53.
[2] See the references in Schoepperle. A free versified adaptation in English by J. Redwood Anderson was published in 1950 (London, Oxford University Press).

Schoepperle, 395 ff.). In this tale Diarmaid has a love-spot the sight of which fills Grainne with an irresistible passion for him. In order to overcome the resistance to her advances which he maintains throughout the early stages of their flight in the wilderness she resorts, not to a potion, but to a *geis*, a spell or taboo which forces him to lie with her.

F. Whitehead, in an article contributed to the *Pope Miscellany*, accepts as proven Murrell's conclusion that the episode of *Girart de Roussillon* in which Girart and his wife Berthe find refuge in a forest is 'indubitably the source of the Morrois episode in the *Tristran*'. But this is far from proven: it seems to me that most of the parallels cited by Murrell are either very remote or general and are attributable to the general similarity of situation. The one exception would appear to be the hermit scenes (see notes to 1367, 2263), the resemblance of which in *Girart* and in *Tristran* was first pointed out by Bédier (II, 263 n.). Since the only texts in which Ogrin appears are *O*, *B* and *Fb*, it is highly probable that he was introduced in their common source (γ). For the rest, some of the resemblances to *Diarmaid and Grainne* are so close (see, for example, 2050 n.) that one must assume familiarity with it (or a variant) on the part of the author of the *Estoire*. The author of γ may have introduced Ogrin under the influence of the hermit scene in *Girart*, developed and adapted his role, with only partial success, to the narrative he took over from the *Estoire*.[1]

(a) *Manner of life of the lovers and Governal* (1271–1305)

SUMMARY

1271– Tristran and Iseut, accompanied by Governal,

[1] If we accept that *Girart de Roussillon* was composed between 1155 and 1165 (Murrell, p. 25), the hypothesis of borrowing by the author of the *Estoire* requires that he should have had access to an earlier version of *Girart* than the one extant or that we accept (with G. Schoepperle) a much later date for the *Estoire* than that now generally postulated.

1278 enter the forest of Morrois [and pass the first
     night upon a hill].
1279– [Tristran gives proof of his prowess with the bow
  1289 which Governal had taken from a forester and
     shoots a roe-deer.]
1290– Tristran makes a bower, which Iseut carpets with
  1305 foliage, [while Governal prepares the meal. Iseut
     is weary and sleeps by the side of her lover. Thus
     they live their forest-life for a long time].

VARIANTS

O 4328–4360; *R* 360, 22–362, 21; *T* xxvi–xxvii; *G* 16683–17245;
S lxiv, 1–28; *E* ccxxiv–ccxxix; *T.r.* 245, 5–16; *Fo* 859–72; *Fb* 460–1.

In *R*, Tristran and Iseut are directed to the house of a forester, who
declares himself ready to serve Tristran (*qui mainte bonté lui avoit faite*),
shelters them for the night and gives them clothes and palfreys. This was
in the forest of Moroys, the greatest in Cornwall. They leave the forester's
house and at Tristran's suggestion they go to a castle (*qui fu a la sage
demoiselle*). They keep with them only Governal and Iseut's *damoiselle*
(*Lamide*). This castle was made by a *damoisel* of Cornwall for a *damoiselle*
he loved and here they lived and died. The *damoiselle* was versed in magic
and neither the castle nor the lovers could be seen by those who sought
them out, even though they spoke to them. Governal is sent to demand
Tristran's horse Passebreul and his dog Hudein from Mark at Norhoult.
Mark complies readily, but Governal refuses to reveal Tristran's where-
abouts. Tristran gives himself up to the chase and to the company of
Iseut.

G: Tristran accompanied by Iseut and Governal rides off into the wilds
and after two days reaches a cave once discovered by him while hunting.
It was a cave made by giants in olden times and wondrously contrived
in idyllic surroundings as a resort of love, and it was called *La fossiur' a la
gent amant*. It drew its light from small windows set high and was closed
by a brazen door. The way to it lay through a wilderness. Governal is sent
back to report that Tristran and Iseut have returned to Ireland and to
bring them news of any measures taken against them—once every twenty
days. No need to ask how the lovers subsisted: they had each other and
what nature offered them. (The poet gives a lengthy allegorical interpretation of the cave or grotto.) Their time is spent in the enjoyment of
nature, in the retelling of ancient tales of love, in the playing of the harp
and in sweet song.—In *S*, the lovers discover the cave: it is subterranean
and is nameless. No allegorical interpretation is given, nor is Governal
mentioned.—*E* merely relates that the lovers lived happily in the forest
and slept in an 'earthen house' (*erþe hous*).—In *T.r.*, the lovers enter the
grande diserto d'Urgana and find a magnificent house in idyllic surroundings,
thirteen leagues distant from Tintagel (*Tintoille*): Governal is not with

them, but Brengain (*Brandina*) goes shopping each day to Monte Albrano.—*Fo* recalls the life in the forest, the grotto being briefly described.

O: Tristran bears Iseut off to a dark wood. One of the lepers had escaped death and complains to Mark that his master and all his fellows have been killed by Tristran who had escaped with Iseut. Mark promises to share all his wealth with anyone of his subjects who may capture Tristran. All the knights, old and young, seek him in vain. [The bower is constructed, by Tristran and Governal at a later stage; see section (f) below.]—In *Fb* Tristran *fou* recalls: 'En la forest fumes un terme O nos plorames mainte lerme' (460–1); cf. the earlier reference (184–5): 'Je ai . . . en bois vescu de racine, Entre mes braz tenu raïne.'

NOTES

1271 'Tristran departs with the queen.'

1272 *la gaudine* used as accusative of direction: 'through the wood Tristran goes together with Governal'.

1275 Whether or not *Morrois* conceals an earlier name of similar form designating Moray, one of the ancient divisions of Scotland, in our poem it applies to a wooded area lying within the Cornish domain of King Mark (cf. 1275, 1648, 1661–2, 1900, 2090) and not far from his residence at Lancïen. It has been identified by J. Loth (*Contr.*, p. 82 ff.) with the manor of Moresc or St. Clement's, near Truro, but may well have been applied loosely to the general area of Southern Cornwall (Loth, p. 85). From it the lovers flee towards Wales (2125–2132).

1279–84 'In Tristran there was a good archer: right well did he know how to make use of his bow. Governal had taken one from a forester who owned it, and two feathered, barbed arrows he had brought for him.' The interpretation *quil = qu'il* does not yield a satisfactory sense and has been abandoned in M[4]. For the word-order of 1284, cf. 1220; *l'en = li en*.

1291 In *T* and its derivatives the bower is replaced by a marvellous grotto, described in great detail by Gottfried (see the summary above, p. 158).

1292 Iseut's action would have come naturally to her:

the spreading of floors with rushes and herbs **and** flowers, particularly on festive occasions, is frequently referred to in romances; cf. Schultz I, 78–79.

1296 Ironical: 'Much did they have wherewith to play the cook!'

(b) 'Orelles de cheval' (1306–1350)

SUMMARY

1306– [The dwarf, while drunk, offers to reveal the king's
  1326 secret to the barons before the Gué Aventuros, where he will confide it to the hawthorn while they listen.

1327– And there they hear him say: 'Mark has horse's
  1335 ears.'

1336– One day the three barons tell Mark they know his
  1346 secret. M: 'This affliction came to me through the dwarf: he shall die.'

1347– Mark draws his sword and beheads the dwarf,
  1350 whereat many a one is pleased!]

There is not the faintest trace of this incident in any other version. It is quite clearly an interpolation made by the poet, and it is significant that once again he marks a departure from the more or less 'standard' narrative sequence (whether we call that the *estoire* or a less explicit tradition) by a direct address to his audience (*Oiez* . . .), as if to underline the 'originality' or 'novelty' of the interpolation. And once again the vocative *Seignors* (1351) introduces a recapitulatory passage by which continuity of the main narrative is restored after a digression.

We have here in effect an 'etymological' jest evidently invented by someone who knew that in Celtic *marc* (Welsh and Breton *march*) means 'horse'. Similar stories of men with the ears of a horse are found in the Gaelic legends of Scotland, and the 'Midas' tale of Mark became popular in the folklore of Wales and Brittany.[1] According to Bédier (II, 312) the episode is one of the few which may have existed in the Celtic sources but were not used by the poet of the *Estoire*. It may have come to Beroul through oral tradition or through the same 'conteurs' upon whose innovations or departures from the accepted tradition he comments in l. 1267. It is in their hands (or probably in the hands of one of the more clerkly of their number) that the story became contaminated with the story of Midas, as can be seen from the manner in which the secret is divulged: Midas's barber, in order to get the baleful secret off his mind, dug a hole and confided it to Mother Earth; in time reeds and rushes grew upon the spot and at the slightest breath of wind whispered: 'Midas, king Midas, has the ears of an ass.'

Midas's deformity was inflicted on him as a punishment for having preferred the flute of Pan to the lyre of Apollo. It was natural that this should be replaced by some explanation more in accord with medieval lore, and lines 1343–5 furnish a hint which would no doubt be taken up and understood more readily by a twelfth-century audience, the reference being probably to popular superstition that persons having some animal feature owe it to their having transformed themselves by occult means into an animal; the reverse transformation not having been entirely successful, they find themselves endowed for life with some animal feature. Beroul's public would doubtless understand that the dwarf, being versed in astrology and magic, had aided the king in an experiment of this kind with just such a result. (Cf. Schoepperle, pp. 245, 269.) The incident would thus be a compound of Celtic, popular and classical lore, and it

<hr />

[1] Cf. Hertz[3], Anm. 7; J. Loth, pp. 108–110; G. Schoepperle, pp. 269–72; J. J. Jones, 'March ap Meirchion', *Aberystwyth Studies* VIII. For a variant recorded as current in Finistère in 1794, see *Annales de Bretagne* LVI (1949), 203–27 and *Comparative Literature* II (1950), 289–306.

is adapted by Beroul as well as such an incident could be to the narrative.

1306 For the significance of the preposition *de*, see 909 n. and 1110–18 n.

1320 It is at the Gué Aventuros that Mark will receive back Iseut (2677, 2747) and that Iseut will justify herself (3436). It is the same as the Mal Pas (3707) described as being 'un poi deça la Lande Blanche' (3298) and also used to designate the bog at the approaches to the ford (3689 ff.). Mal Pas is identified by J. Loth (p. 79) with the Malpas on the river Truro; see 3268 n.

On the magic significance of ford and hawthorn in Celtic folklore, see R. S. Loomis, *Arthurian Tradition and Chrétien de Troyes* (1949), p. 130.

1325–6 *du segroi* would be normal in view of the following line: 'What I say will be about the secret which I share with the king alone (lit. 'by himself').' The correction to *par foi* made by Muret, at the suggestion of G. Paris, and now endorsed by Reid, would eliminate the evidence for an effective use of *par soi*: see the Introduction, p. 45, and the interesting explanation given by J. Orr in his Taylorian Lecture, *The Impact of French upon English* (1948), p. 37. Cf. l. 3313 and also Marie de France, *Fables* (ed. Warnke), 81, 9: *di par tei* 'say it by yourself, on your own': and 9, 50: *Mielz aim a estre el bois par mei*.

1328 *Frocine*, rhyme variant; cf. 320 n.

1330 According to 1321–2 the hole already existed, and it would appear from this line that it had been made by the dwarf. One might therefore interpret *delivrement* as signifying 'freely', 'at leisure', 'with deliberation'; meanings which are not clearly attested for the adverb but find support in the meanings of the adjective *delivre*.

1333 'To you, hawthorn, and not to any knight'; i.e. he whispers to the roots of the hawthorn (cf. the Midas story), but so that the barons can in fact hear. The expression may well be modelled on some popular locution like 'between you and me and the gate-post'.

1336 The *disner* was the first and principal meal of the day, usually taken about nine o'clock in the morning; cf. Schultz, I, 360.

1336 *S'* = *se* for *si* (<SIC): 'And it happened one day'.

1347 The dwarf thus meets his death as indicated in 1310; for the earlier prediction, see note to l. 270.

1349 *Que* may be rel. pron. (= *qui*) or causal conjunction: 'for'.

(c) *Tristran and Iseut visit Ogrin* (1351–1422)

SUMMARY

1351– [You have heard, my lords, why and how] the
1361   lovers live in the forest, subsisting on venison and
      spending but one night in each place.

1362– Suffering but unrepentant they come one day to
1366   the hermitage of brother Ogrin.

1367– O: ['You are outlawed, Tristran;] but God for-
1380   gives those that truly repent.'

1381– T: 'The power of the potion is such that Iseut and
1386   I may not part.'

1387– O: Without repentance there can be no pardon.'
1392

1393– Tristran will not yield to Ogrin's admonition:
1408   [rather would he live on grass and acorns than
      give up Iseut.]

1409– I: 'It is all through the power of the potion.'
1416

1417– [O: 'May God grant you true repentance.'
1419

1420– That night the lovers lay in the hermitage and
1422 Ogrin served them.]

VARIANTS

O 4702–4723; F*b* 462

In O, the first visit to Ogrin takes place after the discovery of the lovers: hard by the remote combe in which the lovers have taken refuge after being discovered by Mark, there lived a holy hermit (*Ûgrîm*), confessor to the king; Tristran asks him for confession, but the hermit refuses unless he gives up the queen. Tristran is unable to do this and rides away unshriven. (The account of the second visit to the hermit follows immediately after the lines—4724 to 4741—in which the waning of the potion is described; see below, pp. 191-2).

In *Fb*, Ugrin is mentioned between the references to 'Iseut and the Lepers' and to Husdent's release from captivity:

> 'En la forest fumes un terme
> O nos plorames mainte lerme.
> Ne vit encor l'hermite Ugrin?
> Deus mete s'ame a boene fin!' (460-3)

NOTES

1356-7 No lacuna need be assumed, but rather the intercalation by Beroul of the recapitulatory lines 1351-6, marked once again by the direct address to his audience; *Seignors. . . .*

1359 Cf. l. 1305. More than two years they remained in the forest, says Eilhart.

1364 Cf. *Fb* 184: *Et en bois vescu de racine.*

1366 *por* 'because of': 'Neither, because of (the love borne to) the other, feels any distress.' Cf. 1650 n.

1367 The name of the hermit (*B*: Ogrin, *O*: Ûgrîm) is French; cf. the *Augrinus* mentioned in the early twelfth-century document cited by Bédier (II, 124). Bédier concluded that Ogrin was introduced into the story by the common source of *B* and *O*. Eilhart describes him as the king's confessor, and it is clear that for Beroul he is anything but a mere ascetic recluse: he immediately recognizes Tristran, and Tristran evidently knows him well enough to seek him out for more than mere confession and absolution (2282-4). He can not only read and write, but is familiar with the recognized usages of the epistolary art and has available the necessary materials (2428-32). It is significant for our understanding of Beroul that he presents Ogrin as combining the orthodoxy of a court preacher (1377-80, 1387-98) with a casuistry which verges on the cynical (2353–4) and a readiness to advise the lovers to pursue a course of action of more than doubtful morality. His worldliness enables him, on the one hand, to indite a letter of legalistic subtlety and practised advocacy, and on the other, to undertake a shopping expedition, not exempt from haggling, on behalf of Iseut (2733–44). Cf. the discussion of Ogrin's character and role by P. Jonin, pp. 348–59.

1374–6 Jonin (pp. 75–78) cites various customaries to show the penalties incurred by subjects who failed to surrender or delate any person declared an outlaw.

1376 The infinitive depends loosely on *l'ait plevi*.

1380 This line may be taken to depend on the preceding line, *par* having practically the meaning 'in virtue of'.

1382 *Que*-clause loosely depending on *raison*.

1385 *pus = puis*.

1392 The scribal error may have been induced by a misreading of *sanz*.

1398 Emendation proposed by Jeanroy: 'The hermit reminds them insistently of their duty to separate.'

1399 *par grant desroi* 'in great perturbation'.

1403 'My mind is quite made up.' M^4: *De tot*.

1404 In the Prose Romance (MS 575) Iseut expresses herself similarly when she is reunited with Tristran after the leper incident: *Je vueil mieulx estre povre avec vous que estre riche sans vous.* Muret (cf. M^4, p. xi) has called attention to a similar line in a chanson of Jean Bretel:

> Que pour ma dame aim mieus amendiier
> Tout mon vivant . . .

1407 'I would not have anyone speak of my leaving her.'

1415 *pechiez* 'sin' or 'misfortune' (?)

1422 'He did violence to his way of living for their sake', i.e. 'He put himself out for them.'

(d) *Return to woodland life* (1423–1436)

SUMMARY

1423–
1430 The lovers resume their life in the forest as already described.

1431–
1436 [The king has had Tristran proclaimed an outlaw throughout Cornwall.]

NOTES

1428–30 Cf. 1360–1.

1431–6 Interpolation introduced by *Seignors* (?)

(e) *Husdent and his training* (1437–1636)

SUMMARY

1437–
1439 [Now hear the wondrous tale of a dog and his training!]

1440–
1466 Husdent was the name of Tristran's dog and he was sorely distressed to lose his master. [Those who witness his distress exclaim: 'Unleash him, king, lest he go mad; for never shall his like be seen: well does he prove the words of Solomon that a dog is man's best friend.'

1467–
1472 M: 'He is a dog of great understanding, for never in our day, methinks, will there be in Cornwall Tristran's equal.'

1473–
1487 By the counsel of the three barons] Mark has Husdent released.

1488–
1526 But Husdent [is not mad: he runs to Tristran's lodging,] following his master's steps. [From the chamber where Tristran was taken, through the chapel he runs, and as he leaps injures his leg. Into the forest he goes; the king and his knights turn back in fear.

1527– Husdent's joy at finding Tristran, Iseut, Governal,
1548 and the horse.]

1549– T: 'Alas! Husdent by his barking will betray us;
1572 it were better to kill him.'

1573– [I: 'I have heard tell of a Welsh forester in the
1590 time of King Arthur who taught his hound to
hunt without barking. What joy if we could
likewise train Husdent!'

1591– T: 'I will try.'] Husdent is trained to hunt in
1636 silence and serves them.

VARIANTS

O 4368–4517; *R* 362, 21–23; *T* xxviii; *G* 17246–17278; *S* lxiv, 28–31;
E ccxxv; *Fo* 873–6; *Fb* 485–92; *Escoufle* 590–3

R merely says that Husdent (who had been fetched by Governal; see above, p. 158) was taught by Tristran to hunt without barking, for fear of discovery.

G: Hudant (whom the lovers and Governal had taken with them on leaving the court) is taught by Tristran to hunt without barking.—*S* says that Tristran had his favourite dog with him and taught him to hunt deer. (In a later chapter, considered suspect by Bédier, *S* says it is Petit-crû.)—In *E*, both Husdent (Hodain) and Petitcrû (Peticrowe) accompany the lovers and are trained by Tristran to hunt at speed. Tristran, with Husdent, kills a wild animal.—In *Fo*, Tristran recalls that he trained Hudein to hunt without barking and that they lived on the game they took with his dog and his hawk.

In *O*, Tristran's favourite dog (Ûtant) struggles to get free and barks: Mark orders a squire to hang him, but the latter lets him go. He follows the road taken by Tristran far into the wood. Tristran, hearing him, fears that he is being used to track them down. On Governal's advice, Tristran and Iseut depart: Governal remains posted by a tree to meet the enemy, determined to kill the dog and anyone leading him. But he is overjoyed to see the dog come running up alone and showing his pleasure. Losing the track of the lovers, he sets the dog to follow them in silence. Great was the joy of all when they were reunited. They ride deep into the wood: they dare not leave it.

In *Fb*, Tristran recalls how Husdent, having been held for three days, would neither eat nor drink and was about to go mad for his master, and how, being released, the dog rejoined him.

Escoufle, 590–3:

> Tristrans et maistre Govremaus
> Et Yseus et ses chiens Hudains,
> Conment il lor prendoit les dains
> Et les cers sans noise et sans cris.

NOTES

1438 Cf. *Fb* 521: *Au brachet dit*: *'La norriture C'ai mise en toi soit benëoite!'*

1441-2 For the rhyme, see Introd., p. 18. M[4] restores the MS reading here and in 1443.

1444 *Husdent* is perhaps a name of Celtic origin. In *E* (str. cliii) he is with the lovers in the ship when they drink the potion! G. Paris conjectured the omission of several lines after 1444, in which Tristran was described as the master of Husdent. While such an assumption is not necessary, various minor imperfections in the lines 1437-44 suggest that they represent a careless recasting by Beroul of what he found in his source (e.g. the repetitive ll. 1442-3). See Hertz[3], p. 546.

1445 *landon*, a clog, or stick fastened across the neck of an animal to prevent it from straying. *Fb* speaks of *lo bel lïen* (l. 490); its account (485-92) is an accurate though rapid summary of Beroul's. (Cf. M.H.G. *lander*, E. Fr. *lad(r)* 'cross-piece in fence'.)

1446 'The dog looked out from the keep.'

1451 To interpret *guignout*, as a scribal rendering of *geignout*, from *giembre* (*geindre*) is not convincing, in spite of the remote support given by *Fb* 505: *gent* (for *gient*?). *Guignier* can mean 'pull a face', 'scowl'; but the word may well conceal an identical form of more limited (Norman) currency representing a Germanic root related to English *whine*. This meaning seems almost demanded by the context, and its limited currency would account for *Fb*'s deviation. Muret emends to *grignout*, ind. impf. of *grignier* 'grincer des dents'.

1455-6 For this rhyme (which Tanquerey would eliminate by emending *deus* to *torz*), see Introd., No. 15.

1461-2 'Solomon rightly says that a man's friend is his dog.' No such saying can be found in any of the medieval collections of sayings attributed to Solomon; but M. Lecoy (in *Rom*. LXXX (1959), 82–85) considers that the poet has in mind a story which was widely known (though not generally attributed to Solomon) and extant in the *Gesta Romanorum* and in two other versions.

1463–5 According to *Fb* (489), this takes place on the third day.

1467 Tobler's emendation to *a son barnage* is unnecessary: *a* may signify 'according to', i.e. 'he speaks according to the dictates of his heart'; or *a* may here be used with the force of *an* (*en*) (or for *an* minus the titulus): 'in his mind' 'to himself'.

1474 *li* for *le* (obl.).

1479–82 'No sooner will he be released than he will bite something else, man or beast, if he is mad, and will have his tongue hanging out.' That is, they wish to see whether he is pining for his master or is simply mad (cf. 1488).

1480–1 Cf. *Fb* 503–4: *Home de lui ne s'aprima Qu'il ne volsist mangier as danz*.

1486 *li* for *le* (obl.).

1500 'when he was taken and was to be burnt.'

1502 'All urge him to go on.'

1504 The substitution of *apris* for *pris* may have been induced by the scribe's misreading of *traït* as *trait*; cf. 1535.

1505–6 The emendation proposed (which has found favour in M⁴) preserves the scribe's *clarele*, a form which is unattested elsewhere and which might be regarded as a derivative of CLARUS, *faire voiz clarele* signifying 'give forth a clear-sounding bark' (?) Hence: 'And he sets out, leaping and barking loudly.' For other suggested emendations see the earlier editions of Muret.

1524 The correction was proposed by Tanquerey (*Rom*. LVI, 121), who derived *traillier* 'chien de chasse' from *traille* (< TRAGULA). Professor Woledge has drawn attention (in *French Studies*, 1956) to a second example

M

occurring in the thirteenth-century *Vie de S. Eustache* with the spelling *treeilliers* and meaning 'hound'. A careful examination of certain Western MSS led him to conclude that our scribe's model was markedly Western and was probably written in S. Normandy, and that the spelling with double *aa* is one of the dialectal features he preserved. It should therefore have been maintained intact in our text. It would seem to be the same word as Engl. *trailer* 'hound' or 'huntsman' (OED); cf. G. Tilander, in *Studia Neophilologica* I (1928), 114–24. Woledge's explanation is firmly endorsed by Tilander in his *Mélanges d'étymologie cynégétique*, Lund, 1958, p. 174 ff. M⁴: *trallier*.

1529 'He is very pleased with the road he is taking.'

1535 The scribe, having misread *esfroï* as *esfroi*, was not unnaturally induced to insert the erroneous *en*.

1541 '. . . who knew the way'. But, as proposed in M² (and accepted in M³), *sut* might be for *siut* (< *SEQUIT); alternatively, it might be the analogical pret. 3.

1543–4 The scribe appears to have truncated and mutilated the description of Husdent's joy, if we may judge by the fuller and more graphic picture presented by *Fb*, though in another context:

> De venir a Tristan se poine.
> Sore li cort, lieve la teste,
> Onques tel joie ne fist beste;
> Boute do groin et fiert do pié,
> Toz li monz en aüst pitié
> Ses mains loiche, de joie abaie. (511–6)

Beroul may well have written (l. 1544) *conme des ieus se molle*, as conjectured by Acher (p. 722). The same verb is used in l. 3450 and, intransitively, in *Fb* 537 where Tristran, describing his feelings at the sight of Iseut's ring, says: *Mi oil moilloient d'eve chaude*. But there can be little doubt that the scribe interpreted the phrase as *con de joie*, although he was content, as for the preceding line, to transliterate what was either imperfectly legible or spelt in an unfamiliar way in his model. M⁴: *Le chief hoque, la queue crole. Qui voit con de joie se molle Dire....*

1548 'He shows his joy to all, even to the horse.'

1550 See note to l. 720.

1567 Note that it is not only Husdent's responsiveness to training (1437) but his noble nature (*Grant nature*) that excites the poet's admiration; cf. l. 1575 and *Fb* 485: *Estrange nature a en chien.*

1574–5 'The dog barks as he takes his prey, whether by nature or by habit.'

1576–7 *forestier* is clearly a mistake in declension; but it is just possible that *uns seüs* may denote a brace of hounds—in spite of the singular in l. 1583.

1578 *en* refers loosely to the notion of Wales implied in *galois.*

1580 *sagnié* in the sense of 'wounded'.

1582–6 The general sense of the passage is clear, particularly if considered in conjunction with ll. 1613–26, both passages showing a certain repetitiveness which is rhetorically effective: 'The Welsh forester (1577) had so trained his dog that, no matter which course was taken by the wounded stag, the dog followed him in leaps and bounds, nor with his barking would he lose the scent, nor would he pursue the stag so hotly that he would bark or cause annoyance.' I consider the subjunctives *suïst, tornast, atainsist* as parallel and consecutive (dependent on *ne fuïst par cele trace*), while *criast* and *feïst* are consecutive and dependent on *n'atainsist, Ja* being used in l. 1586 to introduce the consecutive clause where one might have expected *Que.*

trace presents no difficulty: it refers to the course or track which will be taken by the stag, just as *sa trace* in l. 1623 refers, strictly speaking, to the track followed by the dog and not to the spoor left by the hunted animal, of which there has been no mention.

faut denotes, in the technical language of venery, a break in the line of scent or a check caused by failure of scent, this and other meanings or uses being better attested in English (OED, s.v. *fault*). As for *torner*, in the sense of 'to cast', 'to turn aside', 'to pass beyond', see G. Tilander, *Nouveaux Essais d'étymologie cynégétique* (1957), pp. 54–61, and the OED; cf. also Littré, s.v. *tourner*, sense 23: 'tourner au change, se dit des chiens lorsqu'ils attaquent un autre animal que celui de meute'. I can find no instance of the linking of these two technical terms and can only conjecture that l. 1584 means: 'for any barking he might do, he would not pass beyond the break in the scent', i.e. 'the dog, barking in his eager pursuit, would not miss the change of direction in the scent and run straight on'. Muret's assumption that the scribe misread the poet's *n'estonast le gaut* is palaeographically credible, but the emendation is really out of context, although undeniably neat. I have hesitated to relegate to the variants what may well prove to have been a technical expression of the chase.

1587–90 '. . . it would be a great joy if one could, by taking pains, cause Husdent to leave off barking, to pursue and hunt his quarry.'

1590 Tanquerey eliminates the hiatus by emending to *Ataindre sa beste et chacier*.

1604–5 The construction is loose or elliptical: 'to ensure that the quarry is taken without any barking'.

1607 *Afaitiez*, perhaps for *Afustez*, as proposed tentatively by Muret in view of a similar use in l. 4373.

1613 *a son seignor* 'by his master's side' or 'at his master's bidding'.

1617–8 Godefroy (s.v. *estortoire*) cites a number of examples, including a detailed description of the *estortoire* from *Phebus*, ch. xlv.

1625–6 'He will not abandon his quarry, however quick and active it be.'

1629–30 The correction to *dain* : *rain* (abandoned in M⁴) is defensible though not essential.

1632 'as it happens that he takes many'.

(f) Sufferings of the lovers (1637–1655)

SUMMARY

1637– [In their distress each of the lovers fears that the
1655   other's resolve will weaken.]

VARIANTS

O 4518–4559; Fb 184–5 and 460–1

O corresponds only very roughly: Governal gathers wood and foliage, and he and Tristran make a bower (*hutte*) while Iseut holds the horses. For a year and a half they live on roots (*gekrûte*) and the game and fish Tristran procures: 'I have been told for a fact that Tristran was the first man to fish with hook and line, and also that he was the first to discover how to train hounds to track down game.' They had a hard life, but it was child's play because of the joy they had of their great love. Governal, methinks, bore the brunt of it: it is a wonder he did not die!

Fb 184–5: Tristran *fou* to Mark: 'Don ne sanble je bien Tantris? Je ai ... en bois vescu de racine, Entre mes braz tenu raïne.' *Fb* 460–1: Tristran *fou* to Iseut: 'En la forest fumes un terme O nos plorames mainte lerme.'

NOTES

1642 'And that the proclamation has gone forth in his kingdom to take him (Tristran), whoever might find him.' Cf. R 363.

1649–55 I take the meaning to be: 'The sufferings of the lovers are shared equally: for neither of them feels their pangs because of the other (i.e. thanks to the company and love of the other), the fear of Iseut being that Tristran should repine because of her, while Tristran, for his part, is distressed that Iseut is embroiled because of him and lest she repent of their misconduct'. (Cf. 1364–6 and 1783–5.) A similar interpretation is given by M[4] (which restores the MS reading and accepts the correction in 1655) and also by E. Vinaver in the thorough examination to which he has subjected this passage (in *Ewert Misc.*, pp. 90–95). T. B. W. Reid (in *Vinaver*

Misc., pp. 280–1) interprets similarly but considers that *Qar* in 1650 is scribal error for *Mais*. Both fail to see the connection, which to me seems clear and effective, between ll. 1651–5 and what precedes, and would replace the colon in l. 1650 by a full stop.

Lines 1654–5 show an effective change of mood, l. 1654 being virtually causal and containing a statement of fact, l. 1655 a subjunctive clause depending directly on *repoise*. The emendations proposed by Reid therefore appear to me uncalled for.

(g) *One of the barons killed by Governal* (1656–1750)

SUMMARY

1656–
1667
[Despite the fear inspired by Tristran, one of the three hostile barons goes hunting in the forest of Morrois.]

1668–
1711
Governal, alone in the wood while Tristran and Iseut sleep in the bower, hears the hounds. [From his ambush beneath a tree he observes the baron coming alone. He overcomes him and cuts off his head.

1712–
1728
The huntsmen find the headless body and think it is the work of Tristran. The news is spread abroad: all avoid the forest in fear.

1729–
1738
Governal suspends the head from the fork of the bower. Tristran awakes in alarm and is reassured by Governal.]

1738–
1750
Henceforth they have the forest to themselves.

This slaying of one of the hostile barons is not found in any other version and it is contradicted by the reappearance of all three at l. 2757. It has been variously interpreted by critics as an interpolation by a scribe or a *remanieur*, partly on the ground of linguistic disparity, partly because of the barbarity of the passage (M⁰, pp. x–xii; Bédier II, 312 n.; Golther, p. 108). It is true, as G. Schoepperle pointed out (pp. 318–9), that in many Irish stories there occur instances of heads as trophies; but it is not safe to assume that because the episode is contrary to the spirit and tastes of courtly society, it is necessarily a survival from Celtic sources or primitive. It probably indicates merely that the age of the rougher *chanson de geste* has not completely ended and that we have here one of a number of manifestations of Beroul's predilection for the earthy and the barbarous. See also 4354–95 and 4435–40.

Röttiger's suggestion (p. 23) that the interpolation may have been invited by the situation described in ll. 1678–9 and 1694–6 (= O 4457–65) was adopted by Golther and (with reservations) by Muret. One might also adduce the reference in l. 1124 to the fear of the hostile barons that Tristran might ambush them.

NOTES

1657 The lovers were in fact to be discovered and delated by the forester (1837 ff.). Or is the poet referring to an earlier discovery of the lovers by the three hostile barons?

1660 *Li* (so M⁴) for *Les* ; *par* 'by reason of' 'because of' and hence encroaching (here and elsewhere in the text) on the functions normally attributed to *por*.

1662 I take the subject of *erent* to be implied in 1661, i.e. 'Those of the land of Cornwall were so shy of the forest of Morrois that not one of them dared enter it.' (Cf. 1719.) For a different interpretation, see M⁴ (*Notes critiques*). Muret's emendation (abandoned in M⁴): *li naïf* for *du païs* receives some support from 2380; but see the glossary of M⁰, s.v. *naïf*.

1664 'They had good reason (or 'were well-advised') to fear.' Cf. 1667: 'They had good reason to desist.'

1675 *qu'il* = *cui il* (?); cf. Introd., No. 54.

1678 *esquoi* is not found elsewhere, and various emendations have been suggested, including *recoi* (Suchier) and *estui* (Röttiger); see Introd., No. 23. Tanquerey proposed: *Governal esteit entrues quoi*; M. Roques, in an article on O.Fr. *enaines* (*Rom.* LXIX, 534–40), proposed to read *enunes quoi* and to see in *enunes* the adv. *enaines* 'alone', 'in isolation'. The MS reading is unmistakably *ert en .i. esquoi*, and it seems safer to regard this as one of the small group of Norman words of limited currency (*besuchier*, etc.) used by the poet, and to surmise that it may therefore be a word of Germanic origin related to Engl. *skulk*, itself possibly of Norse origin. Its meaning is indicated by l. 1708 (*agait*).

1682 *Por* 'on account of', 'by virtue of', an example of the encroachment of *por* on the province of *par*; cf. note to 1660.

1685 *une charire* used as accusative of direction.

1691 *escache* (MS *estache*), dialectal form of *eschace* (: *mace*, dial. *mache*). For a different interpretation see A. Holden, *art. cit.*

1697 'None can turn back (the wheel of) fortune.'

1698–9 'He was not on his guard against the enmity he had aroused in Tristran.'

1702 i.e. 'his ashes scattered to the wind'.

1706 *li cerf* for *le cerf*.

1711 *Li* for *Le*.

1712 *parfait*. G. Tilander (in his *Mélanges d'étymologie cynégétique*, Lund, 1958, pp. 5–11) has demonstrated convincingly that *parfaire* is a technical term of the chase and refers to the action of starting the stag ('L'action de mettre le cerf debout') and that lines 1712–3 therefore mean that the huntsmen who had routed out the stag pursued it as it fled ('Les veneurs qui l'avaient mis debout, poursuivaient le cerf de meute').

1715 Cf. 4408.

1716 'Their flight is measured only by their fleetness

of foot'; lit. 'whoever runs fastest flees the most quickly'.

1719 Change of subject: 'Throughout Cornwall they (i.e. people) have heard . . .'. Cf. 1662 n.

1724 ff. As the MS reading is clearly *out* (and not *ont*), I take this as impersonal: 'There was not much hunting in the wood after that; from the moment when he entered the wood, even if it were only to hunt, each one feared lest Tristran the doughty should encounter him: he was feared in the plain and then upon the moor.' Of the emendations proposed by Muret and by Tanquerey, only that of *pus* to *plus* (l. 1728) would seem necessary.

1725 MS $\bar{q}u$ might be read as $\bar{q}n$ (= *qu'en*). M⁴: *qu'u*.

1733 'Through whom he was to have met his death', i.e. 'who bore him mortal enmity'.

1737 *forche*, the forked piece of wood or tree which supports the frame of the bower (?)

1748 *esfreée* 'fear-inspiring'. For the development of active meaning, see Tobler, *Verm. Beitr.* I, 126. Cf. Engl. *fearful*.

1749–50 For the rhyme, see Introd., Nos. 24 and 32.

(*h*) 'L'arc qui ne faut' (1751–1766)

SUMMARY

1751– [Tristran contrives the 'arc qui ne faut' in such
1766 manner that any creature touching it is struck. It has been well named thus by Tristran and it served them well.]

There is no trace of this in the other versions. A remote analogy is furnished by the lines in *O* (4538–4545), where Tristran is averred to be the first to have fished with hook and line (see above, p. 173).

NOTES

1752 While Tristran is credited in other versions with

inventions and accomplishments of various kinds, Beroul alone describes him as having invented *l'Arc qui ne faut*. This device is mentioned by Geffrei Gaimar in his *Estoire des Engleis* (1147–51), where the death of King Edmund (in 1016) is described as due to an *Arc qui ne faut* set up by the traitor Eadric (ll. 4409 ff.); from this it appears that the device consisted of a bow and arrow so arranged that when any object touched the cord the arrow flew against the object so touching it. We have here, therefore, an independent addition made by Beroul from oral tradition or a written source. It is possibly through him that it reached Jean Bretel d'Arras (cf. M⁴, p. xi). For further references, see M. D. Legge, 'The Unerring Bow', *MAe*, XXV (1956), 79–83: cf. J. Szövérffy, 'The Unerring Bow and Petrus Olavi', *MAe*, XXX (1961), 102–3.

1764 Having regard to what we are told in ll. 1755–60, the emendation to *qu'il ne fire* is gratuitous. Interpret: 'The bow is well named, which does not miss any thing which may strike (make contact with) it, high or low.'

(i) The sorely-tried lovers are discovered by the forester (1767– 1942)

SUMMARY

1767– Never did two lovers love so deeply [nor pay for
1792 their love more dearly]: such is the testimony of the 'estoire' [read by Berox].

1793– [Tristran returns to the bower to seek his rest,
1810 and] the lovers lie fully-clad with Tristran's sword between them.

1811– [Iseut's wedding-ring all but slips from her
1815 emaciated finger.

1816– As they lie in each other's arms, the sun's ray falls
1830 upon Iseut's snow-white face.

1831– Governal had gone into the wood with his horse.]
1834

1835– A forester finds the lovers and runs in fear to the
1870 king's court [—a full two leagues, methinks].

1873– M: ['What ails you?] What have you to say?'—F:
1914 'I have found the lovers.'—M: [Where are
they? Tell me privily.'—F: 'In a bower in the
forest of Morrois.'—M: 'Go and await me at
the Croix Rouge.'

1915– The forester goes and sits at the Croix Rouge. A
1920 curse upon him: he will die a shameful death, as
you shall hear anon!

1921– The king refuses an escort, saying: 'A maiden has
1942 bidden me to go and speak with her.']

VARIANTS

O 4560–4616; *R* 362, 8–11, 23–365, 4; *G* 17279–17488; *S* lxv; *E*
ccxxix–ccxxxi; *T.r.* 245, 16–246, 13; *Fo* 877–80

R, having described the fear inspired by Tristran in the king and those
of Cornwall, tells how Mark riding with a large following in the forest
of Moreis, is informed by four shepherd boys that Tristran with a lady,
a maid and a squire are in the house of the 'sage damoiselle'. They find
Iseut and her maid alone and carry them off. Mark has a ban cried against
Tristran, and those of Cornwall seek him. In the meantime Tristran is
found asleep by a varlet (whose father had been killed by Tristran), is
wounded with a poisoned arrow as he awakes, and finding Governal,
proceeds to their abode and discovers the loss of Iseut. On the morrow
he meets a 'damoiselle', a kinswoman of Brengain, who tells him that
Iseut is imprisoned in the tower and that his only hope lies in counsel
from Brengain. The latter comes and advises Tristran to seek out Yseult
aux Blanches Mains in Brittany, who is famed for her knowledge of
medicine.

G: Mark goes hunting in order to forget his wretchedness. A wondrous
white stag is pursued by the hounds and escapes in the direction of the
lovers' grotto. The noise of the hunt fills the lovers with fear. On the
following day, after their daily outing, they retire to rest and on Tristran's
advice lie with their backs to each other and separated by Tristran's unsheathed sword. The chief huntsman, who had set out alone at daybreak
in search of the stag, comes to the grotto and, finding the door barred,
discovers a small window at the top of the grotto and looks down upon
the lovers. In fear he reports to Mark what he has found, and Mark asks
to be led there.—*S* relates the hunting of the stag (it is merely a powerful
stag) in much greater detail and adds that the chief huntsman's name was

Kanves. He looks through the door and sees Tristran and Iseut lying at opposite ends of the grotto. He is overcome with fear, for a mighty sword lies between them; he tells Mark what he has found, saying that he does not know if the beings are celestial or human or faery.—*E*: Tristran having gone hunting one day with Hodain, returns with his game and lies down by the side of Iseut, placing his sword between them. Mark's huntsmen, while pursuing a stag on that same day, see Tristran and Iseut and the separating sword. They report this to Mark.— *T.r.*: Tristran and Iseut were wont to rest at midday, not in a bed but, because of the great heat, on a *grande tavola d'arcipresso* ('cypress') with Tristran's naked sword between them—out of fear. Mark laments his wretchedness. One feast-day he goes hunting and after four days he and one of his barons pursue a stag all day and, stopping to drink from a stream, follow it and find the sumptuous dwelling of the lovers.—In *Fo* the dwarf[1] is said to have brought the king to the lovers' retreat.

O: The lovers and Governal suffer great hardship: they lack fire, bread and clothing. More than two years they lived thus in the forest and saw neither town nor village—so says the book and so people declare. It was Tristran's practice to place his sword between Iseut and himself when they slept. The king's huntsman, coming stealthily to the bower (*hutte*) one morning, sees them and identifies Tristran by the sword. He goes to Mark and tells him.[2] The king asks him to say nothing and to lead him there: you may wonder with what intention; I could not tell you!

NOTES

1767 A similar error in l. 4103 would suggest that the scribe was unaccustomed to *estre mestier*, although familiar with *avoir mestier*. He is, however, not led into error at 3589.

1771 'He (Tristran) remained a long time in this exile. He was of wondrous good resource (i.e. he provided for them wondrously)'.

1774 ff. Cf. *Fb* 200: *Chaut faisoit con el tens de mai* (cf. l. 1794).

1780 *Çaint*, past participle with active force (cf. 1748): 'having girded on his sword'.

1783 'Before he came back (from hunting)'. Cf. 1798– 1800.

1785 *se* (for *le* neuter) is probably a scribal slip; but it

---

[1] Hoepffner (edn., pp. 130–1) suggests that there may have been confusion with the discovery of the lovers in the orchard—in the scene introduced by Thomas (Bédier I, 247–53).

[2] No distance is mentioned; there is no direct speech.

is defensible: cf. *Por celi muir qui ne s'en sent*, Gontier de Soignies (Scheler II.8, vi, 3). 'But neither feels it because of the other (i.e. because they have each other); they had their solace. Never from the time when they were in the wood together did two persons drain such a cup (of sorrow)'. Cf. 1649–55 n.

1790 'Never' is a sweeping assertion, and the poet finds it necessary to substantiate what he avers by reference to an authority, *l'estoire*; cf. the note to 1257–70. Note that, as at 1264, Beroul refers to the *estoire* as a source which he had consulted at some time in the past and cites from memory. See the note to 1259–70. *La ou*] MS *lon* (or *lou?*).

1802–3 'From side to side the foliage was stretched and the ground was well covered with leaves.'

1805 Cf. *Fb* 195 ff., where it is said that Tristran being afraid to flee, pretended to be asleep.

1806 On the separating sword, see the note to 2050.

1807 *out vestue*, with the original force of the compound form: 'she had it on'.

1809 'A dire mishap would have befallen them.'

1813 *planteïz*, analogical obl. pl. of *planteïf*, *plenteïf*.

1816 *Oez* serves once again to introduce a passage peculiar to Beroul and presumably added by him.

1827 Cf. 2034–42.

1834 The supernumerary line may be an alternative reading (to l. 1833 ?) which the scribe has incorporated in the text. One may assume that the *forestier* here mentioned is Orri, who was well disposed to Tristran (cf. 2817).

1835 Repeated verbatim at l. 4351.

1835–6 Cf. *Troie* 16231–2.

1838 *fulliers* (var. *fuellier* 1840) is of uncertain meaning. M^0 glossed it 'Endroit feuillu, ombragé', and M^4 'fourré', associating it no doubt (as well as *fullie* 1291, 1673 = *loge* 1735) with *feuille* (<FOLIA). Alternatively, the word might be related (cf. Tobler-Lommatzsch's 'Eindruck') to *fouler* (<*FULLARE) and interpreted as

denoting the trace (flattened undergrowth?) left at the
halting place or places by the fugitives. The former seems
more likely in view of the context and more specifically
the wording of l. 1840. The Glossary's rendering 'bower'
is incorrect and should be replaced by 'dense wood',
'thicket', in reference to the more impenetrable area of
the forest of Morrois in which the lovers seek safety, and
perhaps to the *espoise* mentioned in l. 1537.

1842 *aünee* 'gathering', and by extension 'gathering-
place', 'rendez-vous', 'abode' (?)

1850 The scribal error induced by the preceding line.

1854 *Qui* (< *CŪGITO), 'methinks'.

1873 *soiz* = *ses, sais*; *toz* = *tost*.

1877 M⁴: *hom qui ait*.

1880 'Has any man refused you his fine (or fee)?'

1889 Muret emends to *Se nel t'ensein . . .*, but the line
may be a question inspired by the forester's fear that the
news may so anger the king that he will lay violent hands
on him.

1892 It would no doubt have been more prudent to
adhere to the reading of the MS with the minor correction of *poie* to *poi a* (as in M⁴) rather than to assume a
homoeoteleuton. See the note in M⁴.

1901 Jeanroy's emendation implies the adverbial use
of the adjective *estroitet* (one example in Godefroy III,
657), which receives support in the use of such forms as
souavet (3105), *petitet* (1439, etc.).

1904 'You have no rights (or 'forfeit all claim') in your
own kingdom.'

1905 From this line the scribe jumped to 1910 (misled
no doubt by the rhyme-word) and, having transcribed
1910–12, then realized his error and resumed at 1906
without deleting the three lines already written.

1907 For Mark's motive in insisting on secrecy, cf.
Eilhart 4614 ff. and Lichtenstein's comment (p. cxx).

1908 'Whether (lit. 'however much') he be a stranger
or privy to my councils.'

1909 I had taken *fors* to be the adverb, used, as in l. 1905, with the meaning 'outside', i.e. 'outside the town or royal palace and precinct' (cf. similar uses with the meaning 'out', 'forth' in ll. 902, 1514, 1521, or 'out of doors' in l. 321), although admittedly our text shows no other comparable use of the adverb *fors* after a substantive, and the repetition of *fors* from l. 1905 is awkward. However, J. Frappier (in *Rom.* LXXXIII) proposed to interpret *au chemin fors* as 'au chemin fourchu', 'à l'endroit où le chemin bifurque', *fors* being the nom. sg. (here wrongly used) of *forc* (preserved in the modern *carrefour* < QUADRIFURCUS). The adjectival use of *forc* is not well attested, but M. Frappier cites *un forc chemin* from *L'Âtre Périlleux* 5448 and *forchemin* from *Yder* (ed. Gelzer) 902. It is true, as he points out, that *fors* (<FURCUS) would involve attributing to the poet both a 'mistake' in declension and an 'inaccurate' rhyme of the close *o* of this word with the open *o* of *cors* (<CORPUS); but since both 'irregularities' are found elsewhere in the text, they do not constitute a fatal objection to the adoption of M. Frappier's interpretation.

1916 'May the drop serene destroy his eyes!' The gutta serena or amaurosis was a disease of the optic nerve. Cf. *Fb* 261: *Male goute ait il es oroilles.*

1918 'It would have been better for him to betake himself off!' The reflexive (*son cors* being the common periphrasis for *se*) used here with the same meaning as in 2054 and 2476.

1920 Cf. the prophecy in 2759–62, and the note to 2753–64. In *Fo* 879 it is said that the dwarf led the king to the grotto.

1926–30 'Are you mocking us that you should thus go anywhere unescorted: there never was a king who did not take his precautions . . . Do not stir for any spy's words.' For the use of the infinitive with pronoun subject, see 891 n.

1932 Perhaps the stock 'damoisele' of romance, of

uncertain status, function and identity, who appears at frequent intervals in the Prose Romance.

1935 The scribe appears to have misread *sor* under the influence of the preceding *seus*.

1939 A spurious reference to the *Disticha Catonis* or their medieval French translations.

1942 'Let me have my own way a little.'

(*j*) *Mark finds the lovers* (1943–2062)

SUMMARY

1943– [Mark, thinking only of his revenge and trusting
1990 in his sword, follows the forester to the bower. He enters with drawn sword and beckons to the forester to withdraw.]

1991– When he sees how they lie, he hesitates, relents
2038 and resolves to leave them a token of his coming: 'I will exchange the [ring upon Iseut's finger with that upon mine and the] sword which lies between them with mine, and with my glove I will cover the sun's ray which burns upon the face of Iseut.'

2039– Thus he does, and bidding the forester be gone,
2062 he returns to his city; nor does he tell of his errand.

VARIANTS

O 4617–4646; R (see under (*i*)); *T* xxviii; *G* 17489–17630; *S* lxvi, 1–17; *E* ccxxxi–ccxxxii; *T.r.* 246, 13–247, 4; *Fo* 881–892; *Fb* 194–207; *Escoufle* 594–616; *Poire* 142–160

G: Mark dismounts and looking through the small window of the grotto, is filled with fear, sorrow, joy and doubt. At last, overcome by Iseut's beauty, he notices that the sun's ray falls upon her face and stops up the window with foliage and flowers. Weeping, he blesses her and returns to his followers: he calls off the hunt, ordering them to return to the royal palace so that none may spy out the lovers.—*S*: Mark goes to the grotto and recognizes the sword as one he had possessed himself. He is convinced of their innocence. He admires Iseut's beauty, goes to her and places his glove upon her cheek to protect it from the sun's ray.

He commends her to God and departs; the hunt is called off and no one accompanies Mark as he rides to his tent.—*E* merely says that Mark saw the lovers and the sword; he places his glove over an opening through which the sun's ray falls upon Iseut's face. He is angry and asserts their innocence. The knights say: 'For true love it is.'—*T.r.*: Mark dismounts and, entrusting his horse to his companion, he goes to see if the dwelling is inhabited: in the lower room he finds Tristran and Iseut asleep on a *tavola* and the naked sword between them; he regrets his unfounded suspicions. He marvels at Iseut's beauty and places an ermine glove on the place where the sun's ray falls; he kisses her tenderly. He returns, mounts his horse and with his barons returns to Tintagel (*Tintoille*).—*Fo*: Tristran *fou* recalls the finding of the lovers with the separating sword and lying far apart, Mark's placing of the glove upon Iseut's face and his departing, convinced of their innocence.

Fb: Tristran *fou* reminds Mark of his fear when he found the lovers in the bower with the separating sword: 'La fis je sanblant de dormir, Car je n'osoie pas foïr'; how Mark placed his gloves over the opening against the sun and departed.

O: Mark, guided by the huntsman, comes to the spot, leaves his horse with his attendants and proceeds alone to the bower. He takes Tristran's sword and substitutes his own. He places his glove on Iseut without waking her and, returning to his horse, rides away.

Escoufle: The sword with the *oche* (*o tout l'oche*) is found between them both *tos nus*. Mark is filled with pity and does not wake them. The sun's ray comes *parmi la raime* (although in l. 595 the bed is said to be *en la roche*). He places the glove beside her ear. He saw them *sos les rains*.

Poire: Mark goes hunting (no mention being made of the forester). He stops up the hole with his glove. Tristran had built the bower. Mark repents of his harshness, saying that he was deceived by evil counsel. The lovers pretend to sleep; the sword is between them. *Puis tornames noz vis Ireuz et engoisseus.*

NOTES

1944 *çaint* is here 3 pr. ind.

1945 The emendation *la cuvertise* satisfies the context (cf. 1956) and a misreading of this word might readily account for what the scribe wrote. Acher had suggested *la grant feintise* and M. Roques (*Rom.* XXXIX, 409) *la covoitise*.

1970 The *marc* was a unit of weight for precious metals. (M⁴: 'le marc d'argent fin pesait 245 grammes et valait 10 sous'.)

1971 The Glossary proposes 'to (the scene of) his misdeed', i.e. where his treachery will be accomplished; but it is possible and more likely that *forfet* here has the meaning 'forfeit', 'bargain', and that the poet meant: 'to the (place of the) fulfilment of his bargain, or the redeeming of his pledge or promise'; cf. 1972–3. Tobler-Lommatzsch takes *forfet* as a past participle adjective, 'he who had done wrong', i.e. Tristran.

1980 *por qu'il* = *por qu(i) il* (cf. Introd., No. 54), or possibly *por qu(e) il*.

1985 *S'en torne* makes satisfactory sense: 'In anger he turns away (from the spot where he had left his horse)', or simply: 'he proceeds'.

1991–2000 This passage has attracted the attention of a number of critics who have shown a singular reluctance to take the text as it stands. A. Henry[1] regards *descendist* (1993) as an example of a 'subjonctif d'imminence contre-carrée', followed by *Quant* (1995), the meaning being, as Miss Hackett indicates,[2] 'the blow would have fallen . . . but for his seeing . . .', and he repunctuates the passage accordingly. But, having regard to the idiosyncratic style of Beroul, it might be more accurately interpreted as a 'subjonctif d'imminence suspendue' or a 'phrase conditionnelle à condition sous-entendue', and be related to such uses of the past subjunctive as we have in ll. 87, 143, 985, 1918, 2173, or (with 'exclamatory' force) in ll. 1253 and 3820. The poet here tells us, in his usual vivid manner, how Mark raised his unsheathed sword in anger, but how his strength fails him (*se tresva*); the blow all but descended upon the lovers (= 'le coup descendait déjà sur eux'); had he killed them, it would have been a grievous thing. When [having recovered himself] he saw that they were clothed . . . and separated by the sword, he was perplexed, saying: 'Ce que puet estre? . . . ne sai que doie faire.'

There is therefore no need to resort to repunctuation

---

[1] In *Rom*. LXXIII; *Chrestomathie de la littérature en ancien français*, 1953, II, 52–3; *Études de syntaxe expressive*, 1960.
[2] In *Vinaver Misc.*, p. 163 and note.

and correction. B. Blakey's proposal[1] to read *tresua* as *tresüa* (cf. 4431) involves the introduction of a stylistically inappropriate preterite and the creation of a hypermetric line (it is not clear what he means by 'the second hemistich' in this connection). A. Henry's proposal to read *Ire* as a substantive instead of an adjectival form (*Iré*) is plausible, although one would expect something like *Ire li fist faire* (cf. 1985). The fact that elsewhere in this text the adjectival form appears as *iriez* or *irié* proves nothing, given the scribe's confusion of *e* and *ie*. Moreover, the undiphthongized form is well attested by rhymes in such works as *Aliscans* (l. 682), *Huon de Bordeaux* (l. 5921) and the *Chansons* of Conon de Béthune (III, 20).

For a general note on this passage, see Introd., pp. 43–44.

1993 'The blow all but descended upon them.'

2009 M⁴: *Entrë eus deus n'eüst espee.*

2020–4 'It will provide them with such proof before they awake that they will know for certain that they were found asleep and that one has had pity on them.'

2021 M⁴: *Que, ançois qu'il s'esvelleront*—which hardly makes sense.

2032–3 Nowhere else is there a suggestion that the gloves were brought from Ireland. *T.r.* specifies that the glove is *uno guanto d'ermellino*. It is clear that the scribe has misread l. 2032 and that he was content to copy more or less mechanically what he had before him, which may quite well have been *Uns ganz de vair rai je o moi*, as conjectured by Muret (Mussafia had proposed *vair ai je*). The absurdity of the scribe's *voirre* ('glass') would therefore be exactly matched by the more modern, though now questioned, transformation of Cinderella's *souliers de vair* into *souliers de verre*. *Vair* denoted the animal (of the squirrel species: mod. *petit-gris*) and its fur. In l. 2075 the gloves are said to be adorned or trimmed with ermine.—One is tempted to suspect some material defect

[1] In *French Studies* XXI (1967), 99–103.

at this point in the model followed, in view of the further misreading in l. 2034 and possibly also in l. 2038.

2038 *blos* is what the scribe finally wrote, and the sense would seem to be 'wherewith the Morholt was beheaded'. The adj. *blos* (<Germ. *bloz*; cf. *REW* 1161) means 'bare', 'deprived (of)', 'bereft', and adverbially 'solely', 'to the exclusion of all else'; and unfamiliarity with this rather uncommon word may have induced the scribe to misinterpret an original *Dont le Morholt fu del chief blos* (emendation since adopted in M[4]); cf. *Ruste ert le coup e merveillus A poi ne l'out fet del chief blus.* (*Ipomedon* 4907–8) and the examples given in Godefroy and Tobler-Lommatzsch. It might be objected that this is at variance with the account given of the Morholt fight (in the other versions). Tristran is described as cutting off the Morholt's head in *G* (7088–9), which here almost certainly deviates; in *O* (904–6) it is his hand that is cut off in the course of the combat. But there are signs of some confusion in the mind of our poet between the details of the Morholt battle and the dragon episode (cf. 485), and it would therefore be safer to regard this as one of the poet's inconsistencies or lapses than to emend (as suggested by Jeanroy) to *Dont el chief Morholt fu* (or *mest*) *uns tros* ('a fragment'), or (as suggested in M[2]) to *Dont au Morholt fu el chief tros.* For other suggestions, see Tanquerey and M[2].

2041–2 *Fb* is more explicit: *Tes ganz botas el pertuis* (l. 204); ll. 2075–6 suggest that Beroul's words are to be interpreted in the same sense.

2044 *il* refers to *doi*; there is therefore no need to regard it as a mistake for *el* (cf. M[4] notes): the following lines make this clear.

2050 On the separating sword, see G. Schoepperle, pp. 430–1, and Hertz[3], Anm. 124. Eilhart finds it strange (l. 4592), but neither he nor the other poets offer an explanation: one must assume that it is a relic of Celtic tradition. A similar episode, with a stone instead of a sword, is contained in the Old Irish story of *Diarmaid and Grainne*. The substitution of the sword, on the other hand, is a popular motif with many parallels in medieval romance and in popular tradition (Schoepperle, pp. 262–5). The substitution is suppressed in Thomas, who transforms the bower into a grotto. In *Fo* we have an account as in Thomas, but the king is accompanied by the dwarf (l. 880). In Eilhart it is found without the exchange of rings.

2055–6 Cf. *Fb* 205–6: *Si t'an alas, il n'i ot plus Ne je ne voil outre conter*.

2058 *out* impers.: 'It was asked'; but the scribe frequently writes *u* for *n* and *n* for *u* (cf. *On* for *Ou* in the very next line), and one might read *ont* 'they asked', particularly in view of *lor* in l. 2060. (M⁰ interprets this *lor* as 'then'.)

(*k*) *Iseut's dream* (2063–2076)

SUMMARY

2063– [Iseut dreams that she is in a fair pavilion in a
2076 great wood. Two lions approach, who, when she is about to cry for mercy, each take her by a hand. She wakes with a cry and finds that the gloves have fallen upon her breast.]

Once again a digression and deviation from received accounts is introduced by an address to the listeners or readers: 'Hear now about the sleeping lovers . . .'. Beroul did not lack precedents for the introduction of a dream at this juncture (cf., for example, the dreams or visions of Charlemagne in the *Chanson de Roland* (717–36, 2525–69) and of Arthur in Wace's *Brut* (ed. Le Roux de Lincy, 11526–59)).

Here, as in the scene of the Tryst under the Pine Tree, Beroul tends to reserve the principal role for Iseut, whereas in the other versions the lovers simply awake and discover the king's glove. He leaves us to conclude that the dream is related to, and in fact inspired by the sufferings and perplexities of Iseut, and at the same time it serves to explain and dramatize the awakening of the lovers. Line 2076 is descriptive and not narrative. In Beroul (and also in the account preserved in *Poire*) Mark had placed his gloves over the opening through which the sun shone and fell upon Iseut's face (2041). Only according to this version could the gloves have fallen upon the sleeping Iseut and thus induced the interruption of her dream and the uttering of the cry which awakened her (both phenomena with which all dreamers are familiar). It was Iseut's cry that awakened Tristran also (2077).

As for the interpretation of the dream or its symbolism, it is reasonable to suppose that the poet meant the two lions 'seeking to devour her' to figure Mark and Tristran, and the *esfroi* of Iseut to have been induced by the fear and perplexity to which she had become a prey in her waking life. We have here, then, a development imagined by Beroul which serves to characterize his gifts of observation and psychological penetration. P. Jonin published in *Le Moyen Age* for 1958 a Freudian analysis of Iseut's dream, which was sharply criticized by P. Cézard in *Rom.* LXXXI (1960), 557.

(*l*) *The lovers' flight* (2077–2132)

SUMMARY

2077– The lovers, discovering the signs of the king's
2100 coming, resolve upon flight [toward Wales].

2101– [Governal returns and is told of this.]
2121

2122– They flee [toward Wales].
2129

2130– [Three full years] they suffered travail: they be-
2132 come pale and weak.

VARIANTS

O 4647–4701; *T* xxviii; *G* 17631–17662; *S* lxvi, 17–21; *E* ccxxxiii

G: The lovers awake to find one of the three windows of the grotto stopped up and footprints round about. They think Mark has come and console themselves with the thought that they were found lying apart. —In *S*, Iseut finds the glove; they do not know what to think, but are relieved that they were found as they were.—In *E*, they find the glove and are glad that Mark has seen them; whereupon 'worthy knights come to fetch them'.—In *T.r.*, nothing is said about the lovers until they are sent for by Mark (see below, p. 213).

O: Tristran awakes, sees the glove and asks Iseut whence it came. Then he recognizes the king's sword: 'We are doomed, the king is near.' Tristran calls for Governal and his horse. They flee deeper into the wood, where they take refuge in a remote combe and live on herbs.[1]

NOTES

2081 This detail of *l'osche* produced when a piece of Tristran's sword remained embedded in the head of the Morholt (see above, p. 63, and *Fb* 408–13) is not mentioned by Eilhart, who merely says that Tristran recognized the king's sword.

2091 Unusual word-order for *molt par li*; M[4] tentatively suggests reading: *molt li parsomes*.

2095–8 Cf. *G* 18260 ff.

2122 'There was in them no (thought of) tarrying. If they are afraid, they cannot help it.'

2124 *Li rois* for *Le roi*.

2126 *Li roi* for *Le roi*.

2131 *Trois anz*. This line indicates that the lovers' wretched woodland life lasted three full years (cf. also ll. 3759–60); but ll. 2140, 2143 and 2148 suggest that the period of three years dates from the drinking of the potion. In *O* the lovers' woodland life lasts more than

---

[1] There follows Tristran's visit to the hermit; see above, section III(c). *O* makes no mention of Wales or of the passage of time.

two years (l. 4578), while the full power of the potion
lasts four years.

IV. WANING OF THE POTION AND RETURN OF ISEUT TO
MARK (2133–3010)

(a) *The potion wanes*: *Tristran proposes restitution* (2133–
2262)

SUMMARY

2133– [My lords, you know of the potion, but not of its
 2142 duration: for three years of love it was brewed by
       Iseut's mother; for Mark and her daughter she
       made it: another tasted of it who suffers for it.]

2143– For [three] years the potion held Tristran and
 2146 Iseut in its thrall.

2147– [Upon the morrow of St. John, Tristran was in
 2160 pursuit of a wounded stag when the anniversary
       fell, and straightway he repented:

2161– 'For three years I have suffered distress and for-
 2199 gotten chivalry when I should have been in royal
       service. And for Iseut I grieve, whom I give a
       bower when she might live in royal splendour.
       God grant me to repent! Gladly would I make
       amends if she might be reconciled with Mark, her
       lawful consort.'

2200– In like manner Iseut laments and blames Brengain
 2220 who failed to guard the potion.

2221– T: 'Gladly would I make terms with Mark if he
 2262   would accept our defence; and if any of his
           knights charged us with a sinful love, he
           would find me armed upon the field. Gladly
           would I serve him then; but if he refused my
           service, I would go with Governal to the king

of Frise or to Brittany. Yet would I not seek
our parting, were it not for the distress you
suffer through the potion given us upon the
high sea. Counsel me!']

VARIANTS

O 4724–4741; Fb 171–5, 306–20, 343–5

O: Tristan, having left the hermit, is constrained by love to remain
with Iseut until the force of the potion abated (*vorgi*). As those say who
have read the book (and it is true), when four years had passed from the
drinking of the potion, Tristran and Iseut began to feel the hardships
they suffered in the forest and could not bear the suffering a day longer.

In *Fb*, Tristran *fou* describes how completely he remains under the
influence of the potion (*Mon san ai en folor changiee*) while Iseut does not
feel it (*Je muir por li, ele nel sant* : *N'est pas parti oniement*);[1] he would appear
to attribute this diversity of effect to the manner in which the potion was
prepared (316–7; cf. Hoepffner's note); he blames Brengain for having
brought (them) the potion.

The significance of the potion and the divergent treatments of it in the primary versions have never ceased to
claim the attention of critics. Miss Schoepperle maintained, with some show of reason, that although the
motif is traceable to ancient classical sources, the form
which it takes in the Tristran romances corresponds very
closely with the Old Irish geis (or spell or taboo or
charm), of which a striking example is furnished by the
story of *Diarmaid and Grainne*, and that it may have been
given the form of a potion by a French poet as being
more familiar or intelligible to a French audience than
a geis or a love-spot.

[1] He returns to the unjust discrepancy between his sufferings and those
of Iseut in lines 343–9 and 437–8. Cf. R 376, 27–33, where Tristran *fou*
says to Iseut, who has just struck him: 'Certes, dame, fol sui je. Et sachiés
qu'il a passé huit jours que ne finay de foloier pour vous; mais se le mal
fust a droit parti, vous foloyssiez aussi comme moi. Et si vous pry pour
Dieu et pour l'amour de Tristran a qui cœur vous avés que ne me touchiés
plus, car certes, le boire que vous et luy beüstes en la mer ne vous est
pas si amer au cœur comme il est au fol Tristan.'

A more definite cleavage of opinion arises over the duration of the potion. In *O* it retains its full potency for four years and thereafter a diminished potency. According to *B*, it retains its potency for three years. *T* and *R* say explicitly that there is no limit to its power, and in *Fb* (307 ff.) there is a presupposition to the same effect. Miss Schoepperle considered that the diminution after a period of years existed in the *Estoire*, but the weight of evidence seems to favour Bédier's conclusion (II, 236–40) that the diminution is attributable to an intermediate version (γ), the source of both *B* and *O*, and that the latter, as usual, follows γ faithfully, specifying that during the first four years the lovers must be together daily: after that they must continue to love each other with all their might for ever. Beroul undoubtedly had the same idea in mind. He makes the period three years but does not say definitely that the potion continues to exert a diminished influence. Yet we are faced by the fact that in the later portion of the poem the lovers still seem to be under the influence of the potion. Miss Schoepperle's explanation is that the second part is the work of a continuator who ignored the three years' term. However, it seems more satisfactory to assume that Beroul did have in mind the same idea of the potion as Eilhart, but (*a*) failed to indicate the nature of the diminution, or (*b*) did so in a portion of the poem lost to us; and we are led to this conclusion by his procedure as we can observe it in 2133–8 (and also, incidentally, by his treatment of the hostile faction). These lines do not appear to me to signify that Beroul is presenting a version different from other versions known to him or to his audience (as some critics, including Bédier, have it), but that he means to say in substance: 'You will remember, my lords, what you have been told about the potion, by whom it was brewed and how the lovers drank it: but I must now tell you something which I did not say then, yet which is a necessary detail for the understanding of what is about to happen.' He then mentions the term of three years, but neglects to say that the potion continues to act with diminished power, in the same way as he had neglected to mention the three years term in the first instance. That the diminution is not the invention of Eilhart (and we may assume the same of Beroul) is shown by his observation to the effect that 'the power of the potion waned, as those say who have read the book— and surely it is true—four years after they had drunk it' (4729–33).

The importance of the potion in reducing, if not completely eliminating, the moral culpability of the lovers stands in marked contrast with its role in *T* and *R*, where it is almost entirely incidental and symbolical of the idea of courtly love.

NOTES

2133 *Seignors*! Once again the poet addresses his public formally in order to indicate a change of subject, a new development or an elaboration.

2134 Cf. 909 n.

2136–42 'But you do not know, methinks, to what length of time it was limited, the love-philtre, the potion: Iseut's mother, who brewed it, made it for three years of love (i.e. to last three years). For Mark she made it and for her daughter; another tasted of it and suffers for it.'

2138 *lovendrins* (MS *loucuendris*) and *lovendrant* (2159) are adaptations of English *love drink*, which occurs in *Sir Tristrem*, l. 1710. The potion is also called *le boivre d'amor* (2218), *li vin herbez* (2138) and *un herbé* (1414). It is not easy to see why a Continental poet should have resorted to the English name. Bédier considered it likely that it is a trace of an episodic poem with a bilingual title. It is not impossible that Beroul picked it up on the Continent, but a similar familiarity with bilingual and trilingual titles of *lais* on the part of Marie de France suggests the possibility that Beroul too may at some time have enjoyed an insular domicile.

2146 What the scribe wrote would seem to mean: 'Wretched, I flee!' 'A wretched fugitive am I!'; but this does not fit the immediate context, which demands rather an indication of the lovers' continued subjection to the potion and therefore of their contentment with their lot. Muret's emendation to *Las n'en sui* is therefore plausible, and these words could easily have been misread as *Los m'en fui*.

2152 Raynaud de Lage (in *Rom.* LXXXIII) sought to explain *doitie* as 'un complément circonstanciel de lieu sans préposition', meaning 'une piste, une coulée de gibier'. This is hard to accept since the verb *traire* is surely used here in the sense of 'to shoot' (cf. 1286) and *doitie* would therefore seem to denote a shaft or missile: but no other example of the word is attested.

2158–9 'The hour (i.e. the anniversary) returns when he had drunk the potion, and he stops in his tracks.'

2162 *riens* is adverbial: 'in any way' or 'in any degree', and the phrase *que riens n'i fal* means 'as I mistake not', 'I make no mistake in my reckoning', and the whole adverbial clause introduced by *que* signifies 'without the possibility of error', 'to a day'.

2162–6 'To-day it is three years, to a day, that distress has not been a stranger to me, neither on holy-days nor on working-days. I have forgotten knighthood and the frequenting of court and baronage.' The poet wishes to convey that, though the lovers were throughout the three years fully conscious of their physical suffering and other privations, their love enabled them (thanks to the potency of the potion) to bear them without repining until precisely the third anniversary. From that moment their regrets begin, and they are retrospective.

2169 'I am not at court with (other) knights' or 'I am not at a knightly court' (cf. 2173).

2168 *gris*, the name given to the grey fur from the back of the *petit-gris*; cf. 2032.

2175 'Who would serve me in order to receive their arms and render me their service.'

2179 Cf. 1110–18 n.

2180 'Whom I give a bower instead of a tapestried room.'

2190 Note the insistence on Tristran's innocence. Or is this a hint that the power of the potion has not completely vanished?

2192–4 'to whom she was wed, alas! before the eyes of many notables, according to the manner prescribed by the Christian religion.'

2197 *qui* obl. = *cui*.

2200 *estoit* for *estot*, impf. ind. 3 of *ester*. Cf. 973.

2203 *com autre serve*, 'like any other serving maid'.

2206 *ma poison*, i.e. the potion brewed for me.

2208 According to *Fb* (as in *E* and *S* and *L'Escoufle*) Brengain herself brought the potion to Tristran and Iseut; in *O* it was a *jungfrauwelin* and in *T* a *valet*, as also in *Fo* (which adds that nevertheless Brengain was to blame because she had been put in charge of the potion); in *R* Brengain and Governal together bring the potion to Tristran and Iseut. Beroul implies that it was in Brengain's custody (*qu'i dut garder*) and she was responsible (*Ce fist Brengain*) in that she failed to guard it (2209); consequently she could not mend matters because, the potion having been brought, Iseut had already drunk too deeply of it (2210). Muret's emendation corrects the imperfect rhyme but alters the meaning in such a way as to fit a wider context, but not the immediate context of Beroul's narrative; it does however find support in *Fb* 433: *Ele mesprist* (MS *me prist*) *estre son voil*. For *qu'i = qui i*, see Introd., No. 54.

2216 *por bien* for *par bien* (?)

2232 *Lidan* (which occurs also in 3562) is to be identified with Eilhart's *Litan*, the fief of Dinas; see note to 1085.

2237 *deresnie*, pp. fem. For the use of *avoir* with reflexive verbs, see Nyrop, *Gram. hist.* VI, pp. 214–5, and Sneyders de Vogel, *Syntaxe*, §§ 168–74.

2242 *soufrist*, corrected by Muret to *servist*; but it is possible that we have here an extension in the meaning of *soufrir* from 'bear with', 'abide by someone's will' (cf. 796) to 'serve', *de sa gerre* meaning 'in respect of his war'. See in this connection the interesting discussion of the meanings of *souffrir* by E. Vinaver in *Cahiers de Civilisation Médiévale* XI (1968), pp. 6–8.

2244 The alternation between *a* and *de* after the same verb is well attested and the 'normalizing' correction to *degerpir* (adopted in M⁰, and favoured by Reid, but abandoned in later editions) is unnecessary.

2246 Tristran envisages the possibility that Mark might be prepared to receive back the queen, but would require him to quit the kingdom, to go into exile or, as it is put several times, to go oversea. Iseut had already described Tristran as preparing to go oversea (443; cf. also 2630), and in the letter indited by Ogrin this is reduced to two alternatives: Brittany or (with a clear preference) Scotland, *outre la mer de Frise* in this context having the same meaning as *ultra mare Fresicum* (or *Frenessicum* according to the text given by Faral, *Lég. Arth.* III, 29) in the *Historia Britonum* attributed to Nennius, viz. beyond the Firth of Forth, but used loosely to designate the northern lands inhabited by the Picts and Scots. Thus, at ll. 2310 and 2868 it is to *Loenoi(s)* (= Lothian), while at 2631 it is to *Gavoie* (= Galloway) that the Cornish barons advise that Tristran is to go and take service with the 'riche roi . . ., a qui li roiz escoz[1]

---

[1] I have had no hesitation in adopting the emendation proposed by Muret in the glossary to M⁰ and introduced in his subsequent editions. He considered that there was here perhaps an allusion to the protracted hostilities in the twelfth century between the kings of Scotland and their vassals, the princes of Galloway (*Gavoie*).

gerroie' (2631–2); at ll. 2408–9 Tristran is to cross the 'mer de Frise' to serve 'un autre roi', while at 2246 and 2610 he proposes to serve the 'roi de Frise'.

We are hardly entitled to conclude from these divergent indications, with Bédier (II, 109) in his discussion of Beroul's *Gavoie* and Eilhart's *Ganôje*, that the poet was merely concerned to indicate vaguely and with some inconsistency an oversea country to which Tristran would pretend to retire. The 'vagueness' may reflect the readiness of Tristran to serve one or other of the warring kings or chieftains, and it is conceivable that Beroul's Scottish king (probably the same as the 'roi de Frise' of ll. 2246 and 2610) who engaged in war against the king of Galloway (2631–2 and possibly 2926) owes something at least to a dim recollection of Malcolm the Maiden (d. 1165) who subdued, at least momentarily, the notoriously warlike and restive Celts of Galloway.[1]

2251–5 'I would not desire our parting if we could remain together, were it not for the great privation you suffer and have ever suffered for my sake in the wilderness.' Muret's *Tanz dis* (2255) is an improvement on the text, but it is difficult to justify in the face of the very similar use of *toz tens* in l. 2594.

(b) Second visit to Ogrin and sending of letter (2263–2509)

SUMMARY

2263– [I: 'Since by God's mercy you repent, let us seek
2275   counsel from the hermit Ogrin.'
2276– T: 'Let us return to him and with his help send
2284   a letter.'

[1] The connection between *Frise* and Dumfries (favoured by Muret, M⁰, s.v. *Frise*) or Dumfriesshire (conjectured in M⁴) is difficult to maintain. In any case it is not the Firth of Forth but the Solway Firth that would have to be crossed to reach Dumfries.

2285– Iseut agrees and they find the hermit reading:
2294 they enter the chapel.]

2295– O: 'Repent of your folly.'
2299

2300– [T: 'For three years we have suffered. Give us
2318   counsel so that I may be reconciled with the
        king; and I will either go to Brittany or
        Loenois, or, if the king so desires, bide in his
        service.'

2319– Iseut falls at Ogrin's feet and beseeches him to
2330 reconcile them with the king: 'I do not repent of
        loving Tristran, but there shall be no carnal love
        between us.'

2331– O: 'God be praised for this repentance. He for-
2409   gives the penitent. Yet, in order that shame
        may be concealed a fair lie may be told. A
        letter I will write which you shall send to
        Lanïcen to greet the king and offer reconcilia-
        tion and ordeal by battle (if anyone should
        accuse you of a sinful love). Of all that passed
        since Iseut was brought from over the sea by
        you shall the letter speak and offer him your
        'escondit' and service at his court or in a
        foreign land.']

2410– T: 'I grant it; yet, since I may not trust him, let
2427   him leave his answering letter at the Croix
        Rouge.'

2428– Ogrin writes the letter, [and Tristran insists that
2448 he himself shall take it, accompanied only by
        Governal.]

2449– Tristran takes the letter to the king's hall at
2470 Lancien and calls softly at his window and tells
        him of the letter.

2471– Mark calls Tristran, but he hastens away [with
2509 Governal to the hermitage where they are re-
        ceived with relief and joy by Ogrin and Iseut.
        Tristran recounts his errand.]

VARIANTS

O 4742–4840

O: Tristran rides to Ogrin with Iseut and expresses regret that he had not heeded Ogrin. The latter receives his assurance that he repents and will return Iseut to the king. He writes a letter and sends it to the king by Tristran, there being no other messenger. He bids the king in God's name to do what is in the letter. Tristran rides to Tintagel and enters the orchard in which the king hid in the tree and ties his horse to the same linden-tree. He speaks through the wall of the room in which Mark lies, asking the king if he sleeps. 'Yes, if I were allowed to.'—'I tell you truly you must remain awake for a time.'—'Why?'—'I would gladly say if I dared.'—'Speak up!'—'Ogrin sends you his earnest prayer.'—'God reward him,' says the king, and bids Tristran speak on. Then Tristran throws the letter on the king through the window in the wall and says: 'Ogrin sends this letter and remission of your sins. To-morrow you shall cause to be written a letter giving your decision and have it suspended from the cross at the fork in the road by the tower before the town, whence your confessor will have it fetched.' Mark recognizes Tristran's voice. 'Remain,' he cries, 'I wish to speak to you.' Tristran pays no heed. Mark runs after him through the door but does not pursue him. He is impatient for the night to pass.

It is significant that in both *B* and *O* the second visit to the hermit is linked with the waning of the potion, a fact which strengthens the view that both were introduced by γ (see the general note at l. 1271). In *B* the lovers are described as having come to the hermitage of Ogrin on the first occasion 'par aventure' (1363) after having wandered in the forest for a long time, and it is Ogrin who counsels repentance and confession; but the lovers declare themselves enslaved by the potion. It is only after they are joined by Husdent and after his training and the killing of one of the hostile barons by Governal and further dire sufferings that *B* recounts the discovery of the lovers in their bower and their panic flight (towards Wales). It is at this point that *B* describes the limitation of the power of the potion to three years and the remorse of the lovers, and at Iseut's suggestion they return to the hermitage of Ogrin (2289–91) and seek his advice.

o

The first visit serves to underline the overpowering influence of the potion against which admonition and entreaty are of no avail, and even the further sufferings of the lovers, their regret and their fears of retribution (which motivate the second visit) would have been without effect had it not been for the waning of the potion. The development which Beroul has given to these scenes illustrates once again his sense of the dramatic as opposed to mere narration. The potion becomes an exteriorization of the role of passion in the human dilemma of the lovers caught up in the triangle of conflicting loyalties.

NOTES

2270–2 'If you had then repented, it could not have come more opportunely.'

2283 *a* 'according to'.

2284 *briés* for *brief*. 'By letter without any other message', i.e. solely in writing.

2299 *queles*, contracted form of *kaëles, chaëles*, a hortatory exclamation derived (according to Meyer-Lübke, *REW*) from *catella* used as 'a term of endearment addressed to women'. It occurs also in *Fb* 486, 557 and (in the form *cheles*) in *Fo* 617.

2302 Cf. *Fb* 54: '*Ha, Deus!*' *fait il*, '*quel destinee*'.

2303 Literally: 'provided that I make no mistake about it', i.e. 'if I mistake not'. Cf. 2162 n.

2308 *a seignor* 'as my liege-lord'; or does the description refer to Tristran's position at court, 'as a baron'? Cf. 162.

2310 *Loenois*; cf. 2246 n and 2868 n.

2315–8 I assume that in the scribe's model there were two successive couplets with the same rhyme (cf. Introd., p. 4) rather than that one of the three lines he wrote was a variant which he wrongly incorporated. M[4] assumes omission of a line between 2313 and 2315.

2319–20 Cf. 909 n.

2328 *amis* for *ami*.

2329–30 'Of the mutual possession of our bodies we are entirely free', i.e. 'We no longer love each other with a carnal love.'

2346–7 There is no doubt about the reading of the MS, and I take *anz* to be the scribe's graphy for *ainz* 'beforehand', i.e. before they claim absolution. For the use of *aus* (= *eus*) as subject of the verb, see L. Foulet's article in *Rom.* LI (1935), 437.

2353–4 See note to l. 1367.

2356 'without fixing a time', i.e. 'without delay'.

2359 *Lancïen* appears only in Beroul and in *Tristan Menestrel*[1] as the residence of Mark. It has been identified by J. Loth (*Contrib.*, p. 72) with Lantyan on the west bank of the Fowey, in the parish of St. Samson (cf. 2973 n). For Beroul it would seem to have been Mark's principal residence (although there is no mention of it after l. 2453), if not his capital—by implication at l. 1155, but more definitely at ll. 2359, 2438, 2453, while according to l. 2394 it was at Lancïen that the marriage of Mark and Iseut took place. It was introduced by Beroul or his immediate source as part of the localization of the legend in Cornwall.

2362 *lui* for *li*.

2364 'You would do the like for him' or 'You would do this much for him, [viz.] go to his court . . .'.

2366–70 For a strikingly similar construction in *Girart de Roussillon*, see W. M. Hackett, in *Vinaver Misc.*, 162. The hermit advises Tristran to declare in effect that if, having presented himself at Mark's court, he cannot defend himself against a charge of sinful love, whoever the accuser, then let Mark have him hanged.

2386 *Costentin*. See Introd., p. 32. Muret identified this with le Cotentin, but J. Loth (*Contrib.*, 85–86) produced strong arguments for preferring the Cornish Constantine

[1] Cf. Introd., pp. 32 n and 39.

(written *Custentin* in the tenth century), situated halfway between Falmouth and Helston. Note that *Fo*, in a different context, has Tristran say: 'Ne dutai par mun cors nul home Ki fust d'Escoce tresk'a Rume' (407-8).

2394 *Nocie*, dial. for *nociée*.

2395-6 'It ill became you to fail her: you preferred to flee with her.'

2401-2 These lines are parenthetical, and *vos* in l. 2402 would seem to be a scribal error for *ses*: 'when, in the judgement of his vassals you will be his loyal subject', i.e. 'when your loyalty is established'.

2403 *Preïst*, impf. subjunctive because it is part of the request to be contained in the letter.

2408 *Frise*: the emendation would seem to be justified by reference to ll. 2246 and 2610.

2411-4 'However much is put in the letter . . . I dare not trust him.' Tristran's fear and distrust of Mark find their justification in the fate reserved for him in certain other versions; cf. 2772-4 n and 4485 n.

2420 'So let him command it.'

2426 *la queue*, the tag of parchment to which the seal was affixed.

2432 'He pressed the stone upon the wax.'

2433 *Tristran* is the indirect object.

2445 *a* 'there is'.

2449 Reid (p. 283) proposes correction of MS *Qanuit* to *La nuit*.

2459 *estre mis en fort* 'reduced to a state of anxiety'; cf. 3073.

2462 'He is not minded to utter a halloo.'

2480 *destoletes* 'side-roads', accusative of direction; for examples of *destoute(s)* with the same meaning, see M^0 glossary.

2491 *li* for *le*.

2495 *lor* 'then'. Lacuna?

2503 *briés* for *brief*.

(c) *Mark's reply* (2510–2680)

SUMMARY

2510– Mark has the letter read to him [by the chaplain].
2520 Great was his joy, for he dearly loved his wife.

2521– [Mark summons his chief barons and asks for their
2530 counsel after they have heard the letter read.

2531– Dinas proposes that this be done and the barons
2612 agree. The chaplain reads the letter aloud: (ll.
2556–2618).

2613– ... 'If reconciliation is refused (it concludes), I
2618 will take Iseut back to Ireland where she was
queen.'

2619– The Cornish barons counsel acceptance on con-
2638 dition that Tristran goes to the king of Gavoie.]

2639– Mark commands [the chaplain] to write the letter
2680 promptly. It is taken to the Croix Rouge. Tristran
takes the letter, to be read by Ogrin: within a
space of [three] days Iseut is to be returned to
Mark [at the Gué Aventuros].

VARIANTS

O 4841–4901

O: As soon as day breaks, Mark has the letter read to him: 'Ogrin bids you take back your wife. Tristran shall bring her to you unaccompanied. You shall receive her lovingly and restore Tristran to favour: *daz mag her wol vorschuldin | mit sime libe swâ he sol.* I ask this of you for God's sake and my own.' Mark tells his counsellors how he found the lovers and swears that Tristran shall never have Iseut to wife. He has a letter written offering to take back Iseut in four days' time, but refusing Tristran his favour because he had done him so much harm and forbidding anyone to ask that he be allowed to remain in the land. He grants Tristran his peace if he brings the queen to the town which he names. At nightfall the letter is hung where Ogrin's messenger had indicated. Tristran fetches it during the night and Ogrin tells him what it contains.

NOTES

2512 The scribe's *qui* might be interpreted as a parenthetical *qui* (< *cūgɪto) 'methinks'.

2514 *Li roi* for *Le roi*, i.e. the name of the king.

2529-30 Cf. the almost identical ll. 631-2.

2531-2 See Introd., Nos. 28 and 31.

2542 *Sel = se* (for *si*) *le*.

2558 *Horlande* is perhaps a scribal variant of *Irlande*. M⁰ glossary: 'Peut-être NORLANDE, qui désignerait le royaume scandinave de Dublin?'

2564 *que* for *quel* (= *que le*).

2565-80 B. Blakey (in *FS* XXI, 99-103) proposes, by way of emendation, an extensive recasting of these lines, involving no substantial change in meaning but producing a smoother rendering to replace what may well be a characteristic specimen of Beroulian syntax and style. Miss Hackett (in *Vinaver Misc.*, 162) has called attention to a close resemblance in construction of a passage in *Girart de Roussillon* (5650-5) to ll. 2568-74.

2569 *Qui* 'whoever', 'if anyone'.

2570 The infinitive (*alegier*) depends loosely on *gage en donge* and introduces *Qu'onques*: 'I am ready to give a pledge... to exculpate her ... to the effect that never...'.

2574 *lui* for *li*.

2577-80 '. . . then have me outlawed before your host; there is not a single baron that I except. There is not a single baron who, to my hurt, may not have me burnt or condemned.' Cf. *Lancelot* 4927 ff.: *Et Meleaganz dist tantost*: '*Nul chevalier ne vos an ost Vers cui la bataille n'anpraigne . . .*'. The passage is suspect, but the extensive emendations undertaken by Muret (following up a suggestion of Acher's in respect of *laisier*) seem overbold; cf. Tanquerey, *Rom.* LVI, 121.

2589 *G'en(n)*. Professor Woledge has pointed out that the doubling of the consonant is frequently found in Western MSS: it would therefore have been more consistent to maintain the double *nn* here and at l. 732; cf. 1524.

2593 *li* might be interpreted as the tonic fem. pron.; but it may be the atonic dat. (= Yvein, understood) for *la li*.

2604 *estoit* is to be taken as impersonal, followed by oblique *vostre pleisir* used as an indirect object; cf. *soit vostre gré* (2802).

2608-9 'But if you are persuaded in another sense, not to desire my service . . .'.

2631-2 The scribe wrote what appears to be *ganoie*, the form adopted in M⁰; but he clearly intended *gauoie*, the failure to distinguish *u* from *n* being very common in the MS (e.g. *noie* for *uoie* in 2636). It is true that Eilhart describes Tristran, after the parting from Iseut, as taking service with the king of *Ganôje* (4997) before proceeding to *Britanja* (which for Eilhart is the part of Britain over which Arthur rules). But *Gavoie* is certainly to be identified with the *Galvoie* of Chrétien's *Perceval*, which is the French form of *Galweya* (modern Galloway), and the emendation of *cornoz* to *escoz* is necessary. See the note to 2246 and Loomis, *Arthurian Tradition*, p. 457.

2634 'And you may have such reports concerning him that you will summon him to come back: otherwise we shall not know whither he goes.'

2653 *La Blanche Lande*; see the note to l. 3268.

2658-62 Note that Iseut is pardoned, but not Tristran: for the legal implications, see Jonin, p. 77.

2664 *rois . . . a*. Muret's emendation appears reasonable; the scribe may have omitted the titulus over *a*, but *croire a Deu* is acceptable and has been adopted in M⁴.

2679 *La* is the adverb 'there'. The direct pronoun object pronoun (*la*) is understood; but *li* may be the tonic fem. form used as a direct object. Cf. 2593 n.

(d) Preparations for the restitution (2681–2744)

SUMMARY

2681–   [Tristran regrets their parting and proposes an
2693   exchange of pledges.

2694– Iseut asks for Husdent and promises her ring: she
 2724 will obey the summons of any messenger bearing
       it.
2725– They make the exchange and Tristran kisses Iseut
 2732 in token of their pledges.
2733– Ogrin proceeds to the Mount to purchase raiment
 2744 and a palfrey for the queen.]

VARIANTS

O 4902–4913

O: Tristran prepares for the restitution. Ogrin gives him such poor
linen as he can provide. Tristran is now prepared to take Iseut to the
meeting-place.

NOTES

2683–4 'It must be done because of the distress you
have suffered so grievously on my account.' Tanquerey's
defence of the scribe's *fors* is unconvincing.

2704 'Since the law was promulgated [on Mount
Sinai].'

2704–6 In *O* (4984 ff.) Tristran, upon restoring Iseut
to Mark, entrusts his dog to her, asking her to look after
him, to see him every day and to think of Tristran as she
does so. There is no mention of a ring. Iseut takes the
dog in her arms, and it is perhaps significant that it is
subsequently referred to as a *hundelîn* and never named
Hudent. The *hundelîn* reappears later (6343 ff.) when it is
borne in a litter past Tristran and Kaherdin as they lie
hidden. It is taken from the litter and fondled by Iseut,
who had been warned of their presence by Dinas. The
ring is first referred to in this context, Dinas having been
given it as a token of recognition by Tristran, for (the
poet adds) it had been given to Tristran and by Iseut,
and she would be sure to recognize it.—In *Fb* both the
giving of the ring (221–3, 530) and its recognition by
Iseut (538) are related and Hudent, who had remained

in Iseut's keeping, recognized Tristran and convinced Iseut of the *fou*'s real identity. *Fo* is in substantial agreement with *Fb*.

From the fact that in *O* this dog is never called *Hudent* (*Ûtant*), that it is obviously a lap-dog (*hundelîn*) rather than a hunting-dog, and from the role it is made to play subsequently it seems clear that Eilhart has been influenced by Petit-Crû and its role as preserved in Gottfried. In Beroul (as in the two *Folies*) it is Hudent that is entrusted to Iseut, and lines 2702–6 can hardly serve as more than evidence of Beroul's familiarity with Petit-Crû, whose magic bell (according to Thomas) brought joy to all. While it is therefore highly improbable that Beroul's narrative ever included an incident such as that narrated by Eilhart (6343 ff.), he clearly intended (even if he did not carry out his intention) to treat an episode in which the ring and Hudent would serve as means of recognition or identification.

2708 *jaspe vert*. In *Fb* it is an emerald, which may or may not have some connection with the ring 'o esmeraudes planteïz' given to Iseut by Mark (*B* 1813); cf. M⁰, p. lxxv.

2716 Cf. *Fb* 220.

2719 *il* (i.e. the messenger); cf. 2796.

2729 *de gerredon* 'as recompense', 'in exchange'.

2730 'She removes it from her finger and places it upon his.' Cf. *L'Escoufle* 4617: ... *Tristan Qui en ot .i. gardé maint an Por l'amor la roïne Ysont.*

2731–2 *par la saisine* 'as a token of possession', each of the lovers having been given 'seisin' of the token given by the other.

2733 J. Loth (*Contrib.*, p. 87) demonstrated that the *Mont* can only be St. Michael's Mount in Cornwall. It was well known for its annual fair in the Middle Ages,[1]

---

[1] However, it should be noted that Eilhart, in another context, relates how Pîloise, having been sent by Iseut to seek Tristran's forgiveness, leaves Cornwall for Karahes, near which town he finds Tristran. In due

and this touch of authentic local colour, taken in conjunction with the knowledge of Cornish topography shown by Beroul, might suggest that he had at least visited England.

2735 *Assés* (so Muret) is what one may expect, but it is not necessarily what the poet wrote; *aprés* is here used with the weakened notion of sequence or succession found in the modern use of *puis* (cf. 2463).

2740 *atornez* for *atorné* (?)

2742 *barate*; cf. M⁰ glossary.

2743 *paile* (<PALLIUM), a precious cloth, generally silk and frequently brocaded; but the term was used very loosely to denote a piece of precious silk worn as a tunic or spread out as a carpet (4135, 4188) or hanging (2968), or a garment made of precious material (2987).

(e) Iseut's return announced and the fate of the hostile faction foretold (2745–2764)

SUMMARY

2745–2752 [Mark announces the reconciliation. All the knights and ladies assemble at the Gué Aventuros.
2753–2764 The four felons had their due reward: two perished by the sword, the third by an arrow; the forester was slain by Perinis with a sling. Thus God humbled their fierce pride!]

NOTES

2745–6 'The king has his reconciliation (*s'acorde*) proclaimed throughout Cornwall.'

2748 'Our reconciliation will take place.'

course he asks Tristan (7378) to direct him to the fair of *Sant Michelssteine*, and Eilhart adds that there is a town of the same name in Cornwall and that both towns have fairs on St. Michael's Day. Pîloise makes his purchases at the fair and returns over the sea (7395). Cf. T. Taylor, *St. Michael's Mount*, Cambridge, 1932.

2749 *an ont* misread by the scribe (owing to the difficulty of distinguishing between *n* and *u*) has induced his *auez*; cf. *Pope Misc.*, p. 95.

2752–64 It is upon these lines, described by Muret as 'vers suspects', that much of the argument for dual authorship turns. For the discrepancy between this passage and what precedes (involving the death of one of the three barons), see the note to ll. 581–648. The discrepancy with what follows consists in the fact that the forester is not killed by Perinis with a sling, but by Governal (4045–54). It might be urged, in exculpation of Beroul, that these lines are not so much a prophecy as an indication of the fate he planned for Tristran's enemies and of the action as envisaged by him at that moment. Nor can his use of the past historic mean that he is relating what happened according to his source or sources. The 'prophecy' is in essence imprecatory and can, to that extent, be associated with other passages in which a fate is foretold or envisaged that is at variance with what in fact befalls the hostile barons (e.g. at ll. 2824, 3198–9, 3331–2, 3337), not to mention the minatory maledictions heaped upon them by Iseut (58–59, 430–1), by the citizens (1082) and, what is more pertinent, by the poet himself (1656, 2754, 2891, 3788).

The shameful end foretold (1919) for the forester who had betrayed the lovers is described more specifically in ll. 2760–2, where we are told that he will be killed by Perinis; but in the event, as indicated above, he will meet his death at the hands of Governal. For a humble forester to meet his end in a knightly encounter, surprising as it is, can hardly be regarded as 'morir a grant honte' (1919) although signifying a 'mort crüele' (2760). It would certainly seem that our author is more concerned with the meting out of condign punishment to the enemies of Tristran than with the precise fulfilment of a prognostication.

2755 *quatre* (not *trois*, as emended in Muret's editions

except M⁴), because the forester is associated with the three hostile barons in the 'prophecy' of punishment to come (cf. 2763).

(f) Parting of the lovers (2765–3009)

SUMMARY

2765– [Tristran, wearing his halberk beneath his tunic,
2776   rides with Iseut towards the tents of the king and
        his court.]

2777– T: 'I leave you Husdent, my lady. [Heed my
2791   bidding if I send you a message.'

2792– I: 'The sight of my ring alone will command my
2802   obedience.'

2803– Tristran embraces Iseut.
2804

2805– I: 'Remain with Orri the forester until Mark's
2836   bearing is revealed. The three barons shall yet
        lie dead in the wood; but I fear them. I will
        send you news by Perinis.'

2837– T: 'Woe betide anyone who accuses you.'—I:
2842   'Now I am content.']

2843– Tristran brings Iseut to the king, [with whom is
2868   Dinas of Dinan, and demands due judgement of
        his case.

2869– Mark speaks to his nephew. Andrez of Nicole
2875   advises the king to retain the services of Tristran.

2876– The queen is left with Dinas.
2889

2890– The three barons persuade Mark to demand
2910   Tristran's departure from the court for the space
        of one year.]

2911– Tristran declines Mark's gifts and departs towards
2934   the sea.

2935– [Dinas, the last to leave Tristran, promises to
2952 watch over Iseut.

2953– General rejoicing over the return of Iseut.
2971

2972– Iseut places upon the altar a rich silken cloth of
2994 which was made a chasuble which may still be
seen at St. Samson; so say those who have seen it.

2995– Iseut is received with festive joy in the royal
3009 palace.]

VARIANTS

O 4914–4997; *T* xxix; *G* 17663–18408; *S* lxvi, 24–lxviii, 6; *E* ccxxxiii–
ccxxxviii; *T.r.* 247

O: When Tristran brings Iseut to Mark, the king rejects all his pleadings
to be allowed to remain, saying that Tristran has harmed him too
grievously and cannot make amends: he must leave the court and the
land. Tristran angrily bids him take the queen, saying that he will fare
forth and never plead again for Mark's favour; but let Mark beware if he
fails to cherish his queen. In sorrow he surrenders her whom he loved
so dearly. Mark takes Iseut back: he loved her for many a year. The
lovers part in sadness. Tristran commends his dog to the queen: let her
care for it and, as she sees it every day, think of Tristran. She takes it
tenderly in her arms. Tristran departs to the court of the king of Gânôje,
thence to Britanja. . . . (All further contact with Beroul ceases from this
point.)

In *G* (17663–18408), Mark, immediately after finding the lovers (see
above, p. 191), summons his counsellors and they give the advice they
see Mark desires: namely that the lovers are to be restored to favour.
Governal is sent to fetch them. But their happiness is now precarious
and Mark does not possess Iseut's heart and deludes himself. He finds
the lovers locked in each other's embrace in a bed in the orchard and
departs to bring his barons as witnesses. Tristran, who has seen him
depart, fears the worst and decides that they must part. They bid each
other farewell and Iseut gives Tristran a ring to remind him of their love
and to maintain his constancy. They kiss and part. Mark returning with
his barons is reproved by them and abandons his vengeful thoughts.—*S*
gives a similar though much shorter account, but there is no Governal,
no bed, and Mark is accompanied by the dwarf who waits while Mark
fetches the barons; Mark scolds Iseut but gives up his anger without
comment by the barons.—In *E*, the dwarf discovers Tristran and Iseut.
The barons intercede for Iseut.—In *T.r.*, the lovers are recalled and the
king abandons his suspicions.—In *T* (Cambridge fragment) the dwarf
betrays the lovers to Mark and accompanies him.

NOTES

2771 *merc* 'boundary stone', here perhaps the stone marking the ford.

2772–4 Tristran takes the precaution of wearing his halberk beneath his tunic (*bliaut*), contrary to the usual practice of wearing the halberk over the tunic when proceeding to combat. In the Prose Romance (Loeseth, para. 546) the suspicions of Tristran are only too well founded, as he is there described as having been treacherously killed by Mark shortly after the restitution of Iseut. In the view of some critics this is the denouement of the primitive version (cf. 4485n).

2773 *de soi* 'concerning himself', 'for himself'.

2776 *li* for *le*.

2780 It is true that Eilhart (4990–1) reads: *ab ich ûch icht lîp sî daz tût an dem brackin schîn*, which would support the emendation proposed by Muret; but *l'amastes* (restored in M⁴) is not necessarily scribal. Translate: 'If ever you bore him affection, show that affection now.'

2794–6 In *Fo* it is the sight of the ring that eventually convinces Iseut of the identity of Tristan *fou* (538–42; cf. 221–3). It is reasonable to suppose, though not certain, that Beroul made a similar use of the ring in a portion of the romance now lost: cf. *Fb* 221–3, 527–37. See note to ll. 2704–6.

2796 *il* (i.e. the messenger); cf. 2719.

2801–2 'According to my honour and loyalty and what I know to be your wish.'

2807 Literally: 'make me, then, to understand', 'make, then, your meaning clear to me'.

2810–46 The repetition of the farewell scene with the exchange of tokens enables the poet (perhaps of set purpose) to introduce a modification, namely Iseut's request that Tristran should remain near at hand for a while, in the 'cellier' of the forester Orri. In doing so, the poet may have had in mind the grotto in which, according to the Thomas versions, Tristran and Iseut sheltered while in the forest (cf. ll. 2820–1); but there may also be some confusion with the role of Ogrin. The forester who in R (pp. 360–2) shelters Tristran plays the role which Beroul appears here to assign to Orri.

2814 *lois*, f. *losche* (Mod.Fr. *louche*): i.e. Iseut desires Tristran to remain in the kingdom until it becomes clear whether Mark will yield to resentment or adopt an equivocal attitude (such as he has shown on more than one occasion). The alternatives are not mutually exclusive or antithetic, nor are they completely so if we adopt Muret's otherwise plausible emendation (*iriez ou voirs*), or Holden's *le roi : coi*, and it is by no means certain that the poet intended them to be so. Cf. J. Bourciez, 'Note sur le couple *lois-losche*', in *Mélanges Roques* I (1950), 21–25.

2815 Acher's emendation to *Get prié* (adopted in Muret's earlier editions) is not necessary: *Gel prié* 'I ask it', the neuter *le* anticipating the following clause; *prier qqch. à qqn.* is possible as late as the seventeenth century (cf. Littré).

2822–7 These lines, interrupting the narrative as they do, may well have been displaced from their original context after l. 2836, as conjectured by Muret. In that case the line originally rhyming with 2821 may have been dropped and l. 2836 may have been substituted for the displaced l. 2822. In the process two or more lines must have been omitted after 2836.

2825 'May Hell open and swallow them!'

2828 *boron*. Tobler questioned the meaning 'cabane'. For *buron, buiron*; cf. *Lancelot* 6447: *Meison ne buiron ne repeire*.

2842 'You have advised me to good purpose.'

2849 *qui = cui* (obl.) or *qu'i* or *qu(i) i*?

2863 *se ge t'en sueffre* 'if I suffer you', i.e. 'your bidding', perhaps with the meaning 'as I . . .', or, with a heavy stop after *cort* (or even after *autrement*), and taking the phrase with the following line: 'If I submit to your pleasure (and in token of it), then burn me in sulphur if I am condemned.' Cf. an identical use of the verb in a similar context in ll. 793–6. Muret's emendation undoubtedly produces a smoother version but alters the meaning. See 2242 n.

2866 Lacuna; or is it possible to interpret this as an elliptical exclamation, the sentence remaining uncompleted?

2868 *Loenoi*. There can be little doubt that (as proposed by F. Lot) for Beroul this is still the traditional designation of the region of Lothian. The possibility that it may at some time have been a name applied to the region of Caerleon (upon Usk) has also been mooted. It was later confused with the region of Léon in Brittany. Cf. 2246 n.

2869 ff. It is reasonable to suppose that the nephew referred to in l. 2869 is Tristran and that the conversation concerns the undertaking Tristran has just given that he will proceed to Loenois if the king does not wish to retain him. A certain Audrez (perhaps to be regarded as the scribe's imperfect rendering of Andrez), a native of Lincoln, advises the king to retain Tristran's services, contrary (be it noted) to the advice tendered by the three hostile barons (2890–2906). It is reasonable also to identify this personage with the Andrez mentioned in l. 3877 (who in company with Dinas attends upon the queen), and, if we accept the emendation, with the Andret of l. 3783.

The fact that in ll. 4035–44 a personage of the same name meets his death at the hands of Tristran in circumstances which suggest that he was a sworn enemy, might therefore appear surprising, although it is not unknown for more than one character to bear the same name in medieval romances. (In *Gaydon*, for example, as many as five bear identical names, and Beroul himself bestows the name of one of the knights of the Round Table (Ivain) upon the chief of the lepers.) In our romance the duality undoubtedly arose from Beroul's familiarity with a version or versions of the Tristran story in which Andret appeared in the equivocal role he plays in Eilhart, where he is the leader of the hostile faction (3157 ff.) and at the same time a member of the queen's retinue and a sort of guardian or lord-in-waiting; see above, pp. 119–20. He is consistently hostile to Tristran, and the fact that they are both nephews of the king and that Andret would presumably be next in line of succession to Tristran may originally have contributed to this, although there is no explicit reference in any version to that effect. But see 126 n.

It is possible, then, that Beroul, baffled by the apparent contradictions in the role of Andret (Antrêt or Antrêd in O), created two characters, one who is well disposed to the lovers and whom he finds it necessary to distinguish by describing him as 'nez de Nicole', the other an enemy, although not a leader or even a member of a faction. It is not clear what significance, if any, is to be attached to the fact that at l. 2870 the scribe clearly wrote *audrez* (which should have been noted in the Variants), and at ll. 3877 and 4035 he wrote *andrez*.

In R, the only other primary version in which Andret (varr. Audret, Sandret) appears, he is a nephew of Mark and an enemy of the lovers, whom he denounces and pursues with relentless hatred. In MS 103 and some other prose versions Andret, when he tried to board the boat which was to take Iseut to Tristran in Brittany, was struck with an oar by Genes, the master of the vessel, and left to drown. In other versions his death is not recounted (cf. Loeseth, p. 380). In *T.r.*, Mark has him killed after the death of Tristran.

In O, Andrêt is not mentioned again after the incident of Tristran *fou* (8772).

If we confine ourselves to what Beroul, deviating once again from other versions, in fact tells us, there is no compelling reason for assuming, with Golther (*op. cit.*

1907, p. 105 n), that *Audrez* in l. 2870 is a scribal error for *Dinas*.

For discussions of the question and the parallelism between Mark, Tristran, Andret on the one hand and Arthur, Gauvain, Modred on the other, see Muret in *Rom.* XVI, 319 ff.; Golther (1907), pp. 34, 105; Schoepperle, pp. 241, 268.

Bédier (II, 120) attributes the name to the Bretons or the Welsh, and Hertz (Anm. 94) regards *Andret* as a corruption of a Breton *Audret*, while for J. Loth (p. 93) *Andret* is English and *Audret* a non-Breton variant. M⁰ reads *Audret*, *Audrez* throughout, while later editions read *Andret*, *Andrez*, but in the Index: 'Andrez *ou* Audrez 2870'.

2873-4 The poet probably used the verb (*asouploie*) intransitively, *le cuer* being used erroneously for *li cuers* (but cf. Introd., p. 20): 'He is very near to granting his request, his heart is greatly softened.' Cf. Godefroy, s.v. *assouploier*: 'Guillaume l'ot, le cuers l'en asouploie' (*Aliscans*).

2875 M¹: *se trait*.

2880-7 For a description of the items of apparel mentioned in this passage (*chape, tunique, bliaut, mantel, robe*) and in ll. 3568-83 (*chemise, cotes, hueses*) and ll. 3725-50 (*paile, sorchauz, aumuce*), see Schultz I, 244-320 and 330-59 (fabrics) and Joan Evans, *Dress in Medieval France*, passim.

2883 As indicated in this line, the *bliaut* was a sort of over-tunic. It was worn by men (cf. 2772) as well as women (1146).

2890 Note that here again the hostile barons are three in number; cf. 2752-64 n.

2909-10 'The barons return [to Tristran] and in the name of the king give his decision.'

2911 For the special appeal of this scene of the parting of the lovers and its exploitation by later writers, see Hertz³, Anm. 127.

2915–6 Jonin (p. 167) calls attention to a very similar description in *Thèbes* 948–9. See also the description of Iseut at the Judgement in Gottfried 15647 ff.

2918 *tant cuer* for *tanz cuers*.

2924 The *malle (maille)* was worth half a denier or 1/24 of a sou.

2925 'I go with the greatest possible joy.'

2926 The reference is clearly to the 'roi de Gavoie' mentioned specifically in ll. 2631–2.

2930–2. Cf. *Eneas* 8385–7 for a very similar description.

2947 'He declares that this is a noble leave-taking.'

2952 Note that Tristran does not go to the king of Gavoie, as the Cornish barons had counselled (2631), nor, as he had undertaken, to the king of Frise (2608–12) or to Loenoi (2868), but first of all towards the sea (2929) and then to the forester Orri, as Iseut had proposed (2917–8). In O (4995–7) Tristran goes to the king of Gânôje, and it is perhaps significant that Eilhart adds that it would be too long a tale to relate what Tristran did there and proceeds to describe his departure for Britanja (5020). After the handing over of Iseut *B* and *O* diverge completely.

2966 *lui* for *li*, the tonic feminine form.

2973 *Saint Sanson*. Lantyan, with which J. Loth identified Beroul's Lancïen, the residence of King Mark, lies in the parish of St. Samson on the west bank of the Fowey. The reference to a chasuble (made from the rich cloth presented by Iseut, 2991) which could still be seen in the church of St. Samson (2992–5) may be of Beroul's invention; but it is possible that the popularity of the legend and its localization in Cornwall had led the church to identify the chasuble with one of the relics in its possession.

The saint, who is Saint Samson of Dol, is commemorated in various place-names in Cornwall, through which he passed on his way from Wales to Brittany. The island on which Tristran's fight with the Morholt took place is called *l'isle saint Sanson* in the Prose Romance (Loeseth, pp. 11 and 20), in Chrétien's *Erec* (1243) and in *Merlin* II, 240. In *Fb* 28, Mark swears 'par saint Sanson de Cornoaille'.

Muret pointed out (in the Index to his CFMA edition) that, when the poet wrote, there was no bishop of Cornwall, the old diocese having been amalgamated with that of Devon in 1040. See J. Loth, *Contrib.*, p. 74 and the references in P. Rickard, *Britain in Medieval French Literature* (1956), 98–100.

2974 The scribe seems at times to represent Iseut as having her own following of knights (*si baron*), and Tristran as also having his (cf. 665 n).

2987 *orfrois* (AURUM PHRYGIUM) 'cloth embroidered with gold'.

2997 *contor*; see 3385 n.

2998 *palais haimçor*, the *palais* being the tallest of the complex of structures which made up a twelfth-century castle. It contained, besides various domestic offices, the *sale*, broadly the 'reception' room, and above it the *chanbre(s)* or private apartments; see 104 n.

V. JUDGEMENT—THE SCENES AT THE FORD—THE OATH
(3010–4266)

(a) Tristran in Orri's cellar (3010–3027)

SUMMARY

3010– [Tristran is sheltered by Orri and receives news 3027 of Iseut through Perinis.]

NOTES

3027 *soit*, scribal variant of *sait* as in 3441, 4458; cf. *soiz* (1873).

(b) The hostile barons rebuffed (3028-3147)

SUMMARY

3028– [One day, while hunting, the three barons propose
3054 to Mark that Iseut should clear herself of the charge or be sent away.

3055– Mark indignantly refuses and threatens them with
3147 the recall of Tristran. They promise to desist, but Mark refuses to heed them and all three— Godoïne, Guenelon and Danalain—retire to their castles with ill-will.]

NOTES

3044 *S'* = *se* for *si* (<SIC): 'and so you are blamed for it'. Cf. l. 316.

3048 *Que on* = *Qu'onc* (cf. *Pope Miscellany*, p. 92): 'They desire her to clear herself [of the charge] that Tristran ever had her love.' M⁴ emends to *Qu'o* in view of l. 130, which does not however present an exact parallel.

3056-9 'For a long time you have not ceased to blame her; now I hear her accused of something which might well be left as it is (sc. 'and not be brought up again').'

3067 'and am I now to drive forth my wife?'

3068-9 'A hundred curses in the teeth of him who bade me part with him!' For the rhyme, see Introd., No. 25 n.

3071-4 'You importune me; this distresses me. How strange it is that there should be such contention! If he did wrong, he suffers for it. You care not for my pleasure.'

3088 M⁴ restores the MS reading: *soz*, and interprets *larri* as 'terre inculte au flanc d'une colline'.

3090 *Li rois* for *Le roi*.

3092 *deputaire* = *de put aire*; cf. *debonnaire*.

3093 *Bien tost* might be interpreted 'perhaps', but 'soon' is the more likely meaning here.

3102 M⁴: *La sunt venu; tost les destot.*

3106 'In an evil hour was this discussion joined', i.e. 'Woe to them that they have come again to importune the king.'

3113 It might have been wiser to preserve the MS reading, since *consentir* was sometimes used, with a personal object, in the sense of 'endure', 'suffer', 'bear with', 'humour', as the examples in Tobler-Lommatzsch show.

3114-6 'A curse upon whatever he has under his belt (i.e. whatever or whoever he be) he who hates you; he will have to leave you—woe to him if he is resentful towards you.' An oblique reference to Tristran (?). Tanquerey (p. 119) finds fault with *o toi* and suggests the emendation *Ja mar est qi s'en m.* or *Ja mal ait qi s'en m.*

3120 'You will see that we keep perfect silence on the subject.'

3128-9 'You were unwilling to present your shield (to fight) and wish to remain on foot (and not to mount your charger).'

3132 *Saint André.* See Introduction, p. 32.

3134-5 'You have planted a pain in my heart which will not depart therefrom within the year.'

3138-9 There can be no doubt that, as F. Lot showed (in *Rom.* XXXV (1906), 615-7), *Godoïne* is Germanic. The name was given by Beroul to one of the hostile barons because of the reputation as a traitor of the Saxon Godwin, who died, after a short period of exile, in 1053 and was succeeded by his son Harold. This might be regarded as further evidence that Beroul was writing for an Anglo-Norman public and may have spent part of his life in England. The occurrence of the name in Continental records (cf. Bédier II, 123 and M⁰ glossary) hardly invalidates such a conclusion.

The second baron owes his name to the arch-traitor Guenelon of the *Chanson de Roland* (cf. Bédier II, 124 and F. Lot in *Rom.* XXXV, 100-1): he earns the special enmity of Gauvain as 'li plus coverz' of the three (3462).

Denoalen is a Celtic name and, according to F. Lot (*Rom.* XXXV, 606) was, to judge from the spelling, borrowed from Brittany. Lot's conjecture that he may have been a personage known as a 'traitor' to the Breton notables established in considerable numbers in England between 1066 and 1203 is very plausible. See also J. Loth, *Contrib.*, p. 99.

The fact that the hostile barons are provided with names so late in the narrative need not surprise us unduly. Beroul's transformation of the hostile faction into principal actors in the drama, with a different role and a different fate from those in his source or sources, is a cumulative process. It is not until l. 581 that they are presented as three in number and, with a minor exception at l. 641 (where one of the barons is described as embracing the dwarf Frocin) and the 'interpolated' killing of one of the faction by Governal (1656–1746) and the prophecy (2756–7), they act and are treated as a group: but in anticipation of their more individualized role (3457 ff.), the poet felt constrained to provide each of them with an appropriate name. The occasion and manner of his doing so underlines once again Beroul's independence and his instinct for giving a lively and even a dramatic turn to his narrative: the attention of his audience is not allowed to flag but is arrested and heightened.

3141 'They could not obtain satisfaction.'

(c) Iseut agrees to her 'escondit' (3148–3282)

SUMMARY

3148– [Mark returns to his 'tower' at Tintagel.
3153

3154– Iseut, judging from his fierce mien that Tristran
3170 has been taken, falls in a faint.

3171– Mark comforts her and tells her of the hostile
3199   barons' importunity and his determination to re-
       call Tristran.

3200– Iseut questions Mark, telling him that he is her
3264   sole protector and agrees to clear herself once and
       for all by a judgement of her own devising, in the
       presence of Arthur and his court.

3265– I: 'The Cornish are treacherous. Summon them
3276   all to la Blanche Lande. King Arthur will not
       fail to come there at my call.

3277– Mark appoints the day, a fortnight hence. The
3282   three barons welcome the news.]

VARIANTS

T xxiv; *G* 15228–15537; *S* lv, 46–lvii; *E* cciii; *T.r.* 236, 28–238, 9

In the Thomas versions Iseut is required by Mark to make her 'escondit' immediately after the discovery of the blood in the bed (see above, p. 135); cf. Bédier II, 251.

G: Mark, finding the blood in Iseut's bed and in Tristran's, but no footprint on the floor, is perplexed and sends for his barons. On their advice a council is summoned at London, so that the prelates learned in God's law may be consulted. Mark asks the assembled barons to help him put an end to the scandal which is being bruited about. As they deliberate vainly, the Bishop of Thamîse, a wise and aged counsellor, gets up and, leaning on his crozier, speaks as one of the peers of the realm: 'Tristran and Iseut have till now been accused only on suspicion and have been convicted of no crime. How can you condemn them and punish them in their honour and in their persons? No one has openly charged them and substantiated the charge according to law and custom. Yet the rumour is so rife that you will not share bed and board with Iseut until she has cleared herself. If she is to be further charged, let her appear before us and let us hear both your charge and her defence.' Mark agrees, and Iseut is sent for. The bishop tells her in the name of the king, regretfully, of the evil suspicions, of the necessity for a hearing and answer, even though she be innocent. Iseut acknowledges the existence of the rumours, but she is not surprised: she is alone, she says, and has no kinsman to help her. She is willing to submit to whatever trial they advise so that she may be acquitted. At Mark's request she solemnly declares her readiness to undergo the ordeal of the red-hot iron in six weeks' time, as demanded, in the town of Karliûne. The council breaks up.

S gives substantially the same account, but the bishop is merely 'an aged bishop' and he refers to the suspicion having rested upon the lovers for more than twelve months; the ordeal is to take place at Korbinburg in one month's time.

E sums up in a few lines: Tristran has fled; in London one day Mark wishes Iseut to clear herself; a bishop is the intermediary; Iseut thinks to clear herself by the ordeal of the hot iron and consents to this.

In *T.r.*, Mark, a prey to suspicion, sends for the archbishop on the following morning. The latter declares it to be unlawful to charge and condemn to death anyone on suspicion; he advises that Iseut be summoned to appear at the Petrone Vermiglio (in the island of Matufer), in which stone are enshrined holy relics and 'la vertudiosa pietra della itropica, la quale non lascia persona mentire'. Upon this stone she shall swear that she never did the king any wrong; but, 'per più certezza', she shall take in hand the red-hot iron. And Mark is to promise that she will not be put to death, if she be found guilty, but condemned to live on bread and water in a prison. The king having agreed, the archbishop informs Iseut and tells her that she is to appear at the said stone in ten days' time.

NOTES

3150 *Tintajol*; see 1040 n.

3155 Iseut waits upon the king, relieving him of his sword.

3157 *Prist l'a la main*; cf. l. 1220.

3162 The king has come to Iseut unaccompanied by so much as a squire; that such a failure to provide himself with an escort or suite was contrary to custom and etiquette is made abundantly clear in ll. 1926–40.

3165–6 Tanquerey (p. 121) is reluctant to attribute the rhyme *denz* : *loinz* to the poet and proposes *denz* : *lenz*. Cf. Introd., No. 26.

3171 If we assume (with Acher) that *Q'* is an erroneous scribal addition, it becomes unnecessary to assume a lacuna; but a more acceptable emendation would be to intervert ll. 3169 and 3170, as Reid suggests.

3173 *mal* for *mals*.

3177 *si* (for *qui*) is no doubt induced partly by *si* of the following line, in which *aseüre* is used intransitively (for other examples of this use, see Tobler-Lommatzsch).

3179 *rest asouagié* (impers. ?): 'then she is once again reassured'.

3188–90 'If I do not give them the lie and do not drive them out of my kingdom, the felons will nevermore fear my hostility (i.e. any threat of punitive action on my part)'.

3193 'My mind is made up'; lit. 'There is no longer any question of changing my mind'.

3220 M⁴: *Par quels.*

3224 'What if I do make it (*l'escondit*)?'; cf. 3235–8.

3227 Iseut proposes some delay (no doubt so that she may warn Tristran); Mark deprecates this, suggesting that any delay will be found long.

3232 'So help me God!'

3233 ff. Jonin (pp. 79–105) has shown how closely the whole of the judgement scene in Beroul accords with custom law and how its various aspects can be paralleled from legal theory and practice, civil and ecclesiastic. Thus, the demand of the hostile barons that Iseut should clear herself of the presumption of guilt which rests upon her is shown to be justified in law, and even her stipulation that she should herself formulate (*deviser*) the oath to be taken and the equivocation with which she invests it, and finally her request for the attendance of Arthur and his suite, as sureties and guarantors, find not only close parallels but actual antecedents in the customaries and other records of legal proceedings. Once again, therefore, Beroul evinces, in addition to a particular interest in the law, a sound knowledge of the legal forms and procedures of his time, a preoccupation which he shares with Marie de France and other writers of the age of the Plantagenets.

3237 'before the end of the third day'.

3240 'because of the distress to which I am reduced'; i.e. once again Iseut reminds Mark that she is without the support of kinsmen and can turn to no one in her extremity except himself (and Tristran). There is no compelling reason to assume (with Muret) that the poet had written *desraignement* (for *desresnement*); cf. Tobler-

Lommatzsch, s.v. *destreignement*. '. . . who because of my distress would stir up war and strife; yet this would please me well.'

3244 'If they demand my oath or if they require trial by judgement, they will not wish it of such a harsh kind (let them fix the term) but that I will perform it.'

3248 ff. Iseut's request for the attendance of Arthur has been shown by Jonin (pp. 85 ff.) to be in accordance with custom and to be merely an application of *la plévine*, in virtue of which a pledge or surety guarantees the carrying out of an undertaking entered upon or accepted in his presence (cf. ll. 3361 and 3445).

3249 *Li* for *Le*.

3251 'If anyone were to wish to calumniate me thereafter, those would be ready to take up my defence who will have witnessed my acquittal.'

3253 In the Prose Romance Mark is Arthur's vassal and seeks his intervention: we have here perhaps a reflection of this when Iseut asks for Arthur's intervention.

3254 '. . . against anyone, be he Cornishman or Saxon.'

3265 For this 'appreciation' of the Cornish character, cf. F. J. Tanquerey, in *MAe*, VI (1937), 1–20.

3268 *Blanche Lande* has been identified by J. Loth (*Contrib.*, pp. 80–82 and 125) with an important manor on the right bank of the Truro river opposite Malpas (cf. 1320 n), called *Blaunchelound* in the earliest document known to him. Loth considers that *Blanche Lande* may be the translation of a Cornish name and that it was one of the residences of the ancient kings of Dumnonia, i.e. Devon and Cornwall. It is attested as the seat of the Alba Landa family in the *Extenta manorum* of 1345 cited by Loth, p. 80.

Tristran crosses Blanche Lande when he bears Mark's letter from la Croiz Rouge to Ogrin's cell. According to l. 3298 it lies a short distance beyond Mal Pas. As the scene of the jousting and Iseut's ambiguous oath, it would be reached by the kings and their company by crossing the Gué Aventuros (i.e. Mal Pas), while Tristran, coming from the direction of Orri's *celier*, would take up his position on a mound on the western side (cf. 1320 n and 2653).

3280 *naïs* 'natives', i.e. native Cornishmen, the three hostile barons. Cf. 1662 n. Corr. *as trois*(?). M¹ and M²: *as trois eschis.*

3281 *Que* for *Qui.*

(d) Iseut sends word to Tristran (3283–3364)

SUMMARY

3283– Iseut sends word [by Perinis] to Tristran asking
3327 him to appear [at the Mal Pas near La Blanche Lande] disguised [as a leper. Let him beg alms and keep them for her.

3328– Tristran agrees and reassures Iseut through
3364 Perinis.]

VARIANTS

T xxiv; *G* 15538–15563; *S* lviii, 1–5; *T.r.* 238, 9–32

G: Iseut, having agreed to the ordeal but being conscious of her guilt, sends a letter to Tristran asking him to be at Karliûne when her ship lands there and to wait for her on the shore.—In *S*, he is to be at a ford in the river (unnamed) and disguised, on the day she names; he is to carry her over the river from the ship and she will then tell him a secret.—In *T.r.*, she sends for Tristran who assures her that he will find a way out. He goes to the house of a friendly citizen, divests himself of all his arms except his sword and crosses over to the island of Mantufer.

NOTES

3295 'at the approach to the bridge': the footbridge consisting of one (3297) or more (3295) planks.

3296 There is no other reference to any such incident.

3299–3302 All the items of equipment of Tristan-*ladre*

are taken from real-life lepers, including the goblet (*henap*) suspended from the neck by a thong (*coroie*).

3301 It is by striking the *henap* with the *botele* that Tristran is to attract the attention of passers-by (cf. 3691-2). Does *dedesoz* imply that he is to have the bottle secreted beneath his cloak, or merely suspended lower than the *henap*?

3311 Other versions refer more explicitly to a mercenary trait in the character of Iseut; cf. 231 n. For another interpretation, see Jonin, p. 119.

3313 *par soi* 'by himself', i.e. in confidence; cf. 1326 n.

3324 *Il dui*; cf. 2938. As a parallel for the rhyme *mains* : *frans*, Muret[3] cites Gottfried, 18713-4: *Isôt als blansche mains* : *Kâedin li frains*. See Introd., p. 14.

3329 'He swears by whatever is within his reach (power): woe to them that they ever had this thought; it cannot fail to come to pass: they will yet lose their heads which shall hang from the gibbet.' For another interpretation see M[4] (Notes Critiques).

3332 *feste*. The word has been translated too loosely in the Glossary. In the present context it denotes the beam or crosspiece of the gallows, which rested upon the two uprights called *forches* because they were forked (cf. 1737). Cf. *La Chanson de Guillaume* (ed. D. McMillan), ll. 341-2:

> Quatre larruns i pendirent bouche a boche;
> Bas ert le fest, curtes erent les furches.

The term *forches* was used, as in this line, in the general sense of 'gallows' or 'gibbet'; also in l. 42.

3340-1 'Tell her that I have contrived everything to save her from [the predicament of] the oath.' Cf. 3565.

3347 *au chief* (sc. *des planches*); cf. 3295.

3349 'I will have his alms, if I can get any out of him.'

3352 Cf. 2820-1.

3354 *moi* 'may-tree, branch of may'. The scribe may have confused the noun with the pronoun *moi* and hence substituted *boces* for *botons*, having in mind the disfigurement referred to in l. 3306.

3362 The interpretation of *greignoient* as the 3 pl. impf. ind. of *greignier* (= *graignier* in Tobler-Lommatzsch) 'grind one's teeth', abandoned in reprints of this edition, should be restored.

3364 'Go with God', 'God be with you'.

(e) Iseut's summons to Arthur (3365-3562)

SUMMARY

3365– [Perinis goes to Caerleon and thence to Isneldone;
3396 there a shepherd directs him to the Round Table where sits King Arthur.

3397– Arthur declares himself ready to serve Iseut.
3410

3411– Perinis tells Arthur, in the presence of his knights,
3447 of the 'escondit' which is now required of Iseut and of her request that Arthur and his followers shall be at the Gué Aventuros to witness it in eight days' time.

3448– His message excites pity and indignation: Gauvain
3494 claims Guenelon as his victim, Gerflet claims Godoïne, Evain (son of Uriën) claims Dinoalen.

3495– Perinis compliments Arthur, who commands his
3519 knights to be prepared on the day appointed.

3520– Arthur and his retinue escort Perinis.
3537

3538– Arthur sends his message to Iseut and reminds
3552 her of a former meeting(?): ll. 3546–3548.

3553– Perinis describes his errand to Iseut at Lidan.]
3562

NOTES

3368 *Cuerlion* is Caerleon-upon-Usk, one of the residences of King Arthur. J. Loth (p. 65) called attention to the existence of several localities called Carlyon in Cornwall, but none of these has ever been connected with Arthur, and it is significant that Tristran describes himself at l. 3758 as 'de Carloon, filz d'un Galois'. In Marie de France's *Chevrefoil*, South Wales is described as Tristran's native country.

3370 'He should fare all the better for it', 'He should have his reward for it.'

3373 *Isneldone* is to be identified with the city variously designated as Snaudune, Snauedoun, Senaudon, Sinaudon, Sinadon. According to Froissart (ed. Kerwyn de Lettenhove II, 313) the fortress at Stirling was considered locally to have been called Sinaudon in the days of King Arthur and to have been a resort of the knights of the Round Table, and the identification of Isneldone with Stirling is defended by K. Brugger (*ZFSL* XLV, 412 n). But Loomis (*Arthurian Tradition*, p. 110 n) maintains that 'there is no evidence whatever that this was an ancient name for Stirling', and he leaves little doubt that Isneldone is the ancient city and fortress of Snowdon (= Welsh Caer Seint), the 'cité' of Senaudon in Wales mentioned by Renaud de Beaujeu in *Le Bel Inconnu* and described by him as 'la Cité Gaste' or 'la Gaste Cités' (3390).

It would seem that the poet pictured Lancïen, Orri's *celier*, Cuerlion and Isneldone as being within fairly easy reach of each other, if we may go by the somewhat loose indications furnished, for example, at lines 3318, 3367-8, 3374-83, 3557-8. The romances show Arthur changing residence with a frequency not unlike that which characterized the Plantagenet kings. It is not surprising, therefore, that Perinis should seek him in vain at Cuerlion and be directed to Isneldone. Our romance shows Arthur successively at Carduel (Carlisle), Cuerlion, Isneldone, and Dureaume (Durham).

3380 *tornoie* 'turns', 'rotates'; cf. J. L. Weston, 'A hitherto unconsidered aspect of the Round Table', in

Mélanges Wilmotte, Paris, 1910, pp. 883–94. Miss Weston concluded that Arthur's Round Table was a Turning Table for certain of the early romance writers, including Layamon, according to whom it was made by a cunning workman of Cornwall.

3385 The *contors* (*comitores*) ranked below the *vavasors*, both being lesser vassals. Cf. B. Woledge, 'Bons vavasseurs, et mauvais sénéchaux, *Mélanges Rita Lejeune*, II (1968), 1263–77.

3396 Assuming that *barnage* is singular, the plural *seoient* is unexceptionable in Old French (agreement according to sense with a collective noun); not so the plural *tuit* (restored in M⁴). One cannot, however, rule out the possibility that, although *barnage*, when denoting the barons collectively, is normally used in the singular, it may here have been intended as a nominative plural and correctly reproduced by the scribe. See, for example, *Li Quatre Livre des Reis* (ed. Curtius), p. 224: 'É li barnages de la terre fírent lur réi de Joáz, sun fiz.' Emendation is therefore uncalled for.

3421 'in respect of fidelity'; cf. 3362.

3422 The authenticity of this line is rendered suspect by the identical rhyme and by the presence of the analogical feminine *tele*; but the repetition of *loiauté* may be intentional and *tele* may be in the nature of a licence, a concession to popular speech. 'Never did any one decide to take up arms in respect of such loyalty.'

3426 *Il n'a = Il n'i a*, with the nom. *frans hon* (cf. Introd., No. 37). *François* is a correction suggested by the form *francier*, which is however perhaps a scribal substitution for *Cornot* (cf. 3254); J. Loth (pp. 70–71) conjectured *Ireis*.

3428 *Ge oi*. For the non-elision, cf. 1534. An alternative interpretation is: *G'oï ja dire . . .* (cf. 1576); but the present tense is normal (cf. *ç'oi dire* 425, etc.).

3428–9 M⁰, s.v. *nagier*, cites a number of other forms of this popular proverb.

3432-3 These lines sum up with admirable brevity the cardinal weakness of Mark as a man and as a king: 'The king has not an undivided mind, now here, now there.' Cf. 4144.

3441 'She knows your court to be so loyal and your household sincere.' M⁴ (which restores *soit*) adopts a somewhat different interpretation and punctuation, and takes *natural* in the technical feudal sense normally applicable to the 'natural' liege-lord.

3443-4 'Before you she will be cleared of the charge, and may God protect her from mischance.'

3445-6 'Because henceforth you would be her protector and would not fail her in any way whatsoever.'

3448 *Plorer en font* is to be taken as a circumlocution of *en pleurent* and may be ranged with some of the examples cited by Tobler in *Verm. Beiträge*, I, 20, under the heading: '*faire* mit dem Infinitiv zur Umschreibung des Verbum finitum'.

3454-6 'May that man never enter Paradise who does not go there [i.e. to the Gué Aventuros] and help her as it is meet, if such be the king's wish.' M⁴ interprets *s'* in l. 3454 as 'un *soi* élidé'; but it would be difficult to find a parallel for this word-order, and it seems more reasonable to see in *s'* the elided form of *se* for *si* (< SIC), which is frequently used to reinforce an optative or jussive subjunctive; *anz* (= *enz*) is here a preposition. Reid proposes emendation to: *Ja ne voie il saint paradis*; cf. 841-3.

3461 'will turn out to the disadvantage of the three felons'.

3462 Cf. 3138-9 n.

3464-5 Kelemina (p. 36) seemed to detect here a reference to the Blades at the Bed incident (cf. 3546-7), but the claim of Gauvain, Gerflet and Evain to have encountered the three hostile barons previously and to know them well is clearly an embellishment contrived by Beroul and not inspired by past events, just as the end here prophesied for them will be belied in the event.

Q

3465 The *bohort* was a short jousting lance without iron, used in a sham tourney called a *tornoi a bohorts*; it is here applied to such a tourney. Cf. Hertz³, Anm. 10.

3470 The infinitive (*pendre*) is once again used loosely as the equivalent of a second finite clause. In this instance it might be partly explained as dependent on *feroie*.

3476 and 3480–1 both indicate the fate Gerflet reserves for himself if the condition postulated in 3477–9 is not fulfilled: 'May God not maintain me in my senses (and may I never embrace a fair lady beneath the bed-cover behind the curtain) if I advance to attack Godoïne and if [in such an attack] the blades of my great ashen lance do not transfix him.'

3483 The poet is too well versed in Arthurian matters to have been guilty of the error (*Dinan* for *Urïen*) shown by the MS. According to Wace, *Brut* 9619 ff., Urien was made king of Mureïf (= Moray), one of the ancient divisions of Scotland, by Arthur, and Ewein was his son (l. 10252). See Loomis, *Arthurian Literature* . . ., pp. 269–73.

3489 Cf. 3463.

3499 ff. 'Never was any man from a foreign land menaced at your court but you soon brought the affair to a conclusion, and in the settlement of it, all those who merited it were discomfited.'

3506 *lui* for *li*.

3508 'He was well content that Perinis should hear it.'

3511–2 Cf. 3708 n.

3518 *qui (e)st*; see Introd., No. 54.

3520 Cf. 3653. For other similar uses of *main*, see Godefroy, Littré and Tobler-Lommatzsch.

3525–30 The interpretation of these lines is difficult: *il* of l. 3526 may be taken to refer to Arthur and *parlemenz* to the interview of Perinis with Arthur (3527: 'before he breaks off their exchanges'). Muret emended by substituting *Qui* for *Qu'il* (3526) and *li* for *de* (3527), introducing a full stop at the end of l. 3527 and no punctuation at the end of ll. 3525–6. M⁴ (p. 148) gives the interpretation: 'La belle fera rompre plus d'une lance pour l'amour d'elle dans le tournois qui accompagnera le *parlement*.' This requires that *metra* be treated as the equivalent of *fera metre*, which, while not impossible, derives no support from the examples cited. *Qui*, if adopted, might be interpreted as yet another example of Beroul's bold use of generic *qui*, loosely connected with what precedes: 'All their talk is of the fair one [and of] whoever will splinter a lance [sc. 'in her honour'].' For the use of *astele* in the singular M⁰ refers to *Raoul de Cambrai* 1766 and to Bartsch, *Romanzen und Pastourellen* I, 57, v. 137.

3540–5 'Greet your lady for me from her loyal servitor who comes to her to conciliate; for her I will be full of zeal, she will have cause to favour me greatly.' In l. 3545 G. Paris conjectured *pot ja* (for *porra*) thus linking this line with the following.

3546–7 The incident of which Perinis is to remind Iseut remains obscure. As transmitted by the scribe, the lines appear to signify: 'Remind her of the hurling of the hunting-spear which was embedded in the post', the reference being to an occasion such as that described by Eilhart (7760–825), when Tristran upon his return from exile takes part, at the bidding of the queen, in the games which include the hurling of the *schaft* (hunting-spear or javelin), at which Tristran excels. Thomas also testifies to this in terms which recall our passage: *De trestuz i fud Tristran mestres . . . E si lancerent od roseals Od gavelos e od espiez* (ed. Bédier, 2076–7 and ed. Wind, 804–5); cf. *Fb* 182–3: *Je ai sailli et lanciez jons Et sostenu dolez bastons*. Muret's substitution (proposed by G. Paris) of *d'acier* for *lancier* may have been induced by the interpretation placed upon the following line: it might seem to refer to the Blades at the Bed incident recounted by Eilhart, i.e. to the fixing of sharp scythe-blades into a block of wood (5305), a sort of caltrop, planted at the approaches to the royal bed. (For a full account of this incident, with parallels and analogues, see G. Schoepperle, 213–21; also Bédier II, 158–9, 265, 355–6; and G. Huet, 'Sur un épisode du Tristan d'Eilhart d'Oberge', *Rom.* XXXVI, 50–57.) The emendation, and with it the identification, is accepted by Golther (p. 51) and others, but it is by no means certain: it is possible that Beroul had in mind the type of competition described, for example, in *Cléomadès*, according to which four targets were erected on tall posts (*sor tres hauts sapins*) which knights and squires on horseback sought to hit with their *gavelos* (l. 15981). The meaning may therefore be that the spear hurled by Tristran in the presence of King Arthur (or by the king himself?) embedded itself in the target-post.

3562 Why the plural? The immediate context suggests that it was Perinis and Iseut who spent the night at Lidan, meaning the castle of Dinas, perhaps here confused with Dinan (cf. the note to ll. 1085–1140). Dinas had undertaken to shelter Iseut (2949), and in l. 4301 it is hinted that it was at his castle that the lovers met; but the poet's account is confused and it appears from ll. 4286–91 and 4304–5 that the final scene was enacted in the royal *chambre*.

(*f*) *Tristran at the ford* (3563–3864)

SUMMARY

3563– Tristran, [accompanied by Governal, leaves his
3606 lodging, his sword girt on beneath his rough clothing. He instructs him to bring his white charger well concealed and his lance and sword to the ford so that he may break a lance for Iseut there at the jousting.

3607– Tristran with his goblet and crutch takes his place
3621 upon the mound near the ford, while Governal is ambushed nearby. Round about the land is marshy.

3622– Tristran begs alms from all and sundry. With his
3662 crutch he belabours those who insult him. None
recognize him.

3663– The valets and squires prepare the tents and
3701 pavilions. The knights, misdirected by Tristran,
flounder in the mire while he begs them for alms.

3702– Arthur and his knights come and joust before the
3756 ford. Tristran begs Arthur to give him his leggings, which he does. Mark gives him his hood,
which Tristran hides under his cloak.

3757– To Mark's question Tristran replies: 'I am of
3780 Caerleon, son of a Welshman; for three years I
have lived apart from my kind, a courtly mistress
I had when I was sound of limb: now through
her I am a leper begging alms. Through her I
had this malady, her husband being leprous: the
fair Iseut she is called.' Mark laughs at this con-
ceit.

3781– Arthur enquires for the queen. Mark replies that
3787 she is with Andret. They wonder how she will
get over the Mal Pas.

3788– The three felons are directed into the worst of the
3852 mire by Tristran, who mocks at their discomfiture.
He offers to pull Donoalen out with his stick and
lets him fall back deeper into the mire saying he
can do no more: 'My hands are numbed and my
arms withered by the "mal d'Acre".'

3853– Iseut has come, and Dinas with her, who recog-
3864 nizes Tristran and takes pleasure in the plight of
the three felons: they are constrained to disrobe
and put on fresh clothes.]

VARIANTS

T xxiv; *G* 15564–15568; *S* lviii, 6–10; *E* cciv

G: Tristran comes to Karliûne and waits upon the shore, dressed as a
pilgrim, his face bedaubed and *geswellet* (= swollen? covered with weals?

drawn?).—*S*: Tristran comes to the ford, his face daubed with yellow and wearing a shabby woollen coat under an old cloak.—*E*: The scene is at Westminster: Tristran comes to Iseut as arranged; he is wretchedly clad, no one recognizes him.

NOTES

3565 For this rare use of the infinitive with pronoun subject, cf. 891 n.

3566 'he does not desist', 'he is not laggardly'.

3569 *let*. The glossary is no doubt at fault in glossing this adjective 'broad' instead of 'ugly'. In a different context we read in the Prose Romance (Bédier II, 375): 'A l'andemain par matin fait Tristan tailler une gonnelle d'un lait burel sans pointes et sans gerons, mal faite et mal taillie.' Cf. also Bartsch, *Altfranzösische Romanzen und Pastourellen* (1870), p. 136, l. 18: 'cotte d'un gros burel a diverse roie'.—Why the plural *cotes*? It might seem strange that Tristran should be wearing more than one *cote* (unless *cotes* is used loosely to include both *cote* and *surcot* or the two garments specified in *S*). Cf. note to ll. 2880–7.

3570 'His boots were all in square patches.' Cf. Godefroy IX: *carrel*, 'pièce de soulier'; *carrel de soliers, pictacium* (1464, J. Lagadeuc, *Catholicon*).

3571 'a loose-fitting cloak of coarse wool'.

3572 *enfumee*. Some of the examples cited by Tobler-Lommatzsch indicate an extension of meaning from 'blackened by smoke' to 'old', 'threadbare', 'worn'.

3574 *Malade* is here a substantive, 'leper'; cf. 1155.

3579–80 See Introd., p. 31.

3581–2 'Observe the queen, for she will give no sign or token [of being aware of your identity?].' M⁴: *Qu'el n'en fera semblant et signe.*

3588–9 M⁴ no longer assumes a lacuna.

3592 'You have long been apprised of it.'

3602 *esbaudie*. Neither Godefroy nor Tobler-Lommatzsch give other examples of this word. The usual form is *esbaudise* 'bold act', and the verb (which occurs in l. 1529) is well attested; e.g. *Gormont et Isembart* 138: *La bataille fut esbaldie* ('hotly engaged').

3616 'without more ado'.

3624 Tristran, in spite of his disguise as a leper, is, the poet tells us, neither a dwarf nor a hunchback, *qar il est gros et corporuz*; see the note to 1162.

3625 'He hears the crowd [approaching].'

3628 'In an evil hour did I come to this.'

3633–4 '. . . for he is successful in making everyone give him something: he receives them [their alms?] without anyone saying anything' (i.e. without making any observation indicating suspicion). If Muret's emendation *que mot ne sone* (cf. 3645 and 3122) were adopted, the line would mean: 'He receives them without uttering a word'; but this is contradicted by the context.

3635 *mignon* is here and at l. 3644 a derogatory term signifying, as M[4] proposes, 'probablement déjà un homme qui se prête à la lubricité d'un autre'. Cf. Littré, s.v. *mignon*, sens 6.

3636 The literal meaning would seem to be: 'who is so successful in extorting pickings' (cf. 3632). M[4] translates *guignon* conjecturally 'lopin' and refers to Guilhen Anelier, *Guerre de Navarre*, v. 1163, where the marauding Navarrese knights are described as indifferent to the rights and welfare of their fellow-countrymen: *Antz prenian la terra, qui guinnon, qui carter*.

3637–41 *corlain* for *corlieu*, of which it is perhaps a variant and which occurs also in Wace, *Brut* 5520: *E ses corlieus* ('messengers') *par tut tramist*. Transl.: 'Even the unmounted lackeys, the vagabonds of ill repute who go seeking their livelihood upon the highway, from them Tristran, with bowed head, in God's name asks alms.'

3647 *corbel* (= Mod.Fr. *corbeau*), used as a term of abuse, applied (according to Tobler-Lommatzsch) to an old prostitute; but it has from time to time been applied to various classes of persons, as can be seen from the examples given by Littré. Cf. ll. 3637–9 and 3643–4.

3650 Ironical? 'He helps them on their way with blows of his crutch' (?)

3654 The value of the *maalle* was half a *denier* and double that of a *ferlin* 'farthing', and it should therefore have been glossed 'halfpenny'. The *sou* (*sol*) was worth 12 *deniers*, and 20 *sous* made a *livre esterline*. See the informative details in M⁰, s.v. 1. *sol*.

3658 'With difficulty he can cast it forth' (i.e. the burning sensation).

3661–2 'Not in the least do those who see him suspect him of not being a leper.'

3663–6 'Servants and squires bethink themselves to make haste to find lodgings for themselves and set up the tents of their lords, pavilions of many colours.' Reid proposes the bold emendation: *Passent vaslet et escuier Qui se hastent d'eus alegier.*

3671 'They have churned it up, the mud is soft.'

3679–80 '... for further on there is no mud. When they think to make trial beyond, the bog gives way beneath their feet.'

3683 'Whoever has no boots feels the need of them.' *Hueses* were sometimes worn as overshoes to protect shoes of finer quality or as gaiters to protect the legs while hunting; see Schultz I, 294–5.

3698 *passeor*. The glossary requires rectification. In this line the word denotes those who traverse the ford: 'Those who cross soil their clothes.' In l. 3703 it denotes the crossing or ford.

3708 *escus fres*, 'refurbished, freshly emblazoned shields', which is probably also the meaning of *escu nuef* in l. 3512. Cf. *argent frois*, 'freshly minted silver'.

3710 'All are fully accoutred, from head to foot' (lit. 'both hands and feet'). The scribe's error may have resulted from his misinterpretation of *mens* (or *meins*) as = *moins*.

3723 *rencïene*. Rheims has continued, from medieval times to be noted for the production of fine cloth, particularly woollens. Cf. *Amadas* 1633: *De toile faite en Rentiien*. The hero in *Flamenca* (ll. 5822–3) wears shirt and breeches made of 'tela de Rens, ben faita e sotil'.

3727 *sorchauz* 'gaiters' or 'leggings'; cf. Schultz I, 295 and note.

3738 Could the MS reading *Fait* perhaps mean *Fait que*: 'He contrives to obtain raiment in great quantity...'? This seems a more probable interpretation than Tanquerey's conjecture (in *Rom.* LVI, 121) that *Fait dras* is for *Faiz dras* 'des vêtements convenables'.

3740 *maroi*, analogical oblique form, the -*s* of *marois* having been mistaken for flexional (nom. sg.) -*s*. Cf. Introd., p. 8.

3758 *Carloon* = Caerleon-upon-Usk; cf. 3368 n. In *E* (str. cvi) *Carlioun* is the name of the port from which Tristran sets out on the Voyage of Healing.

3760 *trois anz* might be taken to confirm indirectly that it was not the full effect of the potion that lasted three years, but the sojourn in the wilderness; cf. note to ll. 2162–6.

3763 *boces* 'swellings'.

3764 *plain dolees* 'smooth-planed'.

3772 *joiaus*. Cf. the quotation in M⁰, s.v. *quartier*, from the *Chasse du cerf* (Jubinal, *Nouveau recueil*, I, p. 168):

> Et le cuer donnez aus mesiaus;
> Car ce doit estre lor joiaus.

and Tobler-Lommatzsch, s.v. *jöel*.

3783 *o Andret*; cf. 2869 n.

3786 The subject of *isse* is Iseut.

3797–8 For the rhyme see Introd., No. 25.

3800 *auves*, the two pieces of wood connecting the bows of the saddle.

3806 *done* might be taken as 2 sg. impve. with incongruent *vostre* (cf. Introd., No. 38); but it is more likely that Beroul intended the 3 sg. pres. subj.: 'Let each one [of you] give me something of yours'.

3810 *le mont*, i.e. the high ground at the approaches to the ford.

3835 *aresnement.* Cf. Tobler-Lommatzsch: *araisnier*, 'address', *araisnement*, 'address'. Muret's correction to *desresnement* is reasonable.

3849–50 *le mal d'Acre*; see Introd., pp. 34–36.

3851 *enpiriez* for *enpirié.*

3864 Misprint in variants: *Li* is the MS reading, *Lor* Muret's correction (since abandoned in M⁴). *Li* may be nothing more than a 'mistake' in declension (for *Les*), the article still retaining much of its demonstrative force.

(g) *Tristran carries Iseut through the ford* (3865–3984)

SUMMARY

3865– [Dinas observes that Iseut will soil her raiment at
3878 the ford. He knows her thoughts and, with Andrez, crosses by a ford lower down.

3879– Iseut accoutres her palfrey so that its harness may
3931 not be soiled and sends it across. Richly attired and in all her beauty] she requests the leper to carry her across.

3932– [Astride the leper's back] Iseut crosses [in full
3955 view of all. The leper pretends to stumble; amid the comments of the onlookers he reaches land, keeping his face bent from view. Iseut lets herself slip to the ground.

3956– Iseut refuses to grant the leper's request for a
3981 reward, in spite of Arthur's words, and abuses the leper.

3982– Iseut has her palfrey restored to her. All those who
3984 have arms resume their jousting.]

VARIANTS

T xxiv; *G* 15569–15637; *S* lviii, 10–31; *E* ccv–ccvii; *T.r.* 238, 33–240, 13; *Fo* 817–34

G: When Iseut and Mark approach the shore, she recognizes Tristran at once. She asks that the pilgrim, if he has the strength, should carry her ashore, saying that she does not wish to be borne by any knight. As he carries her in his arms she whispers in his ear that when he reaches land he is to fall with her. This he does, falling with Iseut in his arms and at his side. The king's followers are prevented by Iseut from beating the pilgrim, for which kindliness she is praised; she replies jestingly: 'What if that poor pilgrim should have wished to sport with me!' Mark saw and heard and was silent, and Iseut continued: 'I do not know what is to come of this, for you all see that I can now no longer swear that no one save Mark has ever lain in my arms and at my side.' Jesting in this fashion they all rode to Karliûne.

S: The queen gets into the boat on the other side of the stream and beckons to Tristran. Then she calls aloud to him to carry her ashore. As he carries her she whispers that he is to fall with her when he reaches the sand, and when they had gone a short distance on land Iseut lifted her clothes and straightway he let himself fall on her. She restrains her followers from killing him, saying that the poor pilgrim, exhausted with wandering, did not do it intentionally. They think well of Iseut for this and as they all ride off together they jest about the pilgrim's clumsiness, but Iseut says: 'Would it have been so strange if the pilgrim had desired to make sport with me and touch my white thighs? But now I cannot swear that no man save the king has ever lain with me.' Whereupon they all ride to the king's palace.

E: Preparations having been made at Westminster for the ordeal of the hot iron and Tristan having come, we are told that Iseut is to cross the Thames: she exclaims: 'This man is to carry me to the boat.' Tristran carried her and fell upon her, close to her naked side, for all to see. Iseut saves him from threats of drowning or worse and attributes his falling to his having starved; at her request they give him gold.

T.r.: Mark, the archbishop and Iseut, with a score of abbots and monks, go from the city and when they reach the shore they find a pilgrim heavily disguised; Iseut requests him to carry her ashore. He does so, and when they reach land he embraces her closely, then departs into the forest. Before reaching the *Petrone Vermiglio* they encounter *uno folle*, likewise heavily disguised and with his face bedaubed with divers colours: he too embraces the queen and kisses her when she approaches to kiss the cross he bears in his hand.

Fo: Tristran reminds Iseut how he held her in his arms as she left the ship, having adopted the disguise recommended by her, how at her bidding he let himself fall between her thighs upon reaching the shore, and how she saved herself by the ambiguous oath.

Fb shows no trace of the Ambiguous Oath episode.

NOTES

3868 *siglaton*, originally a silk fabric (cf. *Flamenca* 5825: *Blisaut portet de cisclaton*), but also used (like *paille*) to denote a garment made of that material. Cf. Schultz I, 547–8.

3872 *posen* may be the scribe's misreading of *poi en* or of *poï* (= *poin* for *point*) *en*.

3877 Cf. 2869 n.

3879 *sole*, i.e. apart from Tristran (and Dinas?).

3886 The *sanbue* was the horsecloth placed over the saddle and designed to protect the clothing, particularly of the ladies (cf. Schultz I, 494). It was generally of costly material, richly embroidered and decorated with fringes or tassels, the latter presumably called *langues* because of their shape. 'Strips (of material)' is therefore a more appropriate gloss than 'straps'.

3904 *Baudas*. Bagdad was famed throughout the Middle Ages for the manufacture of precious silks.

3908 'caught up in linen strips over fine gold net'. See Schultz I, 236–42.

3910 *Qui* is the direct object of *empare*.

3912 G. Paris assumed a lacuna after this line.

3920 *Avoi*; see T. Kalepky, '*Avois—avoi—aoi—vois—voiz du papelart!*', in *Arch. Rom.* XIII, 539–43.

3922 For Muret's correction of *boçu* to *bociez* (abandoned in M⁴) see M⁰ glossary. See 1162 n.

3927 *lui* for *li*.

3928 J. Frappier (*Rom.* LXXXIII, 256) interprets *sovent* as 'beaucoup, fortement, longuement', but the meaning seems to me rather to be 'repeatedly'.

3934 *les gardent*. It is possible that the scribe made a wrong word-division and that the poet intended *l'esgardent*, the pronoun referring to Iseut.

3935 It is clear that Tristran carries Iseut astride his back (cf. 3940). What is not so clear is the position of the crutch. It has been assumed by editors that he places it across his loins or, roughly, the small of his back, and hence in l. 3946 they have emended the scribe's *de soz* to *desor*. This interpretation has been defended by J. Frappier in *Rom.* LXXXIII, 256–8; but M. Delbouille, in a footnote to his article, 'Les *hanches* du Roi Pêcheur et la genèse du *Conte del Graal*' in the *Festschrift Walther von Wartburg* (1968), pp. 362–3, considers that Tristran 'a placé sa béquille horizontalement contre son ventre'. If this interpretation were accepted, *sa hanche* in l. 3946 would apply to Iseut and, as Professor Reid has suggested to me, the scribe's *de soz* would have to be restored and the line would be equivalent to l. 3935. This would involve a 'glissement de sens' in respect of *hanche*, for which, it is true, parallels can be found in the denominating of the hip and adjoining areas of the human anatomy (cf. the semantic history of Latin *coxa*, English *haunch*, etc.). I confess to being impressed, though not entirely convinced, by M. Delbouille's argument. Beroul's description tallies with the depiction of this incident on the ivory caskets of Goodrich Court and of the South Kensington Museum (cf. Hertz[3], Anm. 109).

Bédier (II, 265) regarded the whole of this scene of the Ambiguous Oath as 'une de ces végétations parasites qui se sont développées autour de l'estoire', adopted, one assumes, independently by Thomas and (in a modified form) by Beroul, but not by Eilhart and the Prose Romance. Kelemina's assumption that the beggar's falling with the queen was inadvertently omitted by Beroul is ill-founded in view of l. 3955.

3944 *set clochier*; this attenuated use of *savoir* 'know how to' is well attested. Muret assumed a scribal error for *seut*, ind. pr. 3 of *soleir* 'be wont'. The form *seut* occurs (in rhyme) at l. 3776.

3953 Cf. *Fo* 823: '*Le chef teneie mult enbrunc.*'

3954 *païs*, 'terra firma'.

3960 For the expression *donez la li*, cf. L. Foulet in *Rom.* L, 75.

3961 Another example of Iseut's niggardliness (?). Cf. 231 n.

3971 Cf. 3730–4.

3972 *soz*; the *sou* (*sol*) was worth 1-20 of a *livre*: cf. 3654 n.

3973 Cf. 3750–6.

3974 *si*, 'and so'. Acher proposed emendation to *si soit passor* or *soit passeor* and interpreted: 'Iseut, qui feint d'être mécontente des services du faux ladre, dit qu'il achète avec l'argent qu'il pourra se procurer en vendant l'aumuce de Marc, une bone litière ou un âne qui lui permettra de s'établir passeur au marais.' Reid (p. 285) suggests as a possible emendation *berbiz* for *bien lit*.

3978 'He has found someone who is a match for him', says Iseut, implying that she at least is not deceived by the leper! Gauchat proposed to emend to *Trové argent*; but this is just what Tristran has not succeeded in doing, according to Iseut.

(*h*) *Tristran and Governal join in the jousting* (3985–4074)

SUMMARY

3985–
4009 [Governal, his face covered with a wimple of white silk, and Tristran, in black upon Bel Joëor and with Iseut's favour on his lance, come forth upon La Blanche Lande.

4010–
4019 Gauvain: 'Who are these knights?'—Gerflet: 'One is Li Noirs de la Montaigne, the other I recognize by his 'armes vaires': they are enchanted.'

4020–
4035 Tristran and Governal joust but are recognized only by Iseut who stands apart with Brengain.

4035–
4056 Tristran slays Andret. Governal slays the forester who betrayed the sleeping Tristran in the wood.

4057–
4074 Tristran and Governal escape across the ford. The jousting comes to an end.]

The passage extending from l. 3985 to l. 4113 offers a striking contrast with Beroul's normal manner and pre-occupations. The introduction of Arthur may be held to have invited this concession to the taste of the courtly society of the time for scenes of jousting and of courtesy. It presents a very loose parallel with those passages of *Tristan Menestrel* in which Tristran engages in jousting, first as a mysterious foreign knight at Arthur's court, and then (accompanied by a band of Arthur's knights, all disguised as minstrels) at Lancïen, where king Mark has arranged a tournament. Dinas is ordered to look after the 'musicians', and in the evening Tristran plays the *lai de Chievrefueil*, which Iseut recognizes as 'le lai que moi et lui feïsmes'.

Beroul's predilection for the more robust, not to say primitive and barbarous, and for the matter and style of the *chanson de geste* is betrayed by the casual manner which characterizes this passage. It provides him with the opportunity of unceremoniously eliminating Andret from the narrative and despatching the forester, some-what incongruously introduced as a companion of Arthur's knights (4059) and spared the ignominious death prophesied for him (2759–62). He also introduces two unattested Arthurian knights, Cinglor and Coris.

NOTES

3987 *Castele*. The European fame of Castilian horses is abundantly attested. The author of the *Cronica del famoso cavallero Cid Ruy Díaz Campeador* would have us believe that they are all descended from El Cid's famous horse Babieca.

3999–4002 The knight accoutred entirely in black and thus shrouded in an air of mystery (cf. 4019) is a common figure in Arthurian romance, e.g. in *Cligés* 4662 ff., *La Vengeance Raguidel*, *Perlesvaus*, *La Mort Artu*, etc.

4013 *qu'il sont = qu(i) il sont.* Cf. Introd., No. 54.

4021 *pres*. The meaning 'near' hardly seems appropriate (unless signifying that they held their shields close to their persons?), and one is tempted to treat *pres* as a scribal rendering of *prez* 'ready' (cf. 1442, 1458) or as a mistake for *pris*, which is more likely in view of its occurrence in exactly the same context at l. 4037.

4031 *angarde* has been glossed 'outpost', but the context suggests that the poet used it to denote the vanguard or van, the preliminary manœuvre or forward movement of the contending parties in the tournament. Before the general *mêlée* it was customary for each knight to choose a worthy adversary and engage in a hand-to-hand joust (see L. Gautier, *La Chevalerie* (Paris, 1884), p. 679): thus, we find Tristran and Governal engaging Andret and the forester respectively.

4035 ff. *Andret*; cf. 2869 n.

4053-4. Cf. *Thèbes* 4435-6, and *Moniage Guillaume* 1568.

4057 *Tolas*, to be identified with Taulas mentioned as one of the knights of the Round Table in *Erec* 1729, and named 'Taulas de la Deserte' in *Lancelot* 5835. *Gerflet* = 'Girflez le fiz Do', also mentioned in *Erec* 1729 as one of the knights of the Round Table, and 'Gifflet le fil Do' in *Tristan Menestrel* 94.

4071 M^0 and M^1: *Au pas remestrent.* . . .

(*i*) *Courtesy of Arthur and Mark—Preparation for Iseut's 'escondit'* (4075–4182)

SUMMARY

4075– [Arthur and Mark hold their respective courts.
4113 Arthur visits Mark. In the evening they discuss Iseut's 'escondit'. Festivities continue into the night.

4114– Upon the morrow all the holy relics of Cornwall
4136 are displayed upon a silken cloth before the king's tent.

4137– A: 'You are too easily swayed and have been
4169   misled. Iseut shall clear herself by an oath:
       thereafter let no one raise his voice again.'
4170– M: 'So shall it be.']
4182

NOTES

4081 *corbel*. The term does not appear applicable to a
tent or pavilion, and the emendation *cordel* 'tent-cord'
suggested in M⁰ and made in later editions should perhaps have been adopted.

4083 *glagié*; in support of this emendation (substituted
by Muret for an earlier emendation: *flories*) one might
cite *Erec* (ed. Roques) 2308–9: *de jons, de mantastre, et de
glais / sont totes jonchiees les rues*; and *Galeran de Bretagne*
3358–9: *De jonchier ces rues de mente Et de vers joncs et de
jagleux.*

4085 *vestue*. See the interesting note in M⁰ glossary.

4088 *ot* is the 3 pres. ind. of *oïr*; *menee*, the pursuit (of
the stag), and hence by metonymy the sounding of the
pursuit; cf. *Chanson de Roland* 1454: *.vii. milie graisles i
sunent la menee*, i.e. 'sound the pursuit or charge (by
Marsile's forces)' and 3310: *De l'olifan haltes sont les
menees*. Alternatively, *menee* may denote the mort (Fr.
hallali), the note sounded when the stag is at bay.

4090 'Each king held open court (to hear those who
solicit favours, etc.).'

4096–4100 The text seems corrupt. M⁰ conjectured
that 4099–4100 were perhaps interpolated, suppressed
l. 4100 and emended 4099 to read: *Se laine i out, ce fu en
graine*. The MS readings in 4095–4101 are restored in M⁴
with the emendation *vesteüres*. Cf. *Erec* 1352: *De samiz et
de dras an grainne.*

4099–4100 *en graine* 'dyed a scarlet colour by means of
cochineal or kermes'. The fine woollen cloth called
escarlate, when thus dyed was highly prized and the name

R

came to be used for the colour. Schultz I, 354, cites *Perceval* 28637: *Une escarlate teinte en graine*.

4103 'There is no need of anything but it is found there.'

4107–8 Reid proposes the retention of *enseigne* 'charge', 'incriminating evidence' (Tobler-Lommatzsch, III, 513) and the correction of *barnage* to *conpaigne* (cf. 4027, etc.). This seems more acceptable than the adopted emendation: *l'outrage* for *lenseigne*.

4112 'Whoever was that night in the wood might have heard . . .'

4114 'Before daybreak it began to thunder, decidedly'.

4120 *choier* here means 'subside', 'disperse', 'melt'.

4125 *a paile bis* might be interpreted 'bordered or lined with dark brocaded material'; at l. 4135 the reference is simply to *le paile(s)*. Having regard to the very loose use of *paile* (see note to l. 2743 and Schultz I, 332–8), it seemed wiser to adhere to the MS reading than to turn the difficulty by substituting *un* for the scribe's *a*.

4127 'It was embroidered in small stitches with figures of animals'. (?)

4135 Logically this clause is dependent on the negative statement of the preceding lines, but the construction is loose and the clause takes the form of an independent, positive statement of fact.

4143 *sil* = *cil*; cf. 4180 n.

4144 Cf. 3432–3 n.

4146–9 'He prepared a bitter sauce for you who caused you to convoke this meeting: it should cost him dear in his own person and distress him, whoever [it was that] desired to do this.'; *faire* being here used, as in 728 and 2431, without a pronoun object (*le*), with the meaning 'to complete an act'. See also l. 270.

4158 *qui ara tort* 'whoever may be at fault', referring to the preceding lines(?) Alternatively, *tort* might here be used in a sense similar to that with which the word has survived in English legal terminology, the meaning being: 'Whoever shall have a wrong (to bring up and lay to the charge of Iseut), the queen will come forward . . .'. See l. 4470.

4165 'upon which an evil interpretation might be put'.

4180 M⁴ makes the interesting suggestion that *C'a* may be scribal for *S'a* ('if it has been done'), and cites as examples of the scribe's confusion of *c-* and *s-* ll. 996 (*cele* for *selle*) and 4143 (*sil* for *cil*).—For suggested explanations of the expression *sor mon pois*, see M⁰, s.v. *pois*.

(j) Iseut's ambiguous oath (4183–4266)

SUMMARY

4183– [In the presence of the two courts Arthur adminis-
4196 ters the oath.]

4197– Iseut swears that never did any man rest between
4216 her thighs other than [the leper] who carried her over the ford and her husband Mark.

4217– [All declare that Iseut has need of no further
4231 'escondit'.

4232– A: 'King, you have heard the denial. Let the three
4246 felons not raise their voice again; for nothing shall keep us from coming to Iseut's aid.'

4247– Iseut thanks Arthur. Mark promises never again
4261 to believe the traducers of the queen.

4262– Arthur returns to Durelme. Mark remains in
4266 Cornwall. Tristran abides in peace.]

VARIANTS

T xxiv; *G* 15638–15768; *S* lix, i–lx; *E* ccvii–ccix; *T.r.* 240, 13–end

G: In Karliûne there is a great concourse, clerks and knights and common folk, together with bishops and prelates who fulfilled their office and blessed the court (*gerihte*): the iron was in the fire. Iseut presents offerings to win God's favour and attends Mass, wearing a hair-shirt next her skin and with bare feet and arms, exciting the pity of all. The reliquary is brought upon which she is to swear. She commends her hand and heart to God. The barons, including Marjodo, quarrel over the form of the oath: Iseut interrupts to say that it is for Mark to say whether he is satisfied with the oath she takes: 'No man ever had carnal knowledge of me or lay in my arms or at my side save the king and the pilgrim, so help me God to undergo the ordeal without harm.' Mark declares himself content with this oath and bids her take the iron. Iseut bears it without harm. The king is completely satisfied and Iseut is restored to full favour.—(There follows the Petit-Crù incident (*T* xxvi) and Tristran's return to court.)—*G* (16407–16682):[1] After Tristran's return the lovers resume their life of bliss, but suspicion revives and Mark's anger triumphs over his infatuation; he summons the lovers and banishes them from the court and the land. [They leave Brengain behind; Tristran takes twenty marks from Iseut's treasure, his harp and sword, horn, crossbow and bolts and Hudan. His followers he sends back to his father Rual, except Governal who accompanies the lovers into the wilds. Brengain is to further a reconciliation when Mark's anger subsides.][2]

NOTES

4199 *Or escoutez*, identified by Jonin (p. 97) as a recognized 'formule propitiatoire' used in oaths of this kind (= *Hoc audias*).

4201 For the reasons, other than the requirements of rhyme, which may have prompted Beroul to have Iseut invoke Saint Hilaire, see Jonin, pp. 343–8.

4205 Cf. 3935 n.

[1] *S* liv; *E* ccxxii–ccxxiii; *T.r.* 244, 1–245, 5.
[2] The passage in square brackets and the mention of Karliûne are peculiar to *G*. For the rest, *S* agrees substantially with *G*, but adds to the oath: 'Never did I incur guilt or sin through any other man; this I vow to God and all his saints.'—*E* gives a very summary account.—In *T.r.*, where Mark requires Iseut to place her right hand upon the *Petrone Vermiglio* (see p. 243), she adds a phrase to the same effect as in *S*: 'e d'ogni altra persona io sono netta e pura e leale, e mai co' niun' altra persona io non fei mai niuno fallo, se no' se com' io v' òe contato.' Only when she has held the hot iron without harm is Mark's suspicion overcome; he bestows three castles upon her. The fool gives his name as *Tantri*, explaining that if the *tri* were placed before the *tan*, he would be called *Tritan*. (The narrative continues on the same general lines as in *S*.)

4219 M⁴ restores *en*, but still treats *jure* as a substantive 'serment' in the glossary. One might take *fiere* as standing virtually in apposition to the subject (Iseut) and having adverbial force, a use which may be regarded as typical of Beroul's style. Reid proposes to read: *si fiere enjure!* (= *injure*); but l. 559 could hardly be called an exact parallel to this exclamatory use.

4223–5 In other versions Iseut asks whether the oath is comprehensive enough and Mark answers in the affirmative. Kelemina's suggestion that l. 4215 implies the existence in Beroul's source of the ordeal by the red-hot iron is hardly justified. Line 4223 is to be taken with l. 4225: 'Iseut has no need of further exculpation than you, great and small, have heard, other than that in respect of the king (i.e. Mark) and his nephew (i.e. Tristran).' H. H. Christmann (in *Rom.* LXXX (1959), 85–87 and *ZFSL* LXXVI (1966), 243–5) arrives at a similar interpretation, contrary to Reid's (in *Rom.* LXXXV (1964), 366–7); but I take *fors* by itself to mean 'except' and *du* as signifying 'concerning', 'in respect of'; see l. 1012 and particularly l. 202. Reid's identification of the king and his nephew (4225) as Arthur and Gawain respectively is hardly tenable.—M⁴ restores the MS reading, but proposes a somewhat different interpretation which it is difficult to accept.

4231 An elliptical construction: 'Cursed be he [who] ever disbelieves her!'

4232 The MS reading is not clear: *Li mes* could equally well be read as *Lunes* or *Linies*.

4233 *Li* for *Le*.

4237 'Let the three felons see to it that . . .'

4246 *Lui* for *Li*.

4252 The variant should read: *jos aseür* M; see Introd., No. 57.

4264 *Durelme*. Whereas Durham is here a residence of Arthur and is in his kingdom, at l. 2232 it seems to be in that of Mark (as a vassal of Arthur?).

VI. REVENGE (4267–4485)

This closing section presents a number of obscurities and hesitations or contradictions. The king returns with Iseut (4269), presumably to Tintagel, and according to ll. 4286–93, 4305, 4315–8, 4339, 4409, 4414, the final scene is enacted in the queen's *chanbre*. The spy, having assured the hostile barons that he saw Tristran resort to the *chanbre*, adds that the latter was accompanied by Governal (of whom no mention has been made since his departure with Tristran from the scene of the jousting, l. 4069, and who will not again be mentioned). Tristran's hiding-place (referred to by the spy in l. 4284) is presumably still Orri's cellar (3016–27, 3319, 3351–2), of which the hostile barons are apparently ignorant. The further questions of the barons (4300–3) can hardly apply to anyone but Tristran and Governal, and the evasive replies of the spy are mystificatory, and are perhaps intended to be so by the poet. Lines 4298–4303 would appear to be little more than irrelevant embellishment.

A further looseness of terminology concerns the *fenestre* first mentioned in l. 4289, and again in l. 4304. In ll. 4314–6 (if we accept the emendation) the opening is referred to as *un petit pertus* and again in ll. 4327–8 as a *pertuset*, furnished with a curtain which Godoïne moves aside (4413); yet it is through the *fenestre* that Iseut sees the shadow of his head (4428), while Tristran sees it (4461–2) through the curtain. It would seem that in spite of the distinction implied between *pertus* and *fenestre* at ll. 4321–2, the poet hesitated between *pertus* (*pertuset*) and *fenestre* as a designation of the window or window opening, all the more readily, one must concede, since the window would in his day normally have been unglazed. The explanation may lie in the poet's imperfectly maintained distinction between *pertus* as the designation of the external window opening and *fenestre* as the designation of the embrasure or niche (often of considerable depth in castles or other buildings with thick walls) or of the window as a whole.

(a) Betrayal of Tristran and Iseut (4267–4344)

SUMMARY

4267– [A spy offers, for a silver mark, to take the three
 4312 barons where they may have proof that Tristran and Iseut still meet.

4313– 'They may be seen if the curtain which covers the
 4336 opening in the queen's apartment is moved aside with a long pointed stick.'

4337– It is decided that Godoïne shall be the first to
 4344 observe the lovers.]

NOTES

4285 *Malpertis*, the residence of the Fox in the *Roman de Renart* (cf. Introd., p. 34). The meaning is clearly: 'Tristran is very sly.'

4294 'This very night you will see him come, towards morning.'

4295–4312 The dialogue is carried on in a style which is reminiscent of the romances of Chrétien de Troyes and other courtly writers and is perhaps another sign of their influence in the latter part of Beroul's narrative.

4298 *Cil* for *Cel.*

4300 *En haut ostal*, 'in a fine lodging' (?)

4301 In the Prose Romance too (Loeseth, pp. 204–5) the lovers meet secretly in the castle of the seneschal Dinas, where Tristran has found refuge after his return from Arthur's court to Cornwall. Cf. Kelemina, p. 19.

4307 *quant l'en ratent*, 'in such quantity as I expect it'.

4310 'So help you Church and Mass', 'In the name of Church and Mass'.

4313–4 M⁴ questions the lacuna assumed in earlier editions by Muret between these two lines and very tentatively proposes the correction of *Et* in l. 4314 to *Est*.

4317 The *doiz* can hardly be the stream down which Tristran sent the chips (see above, p. 66).

4318 For *jagloiz*, see Godefroy IV, s.v. *jaglel*, and IX, s.v. *glaieul*; and Tobler-Lommatzsch, under *glaioi*, *glaiolé* and *glaioloi*; *espesse* (which should have been included in the Glossary) is here the ind. pr. 3 of *espesser* 'be or become thick or dense'. The emendation to *espés li iagloloiz*, proposed by Reid, is therefore unnecessary. The access to the opening (*pertus*) is barred by the broad stream and the thick growth of sword-grass (*jagloiz*).

4322 'Let no one pass by outside the window.' See the note on p. 254. In the event, Godoïne pays with his life for his failure to heed the warning of the spy.

4323–30 'Make a long pointed stick with a knife, very pointed: prick the cloth of the curtain with the sharp stick of thorn; then move the curtain gently over the opening, since it is not fastened, so that you may see clearly within when he comes to speak to her.'

4328 *estache*, ind. pr. 3 of *estachier* 'attach', 'fasten': 'since it is not fastened'.

4330 *lui* for *li*.

4339 *orlois* not attested elsewhere; *orlage* is recorded in Tobler-Lommatzsch with the meaning 'sexual excitement'.

4340 *demeine* denotes that which is owned as of right or by title. Translate: 'With her who is his very own'.

(b) *Tristran kills Denoalen* (4345–4410)

SUMMARY

4345– [Tristran, summoned by Iseut, sees Godoïne and

4368 lies in wait for him, but Godoïne takes another path.

4369– Tristran surprises Denoalen on his way to hunt a
4410 boar, slays him, decapitates him and cuts off his tresses to show to Iseut as proof of his death. He hides the body under a tree-trunk and goes to Iseut's chamber.]

NOTES

4350 *Saint Lubin.* M⁰ points out that there are several places of this name in the diocese of Chartres and conjectures that it may have been introduced into the narrative by Beroul or a scribe hailing from this district.

4351 Identical with l. 1835.

4357 The narrative is disjointed, the poet adding, by way of an afterthought, the elaborative and somewhat repetitive information that Tristran, setting out from his hiding-place (cf. 3318 and 4284), had hidden in the thicket.

4368 *poine* is scribal for *poigne* (< PUGNA) 'grip, force, effort', which would give a perfect rhyme (see Introd., No. 27). The scribe sometimes writes *poine* for *peine* (3369, 3658), but not necessarily the poet, to judge from the rhymes (525, 1597, 2131, 2163, 3747).

4370 The subject of *demora* is *Denoalan*.

4372 *grant* refers to *Denoalan*.

4386–93 The killing of Denoalen is reminiscent of the killing of one of the hostile barons by Governal (see ll. 1656–1750 and the general notes to those lines). The barbarity of the present passage has perhaps unduly shocked some critics, and Muret (M⁰, s.v. *treces*) goes so far as to speak of the cutting off of Denoalen's tresses as 'la forme adoucie d'un véritable *scalp* dont la mémoire avait été conservée par des récits antérieurs'. Bédier (II, 312) agrees with Muret in regarding the death of Denoalen as primitive and having existed in the Celtic sources but being left aside by the poet of the *estoire*. But there is nothing exclusively or even specifically Celtic about the decapitation of both victims. Unlike Governal, Tristran does not bear away the head, but cuts off the tresses, to be produced as evidence of Denoalen's death when he sees Iseut (4424). The tresses are evidence of the fashion, developed particularly in France in the twelfth and thirteenth centuries, among men of quality, of wearing their hair long and plaited. For a description and references, see Schultz I, pp. 286–8, and in particular the reproduction there given of the late twelfth-century statue of Clothar I from the portal of Saint-Germain-des-Prés.

4391 *chauce* 'long hose' or 'drawers'. See the O.Fr. examples given by Littré, s.v. *chausses*. Cf. J. Evans, *op. cit.*, p. 6 et passim; Schultz I, 294.

4392–3 'so that, when he shall have shown them to Iseut, she may believe him [to the effect that] he has killed him.'

4399–4401 'Had he awaited me, he might have come to know that he would have no better recompense than Donalan, the felon, bears away with him.'

4401 M⁴: *Que Donalan, le fel, enporte.*

4407 The MS reading is *seimet* or *sennet*. M reads *se met*.

4408 Or read: *a tret*(?)

(c) Death of Godoïne (4411–4485)

SUMMARY

4411– [Godoïne takes up his post and sees Perinis,
4419 Brengain and Iseut in the queen's chamber.
4420– Tristran enters, bearing his bow and two arrows
4431 and Denoalen's tresses. Iseut, rising to greet
      Tristran, sees Godoïne's shadow.

4432– Tristran presents Denoalen's tresses to Iseut. She
4456 bids him test his bow and fit an arrow.

4457– Tristran, alarmed, sees Godoïne's head through
4485 the curtain against the light. He prays that his
arrow may hit its mark and shoots Godoïne
through the eye, killing him instantly.]

NOTES

4413 *ot* is not clear and might be read as *et* or *er*; *percie*
appears in the MS as pcie or ptie. It is possible that the
scribe intended: *er[t] dedenz partie* 'was parted within';
but this spoils the rhyme. The reading adopted describes
the action foreshadowed in 4325–6.

4422 *anter*. See Introd., No. 7 n. The scribe's *aucer* may
well be, as suggested in Muret's CFMA editions, a scribal
corruption of *antrer* (for *entrer*) repeated from the preceding line.

4432 *Tristran* for *Tristrans*.

4433 *Se* for *si* (<SIC): lit. 'So may God keep me with
his [elect]'. Cf. 4201.

4441 Against Muret's *s'esteut* one might object that the
MS reads *sestent* and that nowhere else does the form
esteut occur. Tristran tests the bow by stretching it,
temporizes (in order not to alarm Godoïne), and then
stretches the bow again (4443). Cf. also 4473.

4443 M³ abandoned the earlier emendation *sa tente*.

4454 The correction was first proposed by G. Paris.

4458 *soit* = *sait*.

4465 *cest* for *cist*, referring back to *trait* (4463).

4467 *a grant tort* 'with evil intent', 'boding ill'; cf.
4470–1.

4475 *lui* for *li* (or M⁴: *lui* 'se rapportant à un nom de
chose').

4483 For a parallel to the shooting of Godoïne, see
the Old Irish tale of *The Fate of the Children of Uisneach*.

(Published for the Society for the Preservation of the Irish Language), Dublin, 1914, pp. 71–72.

4485 With the death of Godoïne the elimination of the hostile faction is complete, with the exception of Guenelon, and the lovers have nothing to fear except the resentment and any desire for revenge that Mark may harbour. In these circumstances one must ask oneself whether Beroul is likely to have gone on to recount the further adventures of Tristran in exile, to introduce the second Iseut (of the White Hands) and to conclude with the death of the lovers as told by Eilhart, Thomas, and the prose version given by Bédier (in extracts) as an appendix to Vol. II of his edition of Thomas, and as retold so admirably in his modernized version.

The scenes in which the lovers take leave of each other and exchange their parting gifts (ll. 2695–2732, repeated and confirmed in ll. 2777–2802) appear to favour an affirmative reply. Iseut gives Tristran her ring, upon the production of which she will do whatever the bearer requests in Tristran's name (2716–22 and 2797–2802). This would seem to foreshadow the use of the ring to summon Iseut to come to the aid of the dying Tristran, as, for example, in Eilhart (9298–9 and 9326). However, in view of the independent and eclectic procedure shown by Beroul, it would be rash to conclude that he in fact composed a denouement similar to Eilhart's. Nor can the terms in which Iseut asks for the gift of Hudent in return (2695–2706) and promises to lodge him sumptuously hardly do more than suggest that Beroul was familiar with the figure of Petit Crû (cf. the note to ll. 2704–6).

On the other hand, the sequence of events and the tone of the final scenes suggest the possibility, if not the probability, that Beroul's narrative ended, as did the Prose Romance (apart from the version preserved in MS 103), with the death of Tristran at the hands of Mark, who, at the instigation of Andret, finds Tristran in the queen's apartment, performing on the harp a lay he had composed, and wounds him mortally with the poisoned lance which had been given him by the fay Morgain (Loeseth, pp. 383–4).[1] This seems all the more likely in view of the partial though striking parallel to the closing lines of our fragment presented by a passage in the *Tavola Ritonda* I, 495 ff. (quoted by G. Schoepperle, pp. 440–1), according to which Andret, having found the lovers together, betrays them to Mark who, looking through the barred window of the chamber, sees Tristran playing chess with Iseut, hurls the lance given him by the fay and wounds Tristran mortally in the left side. Whether this violent denouement represents an older tradition, before the introduction of the second Iseut and the connected scenes was undertaken (as G. Schoepperle was inclined to think), must remain an open question.

[1] See also the text published by E. S. Murrell, 'The Death of Tristan from Douce MS 189', *PMLA*, XLIII (1928), 343–83.

SELECTIVE INDEX TO COMMENTARY

(References are to line-numbers)

CORRECTIONS AND ADDITIONS TO VOL. I

(1967 reprint)

Line 1605, *replace comma by full stop at end of line*—3501 var., *read:* c. M] chies—3527 var., *add:* parlemenz M] parlomenz—3531 var., *read:* l'out un] senble li, l'a un M—3984, *read:* lors—4314 var., *read:* pertus M—4472 var., *insert* la *before* paroi—

GLOSSARY

acroire. *Add:* 29 *and after* credit *add:* ; *faire a.* cause to believe—**acuellir.** *For* 2153 *read:* 2155—*Add:* **afaire;** *sans autre a.* without more ado 3616—**ainz.** *For* even 3004 *read:* ainz . . . ne never 3004-5—*Add:* **anter;** v. **entier.**—**avoir.** *For* 723 *read:* 725—**bandon.** *Add: tot a b.* with complete abandon, impetuously 2956—**bendé.** *For* bend *read:* string—**cliner.** *For v.n.* bow *read: v.a.* bow—**cointier.** *Read:* **cointoier**—**cors.** *After* 1918 *add:* 2054—**demonstrance.** *Read:* **demostrance**—**desfait.** *After* infirm *add:* , deformed—**el.** *For lc read:* le—*Add:* **el, ele;** v. **il**—**esgarder.** *After* 3267 *add: e. que* see to it that 4237.—**eshahir.** *Read:* **esbahir**—*Add:* **estachier,** *v.a.* attach, fasten 4328—**fors.** *Reword the article:* **fors,** *adv.* out of doors, without 321, 1905, 3658; *f. de* out of, away from, free of, exempt from 723, 1455, 1466, 2051, 2330, 3759, 3846; *prep.* except 24, 1012; *conj.* except that 1848, 3081; *f. que* except 880, except that 111; *f. tant que* except that 763. See note to l. 1909.—**fuellier.** *For* bower *read:* dense wood, thicket(?)—**grenir.** *Restore:* **greignier,** *v.n.* grind one's teeth 3362.—**il.** *After* 2362 *add:* 2574,—**langue.** *For* strap *read:* strip (of material), fringe, tassel—**lores.** *After* 899 *add:* **lor** 2495, 3984,—**mesfaire.** *For* 1103, 820 *read:* 820, 1105—**non.** *After* 1444 *add: par nons* by name 2522; *par non* specifically 3414—**ome.** *After* 89, *add:* 4165, *and for* 2608 *read:* [2608]—**onc.** *For* **dont** *read:* **onques**— *Add:* **pais** 894, **pes** 3293, **pez** 622, *sf.* peace; respite 3367.—*Add:* **païs,** *sm.* country 457.—**passeor.** *Read:* one who crosses 3698, crossing, ford 3703.—**pois.** *Delete* , trifling weight, trifle 780—*Add:* **pois,** *sm.* pea (used as negative complement) 780.—**pooir.** *For* **puis** *in l.* 4 *read:* **puise**—**pres.** *Before* 930 *insert:* near—**que.** *Delete* = *ce que* 519, 2262 *and delete* 38 *and for porce read: por ce*—**qui.** *For* 2061 *read:* 519, 2061, 2262—**quidier.** *For* 123, etc. *read:* , I think 123, 721, 781, 1470, 1854, 2035, 2847.— **ratendre.** *For* 4307 *read* [4307]—*Add:* **saintuaire,** *sm.* reliquary 4202.—*Add:* **savroit** 254, *condl.* 3 of **savoir,** *v.n.* have a savour, be pleasing to one's taste.—**seri.** *For* soft *read:* thin(?)—**si.** Transfer 1509 to preceding line—**tost.** *For* **tos(t)** *read:* **tos[t]**—

INDEX